SAGE was founded in 1965 by Sara Miller McCune to support the dissemination of usable knowledge by publishing innovative and high-quality research and teaching content. Today, we publish over 900 journals, including those of more than 400 learned societies, more than 800 new books per year, and a growing range of library products including archives, data, case studies, reports, and video. SAGE remains majority-owned by our founder, and after Sara's lifetime will become owned by a charitable trust that secures our continued independence.

Los Angeles | London | New Delhi | Singapore | Washington DC | Melbourne

INDIAN DEMOCRACY

INDIAN DEMOCRACY

Contradictions and Reconciliations

Edited by

Arvind
Sivaramakrishnan

Sudarsan
Padmanabhan

Los Angeles | London | New Delhi
Singapore | Washington DC | Melbourne

First published in 2020 by

SAGE Publications India Pvt Ltd
B1/I-1 Mohan Cooperative Industrial Area
Mathura Road, New Delhi 110 044, India
www.sagepub.in

SAGE Publications Inc
2455 Teller Road
Thousand Oaks, California 91320, USA

SAGE Publications Ltd
1 Oliver's Yard, 55 City Road
London EC1Y 1SP, United Kingdom

SAGE Publications Asia-Pacific Pte Ltd
18 Cross Street #10-10/11/12
China Square Central
Singapore 048423

Published by Vivek Mehra for SAGE Publications India Pvt Ltd. Typeset in 10.5/13 pt Bembo by Zaza Eunice, Hosur, Tamil Nadu, India.

Library of Congress Control Number: 2019954518

ISBN: 978-93-5328-980-5 (HB)

SAGE Team: Abhijit Baroi, Vandana Gupta, Madhurima Thapa and Anupama Krishnan

This book is dedicated to

Era Sezhiyan

the great constitutionalist and parliamentarian.

Thank you for choosing a SAGE product!
If you have any comment, observation or feedback,
I would like to personally hear from you.

Please write to me at **contactceo@sagepub.in**

Vivek Mehra, Managing Director and CEO, SAGE India.

Bulk Sales

SAGE India offers special discounts
for purchase of books in bulk.
We also make available special imprints
and excerpts from our books on demand.

For orders and enquiries, write to us at

Marketing Department
SAGE Publications India Pvt Ltd
B1/I-1, Mohan Cooperative Industrial Area
Mathura Road, Post Bag 7
New Delhi 110044, India

E-mail us at **marketing@sagepub.in**

Subscribe to our mailing list
Write to **marketing@sagepub.in**

This book is also available as an e-book.

Contents

Introduction
Arvind Sivaramakrishnan and Sudarsan Padmanabhan   1

Part I: Democratic Principles and Their Applications in India

Chapter 1   Democracy as Antinomy:
             Procedural versus Substantive
             Sudarsan Padmanabhan   9
Chapter 2   Electoral Issues and the
             Constitution of India
             N. L. Rajah   35
Chapter 3   Voter Education:
             Importance and Impact
             S. Y. Quraishi   62
Chapter 4   Proportional Representation
             Arvind Sivaramakrishnan and Chris Terry   73

Part II: Political Processes

Chapter 5   The Election Commission of India
             and General Elections
             N. Gopalaswami   101
Chapter 6   India's Democracy: Lost and Regained
             M. G. Devasahayam   118
Chapter 7   Reforming Politics and Elections
             through Legal Changes
             Jagdeep Chhokar   141
Chapter 8   Voters and Good Governance
             Trilochan Sastry   169

Part III: The Practice of Democracy

Chapter 9   Representing Women: Voting Rights
             and Women Legislators
             Wendy Singer   189
Chapter 10   Democracy as Emancipatory Politics
             R. Azhagarasan   212
Chapter 11   Gender Equity in Education among
             Muslims in India
             *Josephine Anthony and
             Sudarsan Padmanabhan*   231
Chapter 12   Organic Agriculture and
             India's Food Security
             A. V. Balasubramanian   254
Chapter 13   India's New Intellectual Property Policy:
             Passive Sovereignty
             Chamundeeswari Kuppuswamy   268
Chapter 14   The Practice of Democracy:
             Chennai Floods, 2015
             Arappor Iyakkam   289

About the Editors and Contributors   319
Index   327

Introduction

Arvind Sivaramakrishnan and Sudarsan Padmanabhan

This collection is intended to provide an articulated and nuanced understanding of India's enormous achievement in creating and sustaining its own democracy, but to do so without minimising or evading the many serious problems faced by the Indian polity and Indian society. The volume is made up of accessible contributions, respectively, by former Election Commissioners, campaigners for electoral reforms, academic analysts and others with experience of engagement with the systems and process of Indian democracy. The theme throughout is the interrelatedness of the theoretical, procedural and practical aspects of Indian democracy as well as the innate tension between them. The Constitution of India provides the theoretical validation for democratic politics and serves as a reflective and a regulative ideal; during the Constituent Assembly debates, B. R. Ambedkar often quoted the lofty democratic ideas of liberty, equality and fraternity, but he also insisted that the polity create an environment conducive to the realisation of those ideals. Institutions are crucial here, as transparent public procedures are the bulwark of democracy, a constant reminder that democracy is also 'of the people' not only 'by the people' and 'for the people'; democracy needs such pathways to popular sovereignty. Ambedkar, we must note, expressly disavows the revolutionary impulses to overthrow the state under the pretext of class conflict, which he calls the 'Dictatorship of the Proletariat'. He was aware of the cascading effect of structural violence in a deeply divided Indian society, but he also rejected civil disobedience, calling it the 'Grammar of Anarchy'.

The observance of procedures, crucially, prevents the concentration of power and the accumulation of power and authority, and maintains the separation of powers between the Executive, the Legislature, and the Judiciary. This book's material on theory reflects debates in the Constituent Assembly of India between December 1946 and November 1949. Most of these were about federalism and the unitary state, concepts which had been in constant tension during the drafting of the American Constitution between 1774 and 1787. In the Indian debates, B. R. Ambedkar, T. T. Krishnamachari and Alladi Krishnaswami Ayyar made it clear that the American Constitution was an enormous source of inspiration. Those debates continue to rage in India, inside and outside the legislature. While the American debate was mainly confined to the liberal-democratic versus republican social, political, economic and legal philosophies, Ambedkar and other members of the Constitution Drafting Committee had to make decisions in the light of a plethora of considerations, namely caste inequalities, linguistic and ethnic identities, the majority–minority divide, abject poverty, socially ingrained gender biases, the effects of colonial subjection on what might broadly be termed the Indian psyche, and, most of all, the theory, process and practice of democracy itself.

Ambedkar considered constitutional morality not as a natural sentiment but as something which had to be cultivated. His acerbic observations about the infirmity of the democratic credentials of Indian society and his summary dismissal of the Gandhian village republics evoked strong rebuttals even from his fellow Drafting Committee members, such as Alladi Krishnaswami Ayyar. The concept of fundamental rights, the basic structure of the Constitution, the role of political parties, property rights, proportional representation, tyranny of the majority, popular sovereignty, taxation, secularism, separation of powers, limitations of powers, religious freedom, minority rights, gender justice, religious education, personal law and the status of various territories were debated in great detail. As Jawaharlal Nehru said to the Constituent Assembly, there was a need to build upon the unity in the infinite variety that characterises Indian culture and society. Nehru argued that the Constitution should be solid but not rigid; it should be flexible but not piecemeal; and the process of amending the Constitution should be left to the representatives of the people. Hence, the Constitution of India is a document that encapsulates the bonds and tensions between democratic theory and practice. The crucible in which these unfurl is the democratic space in which all the arms of the government—the Executive, the Legislature and the Judiciary—act in the spirit of the Lincoln dictum 'of the people, by the people, and for the people'. Indian democracy, over a period of time, seems to have nurtured institutions such as the Election Commission, the Central Vigilance Commission, the Central Information Commission and the Comptroller and Auditor General, with the courts keeping a close eye on constitutional infringements on the part of the legislature or the executive.

Almost inevitably in democracies, strong tendencies occasionally emerge which in effect reduce democracy to electoral politics as the only authentic form of political activity. Major political parties seem to do this very often, but civil society organisations occasionally take such approaches too. Examples include the Anna Hazare movement, India Against Corruption (IAC) and others. Such an approach almost invariably degenerates into some form of appeal to popular sovereignty. Ambedkar is categorical in decrying revolutionary politics, be they violent or non-violent, or any form of civil disobedience, including *satyagraha*, which he terms unconstitutional. Ambedkar expressly disavows revolutionary impulses to overthrow the state under the pretext of class conflict, which he calls the 'Dictatorship of the Proletariat'. He was aware of the cascading effect of structural violence in a deeply divided Indian society, but he also rejected civil disobedience, calling it the 'Grammar of Anarchy'. Ambedkar refused to engage in a moral debate based on religious and political ideologies, which he held thrive on a sense of moral outrage.

So, what is, in Martin Luther King Jr's phrase, the 'Eyes on the Prize' moment for Ambedkar? It is neither the theory nor the process of democracy, neither 'by the people' nor 'of the people'. For Ambedkar, the nation would be imperilled if the Constitution ceased to be 'for the people'. When democracy remains merely political or formal without being transformed into social democracy, the terms 'of the people' and 'by the people' become ossified, or, worse still, meaningless. Then the Constitution would automatically lose its vitality, as its procedural aspects would have been contradicted by the divorce between what democracy stands for and what people expect from it—and how they themselves engage with it or fail to do so.

In respect of several procedural matters, Indian democracy is in far better condition than it was even two decades ago. Electoral registers are much more accurate, electronic voting machines have strongly curbed—if not altogether eliminated—the practice of stuffing ballot boxes with fraudulent votes, and at polling stations there is far less violence and intimidation than there used to be. During campaigns, the Election Commission's Model Code of Conduct, even though it is not legally enforceable, has ensured that candidates and parties are named for breaches of the Code; the Commission can and does impose penalties in the form of specified restrictions on publicity or the content of campaign speeches. Many of these improvements result from the attitude taken by the Commission since the early 1990s; this body has improved the electoral process at every level, and the Commission is now one of the most trusted public bodies in the country. These procedural improvements are, unsurprisingly, often put under pressure; at the time of writing, the 2019 general election campaign has seen widely publicised and apparently authoritative complaints and analyses of voter intimidation, consequent fraudulent voting and—just as seriously—the alleged removal of up to 70 million voters from the electoral rolls. The Commission has also been publicly criticised on—mainly—procedural grounds in relation to its supervision of candidates' conduct and over the way polling itself has been conducted in several states of India.

The key point here is that the Indian public have steadily grown more demanding of probity in electoral procedures; secondly, improved processes have also strengthened Indian voters' confidence in their democracy as a whole. While very few Indian politicians have openly queried election results, especially those for general elections, by the early 1990s the system faced the much more damaging prospect of public disengagement and loss of confidence even in as basic a feature of democracy as elections. This was far more dangerous than, for example, the problems of legitimacy caused by rigged elections—and sometimes rigging combined with violence—in Kashmir, where the 1987 state elections constituted one of the worst cases so far of interference by the central government.

Fortunately, in respect of elections and electoral processes many of the relevant dangers have not materialised. Other very serious problems, of course, still obtain, including what may well be engineered pre-election violence intended to divide the electorate by caste and community, the widespread and gross abuse of elected office for personal gain or for the corrupt and nepotistic or cronyistic allocation of public funds. Other problems include apparently uncontrollable election spending by parties or individuals, and cash inducements to voters, even though the effectiveness of these is not always clear. These problems severely affect life at all levels between elections, and voters know that most of the time the act of voting provides their only chance to participate in public affairs with any degree of authority. Voters also know that public institutions at all levels are often sclerotic and unresponsive.

Other issues involve the nature of campaigning, with entire castes and communities often targeted or strenuously canvassed for their vote, which if delivered en bloc can decide the result of both state and general elections. Some of this targeted campaigning has to do with the voters' sense of identity or self-identification in a very traditional society. Another key factor here is the electoral system itself; the current Simple Majority system means that small swings in voter preferences can deliver very large majorities at state and central level, and also means that even 30 per cent of the turnout vote (usually between 55 and 60 per cent of the electorate) can result in landslide victories and in what is effectively one-party control of elected assemblies.

This work, therefore, is an attempt to outline the ways Indian democracy has shaped and reshaped itself aped in the last six decades, in the light of the Indian republic's theoretical foundations, institutional mechanisms and certain kinds of political practices. The papers here broadly follow that sequence, starting with theoretical reflections, including an argument for a different electoral system itself. That argument leads into accounts by three former Chief Election Commissioners of the issues they faced, including shockingly low turnouts, and how they addressed those—with often striking success. All these chapters show, among other things, that procedural issues are inseparable from the substantive character of democracy. The demonstration of that creates a path to papers on women's right both to the vote and the right to stand, the latter of which still faces enormous obstacles in a society with some of the most severe social oppression of women in the world. Those obstacles remain formidable despite the fact that 20 states now reserve 50% of all panchayat seats for women, and women continue to be underrepresented at all levels of the system. Public responses to some of those issues are then covered, including India's approach to intellectual property rights and citizens' spontaneous collaborative efforts after natural disasters. As one contributor powerfully shows, the practice of democracy by citizens is the practice of emancipatory politics.

PART I

Democratic Principles and Their Applications in India

Chapter 1

Democracy as Antinomy
Procedural versus Substantive

Sudarsan Padmanabhan

INTRODUCTION

The theory of democracy, the process of democracy and the practice of democracy are imagined in the Indian Constitution as being in a dynamic equilibrium. A perspicacious understanding of confluence of factors is a prerequisite to appreciate democracy. The relationship between the theory, process and practice of democracy is an intricate yet trepidatious relationship. For an effective democratic practice, there is a need for theoretical and procedural understanding. But democratic practice, in itself, is concerned primarily with governance. Governance is about dealing with antinomic factors that are necessarily contingent in nature, for example, due process and popular sovereignty (Turner 2018). The tension between the idea of democracy and governance, on the one hand, and, on the other, between democratic theory and practice are viewed as categorical relations. In this chapter, both antinomic and categorical relations will be treated in considerable detail. The Indian Constitution underscores the antinomic tensions inherent in democracy as practice (Austin 2006: 313–317, 327). Hence, it proffers democracy as process as the via media. Democracy as theory traverses the rarefied realms of formal ideas. Democracy as theory leads the way by anticipating democracy as practice, in which it is validated or invalidated, mediated by democracy as process. Theorization, validation and institutionalization are not linear but asymmetrical processes. Democracy as process is vested with the onerous task of not allowing itself to be either alienated from the people or completely commandeered by the people. In the case of India, this could be seen in the context of the long and yet unresolved debate between the Panchayati Raj system and the Parliamentary constitutional system (Austin 2006: 318–319). Thus, democracy as a process involves institutionalization of the will of the people in the form of various fundamental rights and guarantees. It is also responsible for not allowing the will of the people to trample upon the fundamental rights claiming legitimacy of the majority opinion (Austin 2006: 151–154, 302). Underlying the strong emphasis on the legal due process is an understanding that democratic institutions often need to adjudicate between competing claims of validity and authenticity, which are not necessarily reducible to claims of truth or falsity. There could be many valid claims of equal authenticity, thereby making the entire democratic process asymmetrical and pluralistic. Hence, any attempt to forge a consensus based on symmetrical or idealized principles of culture, society, economy and politics is often not plausible. Thus, the process of democracy ministers to the constant effervescence stirred up by the tension between antinomic factors.

IMAGINING A CONSTITUTIONAL DEMOCRACY IN AN ANTINOMIC POLITY

The imagining of a constitutional democracy, as witnessed during the Constituent Assembly debates (1946–1949) when the Indian Constitution was being drafted under the leadership of B. R. Ambedkar, was not only a contestation of lofty ideas but also a negotiation of antinomies, namely procedural democracy and substantive freedoms, justice and happiness, freedom and justice, freedom and equality, democratic due process and popular sovereignty, and democratic leadership and citizenship, to name a few[1] (CAD 1946).

---

[1] Constituent Assembly of India Debates, Vol. 1, 17th December 1946. Minoo Masani's stellar introduction to the resolution on the aims and objectives of the

According to Stephen Turner, these antinomies are polar opposites and contingent facts which makes confronting them unavoidable in the realm of the political. Turner refers to Michael Oakeshott's remark, 'Democracy is not merely ambiguous but deeply ambiguous—the home of its own antinomic interpretations' (Turner 2015). Other forms of non-antinomic or categorical distinctions, for example, theory and practice, political ideals and governance, do not exhibit the binding and tension of the antinomic because their dissonance is resolvable in the theoretical or practical realms, as Plato and Aristotle attempted to do in *The Republic* and *Nicomachean Ethics*, respectively (Jowett 1892; Aristotle 1893). According to Cynthia Farrar, both in Plato and Aristotle, the realm of politics is neatly elided by a flight of imagination into the realm of theory, especially with reference to the problematic relationship between justice and happiness, and virtue and happiness, in a polis or state (Farrar 1992: 33–34). Many a time, attempts to resolve antinomic relationships might have resulted in revolutionary events where the democratic will of the demos or res publica is manifested in an untrammelled manner. Imagine, for example, a Communist revolution where the socio-economic classes were dissolved. Whereas Plato and Aristotle attempted to resolve this battle in the realm of ideas and political praxis, the American and the French revolutions erupted as republican movements, and the Bolshevik and the Chinese Communist revolutions were, at least in theory, the result of a proletarian uprising. In Machiavelli, it sneaks a peek through civic republicanism (Machiavelli 1882: 37–39). The antinomic nature of politics, per se, has not been transcended. The polar opposite and contingent nature of the antinomic categories continues to remain dormant but rears its head intermittently even in the most liberal of democracies.

Presciently, B. R. Ambedkar does acknowledge such revolutionary possibilities and the very real danger of the abrogation of the Indian Constitution. During the Constituent Assembly debates, Ambedkar discerned a tension between 'of the people, by the people, and for

---

Constitution succinctly encapsulates all the important points mentioned earlier. Dr Ambedkar supports the resolution of Dr Jayakar to wait for Muslim League's participation contrary to the popular mood. He sees Constitutional Drafting process as a unifying endeavour.

the people' while various provisions of the Indian Constitution were being debated. To paraphrase Ambedkar, if the substantive freedoms enshrined in the Indian Constitution were to prove to be too elusive to be realized, that is, if the Executive, the Legislature and the Judiciary fail to translate the formal guarantees of rights enshrined in the Indian Constitution into substantive freedoms, then the term government 'by the people' and 'of the people' would become untenable. Ambedkar warned that people would rather want a government 'for the people' even imperilling the government 'of and by the people'[2] (CAD 1946e–1949). While Ambedkar recognized the antinomic nature of the process of governance, he emphasized the importance of legal due process to negotiate vexatious issues. Gandhi, contrary to generally held belief, did not envisage a concomitant relationship between ethics and politics. Gandhi's claim was a strong normative claim that emerged out of an understanding of the antinomic nature of governance. It is because of such an understanding that Gandhi unflinchingly emphasized the imperative need to categorically pair ethics and politics (Raghawan: 7). It was an ought that was necessitated by Gandhi's understanding of the philosophy of governance as necessarily an adjudication between antinomic categories. Hence, the non-violent means (ahimsa) increasingly became more important than the truth (satya), the end. In this context, Gandhi's earlier claim identifying Truth and God morphs into an identification of Love and God.

Gandhi's claim that duty precedes rights is anathemic to the modern liberal conception of a vibrant and fair political system that emphasizes the paramountcy of individual rights. As a humanist, Gandhi does not dichotomize duties and rights. If he were to choose between duties and rights, he would choose the former[3] (Dalton 1998; Lindley 2006). As a humanist and a moral cosmopolitan, Gandhi would subsume the

---

[2] The entire proceedings of the Constituent Assembly debates from December 1946 to January 1950 is available on the Rajya Sabha website, the Upper House of the Parliament of India. Rajya Sabha is known as the Council of States. Ambedkar's concluding speech directly deals with the importance of the Constitution to be 'for the people' (Vol. XI, 25 Nov 1949).

[3] Dennis Dalton delivered this lecture at the International Seminar on Gandhi and the Twenty First Century (30 January–4 February 1998) at New Delhi and Wardha.

concept of rights under the concept of duties towards not only other human beings but other beings in general. Also, Gandhi's conception of non-injury or non-violence was not only anthropocentric but also against even imagining any harm to any being, living or non-living.[4] So Gandhi, while appreciative of the advantages of a democratic Constitution, was acutely aware of the tension between variegated claimants to individual and group rights, especially in a society which had innumerable schisms due to a long history of hierocratic social structures. Gandhi, who many consider an anarchist, interestingly, did not consider the caste system an antinomic institution in polar opposition with any social or religious system.[5] Rather, Gandhi understood the caste system as a categorial construction that hypostatized into a categorical structure. And hence the contradiction between caste or religion or morality or law or economy was due to rigidification of structures of power and domination. It is to be emphasized here that Gandhi's philosophical, moral and political understanding of the antinomic tension that pervades democracy and his views on the evolution of the caste system should not be viewed in a linear trajectory. What is called the *jati* or caste and *varna* or class in the Indian social history are not interchangeable. Gandhi initially understood the caste system as a deterioration of the class system (Gandhi 1947: 15–18). The class system at least had vertical mobility, theoretically. As Frances Stewart argues, vertical inequality is different from horizontal inequality which is the group-based inequality, which in the Indian case is the caste system that dehumanizes a person based on being born in a particular caste group (Stewart 2001). Gandhi always felt that a system based on a visceral and atavistic fear or revulsion of socialization and fraternization, with ostracized castes, is to be addressed not only politically but at multiple levels. So he constructed parallel social experiments in terms of various farms or ashrams where people lived together, thereby demonstrating that caste and religious injunctions as mere categories to be disbanded. Such experiments were part of Gandhi's demonstration in socio-religious

---

[4] Available at http://www.mkgandhi.org/nonviolence/phil1.htm (accessed on 7 March 2019).

[5] Available at http://www.mkgandhi.org/journalist/ambedkar.htm (accessed on 7 March 2019).

harmony in South Africa and later India[6] (Gandhi 1955, 1962, 2009; Vivekanandan 2002). Gandhi's understanding of the differentiation between what Kwasi Wiredu calls cultural particulars and universals is also very important for his moral and cultural outlook (Wiredu 1996: 174). For Gandhi, knowledge was only possible as a relatively certain truth (Erikson 1969: 241). This is not to say that his views were always incontrovertible or well-formulated. The Gandhian philosophy of ahimsa and satyagraha was based on an epistemological understanding that knowledge has innumerable facets.[7] So it would be facetious to reduce knowledge to only known categories. Negotiation of different facets of knowledge becomes a part of the Gandhian method, therefore, by extension, to an understanding of truth as well. The famous Jaina parable of five blind men and an elephant illustrates the uncertainty or the probabilistic nature of knowledge. So also, in a manner similar to Buddhism, the domain of ethics or conduct becomes very important. Thus, ahimsa and satya assume greater significance. Satya for Gandhi is not only about speaking the truth but also to be truthful to oneself. In Habermasian parlance, there is a coherence between intentions and declaration of intentions (Habermas 1999: 320). More often than not, truth does not only set one free but also enchains, in an embrace of malevolence (Erikson: 234–251). The rancour of certitude of satya is soothed by the gentleness of ahimsa. This also seems to true of both Mahavira and the Buddha.

As Michael Oakeshott, Chantal Mouffe and Stephen Turner emphasize, antinomical relations between competing considerations characterize democracy (Mouffe 2000; Turner 2015). Isaiah Berlin, the doyen of liberal theory, emphasized the concept of negative liberty, in which liberty is characterized as non-interference. Berlin also described republicanism as non-domination whereby a citizen's political rights are guaranteed (Berlin 1958). In a republican conception, individual rights are not inviolable if public order or welfare is under threat. Liberalism utilizes the language of rights to resolve antinomic tensions between

---

[6] Available at http://www.mkgandhi.org/humantouch.htm (accessed on 7 March 2019).

[7] Available at http://www.mkgandhi.org/g_relevance/chap28.htm (accessed on 7 March 2019).

contingent facts. This is done by earmarking territories as private and public spheres. Liberalism devises a system of rights and institutions to govern the public sphere. Such a separation of spheres does not necessarily address or redress antinomic tensions. This separation also creates a false dichotomy between duties and rights, misconstrued as a contestation in the realm of ideas. While Gandhi was very conscious of the due process, he was also acutely aware of its lacunae. Very seldom does due process resolve antinomic tensions. But due process is an institutionalized mechanism to ensure fair administration of laws. In a brilliant and yet laconic reply, as he is arraigned in court, Gandhi points out the discrepancy between fair administration of laws, on the one hand, and justice, on the other. Justice has to be the foundation of law[8] (Gandhi 1962, 2009). Law could merely be procedural, whereas the justice is not only procedural but also substantive hence mindful of the notion of good. The former is based on an understanding of rules, regulations and norms while the latter examines the underlying process of norm formation. The entire liberal discourse hovers around individual rights and due process, whose relationship is ironically antinomical. On the other hand, consequentialist theories such as utilitarianism and socialism, while inimical to one another, attempt to invert the liberal model by emphasizing a more substantive notion of social good (Sen 1983: 131–132). When the antinomic relations exist between the individual and the social, an attempt to emphasize one over the other does not resolve the antinomic contingency. These contingencies cannot be resolved at the realm of ideas (Turner 2015). Hence, Gandhi never constructed grand theories. In his early writings, Gandhi did try to theorize and rationalize India's lattice-like social stratification, the caste system, but without much success. He tried to understand it in terms of social practices and class relationships (Gandhi 1955). But the caste system was an abominable aberration, yet one of *longue dureé*. He then changed his approach to begin his exercise afresh from a humanistic perspective. Earlier, the question was to see whether there was any sort of justification or, intriguingly, a Platoesque ideal state behind the *jati* or *varna* system. Quickly, Gandhi realized that there could be no

---

[8] Refer to two important cases involving Gandhi: (a) Was it Contempt of the Court? (b) The Great Trial.

ethical justification in history or any legal justification in contemporary or modern practice and the *jati* was simply a system of social and political domination based on endogamous relationships and elaborately orchestrated rituals. Gandhi also realized that if he were to dismantle the millennia old and resilient structure of caste system, emphasis on due process or class revolution would not suffice. Since he was opposed to any violent insurrection, an armed revolution inspired by communism was clearly not in his thoughts. He was also not very impressed by the demands of the members of the Indian National Congress for a Constituent Assembly to envision a Constitution for the Indians, by the Indians and of the Indians (Austin 2006: 1). Constitution, whose value he understood, could only be a formal scaffolding. Nehru and many other Congress leaders were unflinching in their demands for the Constituent Assembly to devise the Constitution of India in a consultative and consensual manner among the representatives of various socio-economic, cultural and religious segments of the Indian population (Austin 2006: 1). Ambedkar was also initially against the Constituent Assembly. But Ambedkar, who had been involved in the discussions with Simon Commission, London Round Table Conferences, Lothian Commission and, later, the Constituent Assembly, was able to marshal the Drafting Committee to design an Indian Constitution around the central issues of social justice and social development (Austin 2006: 3). Ambedkar, in spite of being a trenchant critic of Gandhi and Congress, ensured a delicate balance between due process and popular sovereignty. He also inserted a stern warning against unconstitutional defiance of the political process in the name of moral outrage. Thus, he was against civil disobedience, a veiled attack on the model of Gandhian Satyagraha which could be abused for trivial matters, and the communist propensity for struggles to overthrow the state in the name of revolution with scant respect for due process[9] (CAD 1949).

Neither constitutional democracy nor revolutionary Marxism genuinely engaged with antinomic factors inherent to a grassroots model of village republic which was true *swaraj* for Gandhi. Hence,

---

[9] Dr Ambedkar's great speech on 25 November 1949 to conclude the CA session. Available at http://164.100.47.132/lssnew/cadebatefiles/C25111949.html (accessed on 7 March 2019).

there was a need for a more hermeneutical, humanistic, egalitarian, ecumenical and ethical understanding of the social, political, economic and cultural practices of a milieu. This was Gandhi's prescription (Austin 2006: 26–33; Gandhi 1955). Since he understood that the root cause of antinomical vestiges in all conflicts were contingent, he never offered universal solutions. Rather his unconditional emphasis on *satya* and ahimsa anticipates the conflictual and antinomic nature of politics. The contingency of facts that are in antinomic relationship are not considered absolute by Gandhi. In relation to *satya* and ahimsa, all other categories are contingent for Gandhi (Erikson: 241–242). Hence, Oakeshott's claim about the nature of democracy as inherently antinomic is not inimical to the Gandhian thought. Initially, Gandhi attempts to resolve the differences among people created by language, religion, culture and politics not merely through a process of categorical understanding but also through a process of dialogue. But the categories themselves created more impediments to understanding others. And hence, Gandhi, a la Buddha, did not attempt to resolve logical, metaphysical and philosophical conflicts. He addressed human suffering that was abounding due to a lack of virtuous living among the citizens. The Gandhian categories, namely social, political, economic and spiritual, had both a hermeneutical and a causal relationship (Erikson: 260–268).

AN ANCIENT TRYST BETWEEN POLITICS AND JUSTICE: ATHENS AND ROME

Democracy, as a concept, evokes a feeling of participatory political process, a stable polis, emphasis on legal due process, and a deliberative and equitable decision-making model of politics. But an understanding of democracy at the ground level is that of an arena of intense contestation of not only ideas but also conflictual power relationships between various groups jostling for political office. For many of these groups, democratic due process is only a scaffolding to scale new heights of political power and pelf or a necessary protection against abuse of power by one's opponents. So, Glaucon's and Adeimantus' question to Socrates in Plato's *Republic* continues to ring uncomfortably true to any thinker who attempts to deduce a concomitant relation between democracy and justice or for that matter any ideal form of polity and justice (Jowett 1892: 185–192). The consummation of the union is possible only metaphysically or at best formally. Politics and justice seem to have an asymptotic relationship. This is not a question that is unique to the Greeks or the Romans who were much less philosophical about power politics. For the Romans, politics was all about power notwithstanding what many writers on the history of Rome argue about the relation between the fall of Rome and the moral decay of the Romans (Goldsworthy 2009: 16). When many of the institutions of the Roman republic that were invented to prevent anarchy or tyranny failed at one point or another, it was either due to the moral depravity of the rulers or the moral turpitude of the populace. The reason for the fall of the Empire was more due to its failings as an imperium than as a Republic (Gibbon 1906: 89–93). Furthermore, a claim to concomitance between various concepts is a futile attempt to envision politics into a causal science. The only way this has been achieved is to paraphrase the famous Upanishadic negative claim *neti, neti* (not this, not this). From the ancient Greek and Roman scholars to the Medieval and Modern thinkers, and not to mention contemporary theorists, none seem to have discovered a causal connection to the best form of government and justice or happiness. Plato was the progenitor of this enterprise and it was a grandiose attempt that he made in the *Republic* (Jowett 1892: 197). As mentioned earlier, his failures in politics are less spectacular than the successes in the realm of political theory.[10] Hence, in the introductory chapters of *Nicomachean Ethics*, Aristotle raises the question whether the idea of justice is worthier than justice itself (Aristotle 1893: 16–18). The disciple questions his master's methodology rather than his assumptions or conclusions about justice and politics. Aristotle desists from applying a formal logical method that merely tests the validity of Plato's assumptions and conclusions, even some very uncomfortable ones with respect to the Athenian democracy, which was the pride of the Athenians. The virtue of the citizenry assumes more importance for Aristotle (1885: 109). The eternal tussle between the political process and realization of a just state is resolved only in Plato's Ideas or Forms, as the state in idea. Plato seems to emphasize the process more and

---

[10] Before Plato, the Athenians were justly proud of their democratic processes and freedoms though the Spartans had a Constitution much earlier.

hence ends up abstracting justice from the polis. Justice of the polis, which Plato calls the excellence of the soul, also animates Aristotelian ethics and politics (Plato 1892: 186). Plato, instead of beginning with individual notions of justice, which are numerous, contextual and based on individual opinions rather than attributes, changes the order and begins with an idea of a good polis (Plato 1892: 196–197). Then he derives step by step, applying deductive inference, the attributes of a good political person from the idea of a good polis. Hence, in Plato's *Republic* there is no place for a normal person who is considered less informed about Kallipolis, the good city.

Aristotle, while appreciating Plato's vexatious problem, refrains from deducing the particular from the universal, in this case, a good citizen from a good polis. Rather he begins from taxonomy of the particular notions of good and what makes an individual virtuous in character. Aristotle was of the view that very few people would pursue an idea for itself or for that matter virtue for itself. On the other hand, virtue cannot be the final good. It needs to represent something in practice or denote something, the good which one strives to achieve (Aristotle 1893: 15). For Aristotle, virtue denotes a relative mean between two extremes. He also avoids the pure formal understanding by forswearing virtue as a mathematical mean. As a relative mean, virtue is firmly contextualized. But Aristotle also consistently foregrounds *eudaimonia* that is beyond a particular understanding of the mean. *Eudaimonia* is the universal or the state of blessedness or happiness everyone desires but attained through a perfection of a lifelong pursuit of virtuous activity, which is a fine balance between the two extremes of moral excess and deficiency (Aristotle 1893: 30). There is a causal relationship between the individual and the polis but not in an instrumental sense. The causal connection is natural from which it derives its formal character, a la Plato. In *Politics*, Aristotle addresses the methodological issues while explaining why political systems are good or bad (Aristotle 1885: 112). The regulative element is the Constitution, the formal cause. The emanation of a Constitution is an interplay of the four causes, namely, the material cause, formal cause, efficient cause and the final cause (Miller 2012). However much Aristotle wants to relate the individual good and the good of the polis and analogously create a connection between the individual virtue as a good and the good of the polis as a greater good, *eudaimonia* exists on a plane on its own. It is the appeal to this *eudaimonia* that justifies the greater good or the good of the polis (Aristotle 1885: 239; Lane 2014). *Eudaimonia* is also an idea because Aristotle does not establish a concomitant connection between virtuous life and *eudaimonia*. Even if it does exist, there is a normative relationship between virtuous character of an individual and *eudaimonia* at the individual level. Aristotle's claim that there is a connection between the individual and the social understanding of *eudaimonia* is not clearly established. The concomitance is not to be established in Aristotle's ethics as well. An appeal to politics or the master form of all arts or the art that governs the greater good could either be the premise or the conclusion of the categorical syllogism which validates the whole enterprise of virtue ethics if Aristotle followed Plato's model. But Aristotle, as a naturalist, argues that the propensity of the human species to be a rational, political and social animal is a natural attribute. This is more clearly established in his *Politics* when he discusses both successful and unsuccessful constitutions.[11] Aristotle cleverly separates ethics and politics learning from Plato's predicament brilliantly illustrated through the ring of Gyges allegory (Plato 1892: 460).

Plato's *Republic* is a state where the very existence and flourishing of the state is linked with justice. The state where justice is enshrined would be an ideal state. Such a state would also be a happy state by virtue of being a just state where the citizens act according to their understanding of what constitutes justice. There is a clear tension between the particular conception of justice and a general conception of justice (Plato 1892: 25–26). Does Plato think that an understanding of justice as a formal–universal concept could surmount the diversions of a more particular conception of justice? Plato's ideal state is formal but also has a substantive basis. Plato incorporates the positive features of various political systems into his polis. In the storied understanding of the Athenian democracy and the Roman republic, one can find the

---

[11] *The Nicomachean Ethics* is a preparation for the individual to become a virtuous person who could then embark on the path to transform the polis into a virtuous entity. *Politics* is the analysis of the science of polity, what makes a polis virtuous and how to make it virtuous. The answer lies in the formal cause, the Constitution (accessed 7 March 2019).

fear of one, the spectre of the tyrant or dictator hovering above. In the Parmenidian metaphysics, the one is real (Plato 1892: 505). Ironically, one can find an interesting relationship between the Greek metaphysics and politics, both antagonistic and synthetic. Even in Plato, the many seems to be unreal and there is a search for the real one, in this case, the philosopher-king, a perfect anti-thesis of a tyrant. The philosopher is the seeker of the one whereas the king is the seeker of the many. The former seeks the World of Forms/Ideas whereas the latter seeks the World of objects, which represent the realms of knowledge and opinion, respectively. Plato brings them together by constructing a formal-ideal world of *politeia*. The antinomic relationship between the pairs, the one and the many, the philosopher and the king, Forms and objects, and knowledge and opinion seem to fascinate Plato but also defy categorization. The philosopher of the Parmenedian ilk seeks the one whereas the politicians are comfortable among the multitude (Plato 1892: 442). Can justice be sought among the many rather than the one? Could logocentrism be thus a valiant but a foredoomed attempt to transcend antinomic relations? Could justice be an evolute of the particular and scattered understanding of the many or is it the fundamental structure of the one from which the particular understanding of justice evolves?

Aristotle addresses the question slightly differently from Plato. Plato's *politeia* is a state in an idea (Plato 1892: 197). In the case of Aristotle, a polis that promotes the flourishing of virtuous individuals exemplifies the best aspects of a polis. But most people though capable of virtuous life, due to various factors, face difficulties. Akin to Plato's *Republic*, Aristotle has to strike a balance between a life of honour and a life of contemplation. For Plato, the motivation or rationale comes from understanding how justice holds the polis together and hence the particular understanding of justice ought to partake in the universal understanding of justice. The universal idea of justice is based on an idea of good. The dialectic examines various levels of knowledge for correspondence with the understanding of good. So knowledge is a constant search for the good and anything else is not knowledge. Aristotle's understanding of good is oriented not towards the ultimate knowledge or idea but towards untangling the web of relations that pervade the human life. So both Plato's and Aristotle's metaphysics is a constant search for the summum bonum of life, to strive for stability in a world of flux. Plato seeks certainty and hence moves higher and higher in abstraction from the world of opinion to the world of knowledge and correspondingly the world of things to the world of ideas/forms. Hence, one could call Plato's schema of knowledge pyramidal with the knowledge of good at the pinnacle. This is a vertical model. Aristotle, on the other hand, does agree with Plato on the need for justice and a polis that is based on an understanding of the good. He also accepts that particular notion of good needs to be linked to a larger notion of good. Hence, the citizens of a polis should strive to be virtuous in pursuit of good. This particular understanding of good ought to be connected to the good of the polis, which is *eudaimonia*, the human flourishing. But Aristotle does not abstract good or justice from everyday life experience. Hence, justice and good are not only mere abstract theoretical constructs but also substantive praxis, and the path to achieve good and justice varies for Plato and Aristotle. In the context of the Indian Constitution, conception of both good and justice has to be interweaved and mediated through procedural democracy. The role of jurisprudence in a democracy is to negotiate the tension between good and justice, and maintain a reflective equilibrium.

In the Indian context, the concept of *purusharthas* corresponds to virtue ethics. *Purusharthas* comprise dharma, *artha*, *kama* and *moksha*. In some schools, *moksha* is not recognized. Many schools of Indian thought accept *purusharthas* as the end-aims of life. Gandhi and many other freedom fighters used traditional literature and texts such as the Ramayana, the Mahabharata and the Gita to prepare the ground for a shared moral imaginary that would facilitate a transition from a colonized nation to an independent nation in all respects, social, political, economic and cultural. In contrast, Ambedkar analysed every sinew of the very same Indian texts and exposed the contradiction between philosophical idealism and social practice. Hence, he advocated an entirely new paradigm of social mores based on constitutional morality. Gandhi worried that by completely abandoning the language of the masses a vast swathe of rural population would be left behind in the quest for social and political transformation of India. For Gandhi, reinterpretation of the important texts that have interpenetrated the cultural imaginary of Indians was a necessary and unavoidable step towards construction of a humanist moral discourse to address social discrimination, be it caste, gender, religion, region or language.

DEMOCRACY: THE PROBLEM OR SOLUTION?

Is democracy beset by the problem of irresolvable conflicts due to ideological entrenchments? Such ideological entrenchments could wreak havoc with the Constitutional process as well as institutionalization of rights and duties in a democracy. While the process of designing a Constitution involves negotiation and contestation of various ideas and ideologies, it is always guided by the context which enframes the process. To put it laconically, one of the main considerations of a democratic constitutional process is a contestation between two conceptions of liberty, negative and positive. A Constitution broadly defines the contours of what should be justiciable and what should not be (CAD 1946–1949). While the aforementioned definition seems to be narrow, the connotations reverberate at multiple registers. A Constitution is also the harbinger of judicial, administrative, constitutional and legislative legal processes and institutions. The challenge of any Constitution is to be 'of the people, by the people, and for the people'[12] (Lincoln 1863). Abraham Lincoln expertly compounded the seemingly obvious constitutive principles of democracy in his immortal words. But, while those pithy words have never ceased to enrapture millions of people across the planet, it belies the inherent antinomic tension between the 'of, by and for' the people. In addition, there is further tension between the form and substance of each of those, respectively. Hence, a Constitution, neither by definition nor by design, could ever be likened to the holy scriptures of various religions. Even within religions, the interpretation of the sacred word is varied. But, finally, the authority of the word is supreme, inviolable. This inviolability clause is mostly ensured by a threat of force. A Constitution, in contrast, opens up all its assumptions to contestations and negotiations. Thus, one could argue

---

[12] Lincoln's very succinct Gettysburg Address in 1863 carried the famous words 'of the people, by the people, for the people'. Available at http://myloc.gov/Exhibitions/gettysburgaddress/Pages/default.aspx (accessed on 7 March 2019).

that the Constitution has a being and it dwells in its own language that it creates while it is being constructed, simultaneously. A new language with a new constitutional vocabulary for the contestation and negotiation of 'of the people, by the people and for the people' is imagined. With this new language, in which a Constitution is imagined, would also emerge new ethos or mores. This language, to paraphrase Sheldon Pollock artfully, is 'the language of the Gods in the world of men' (Pollock 2009). This language shapes the idea of the Constitution and, in turn, it is also shaped by the Constitution. This language is an ideal language, a formal language, hence cosmopolitan in scope. But the cosmos, in this context, is miniscule. The world of *verna* is the vast and wide world. So the term 'for the people' is more appropriate since the world of *verna* is represented only notionally in 'by the people' and 'of the people'. It is for this reason that popular sovereignty which should theoretically include 'of the people, by the people and for the people' subsumes the other two under 'for the people'. It is because of this that the due process clause becomes all the more important and always under pressure from the advocates of popular sovereignty. So, the most troubling question is whether a formal Constitution could ever substantively represent the vast majority. Finding a convincing answer to this question is pivotal to any democratic system. Many a titanic struggle between the legal due process and will of the people has been fought on these sliding tectonic plates. The history of these struggles dates back several centuries to the Greeks and Romans in the West and various cultures in the Indian subcontinent, for example, the Gana Sanghas and village republics. In India, the situation is extremely complex due to the institutionalization of hierocracy not only in the political sphere but also in the social realm. While most of the committees set up for debating various constitutional provisions had to deal with the issue of the separation of the State and the Church and the issue of representation in the form of a republican or democratic political system. India had to deal with unimaginably complex circumstances, most of them not of her own making (Austin 2006: 308). So, while the process of drafting a Constitution is difficult under ordinary circumstances, the difficulty increases manifold if there is an interpellation of various vexatious issues such as religious, economic, linguistic, social and cultural differences (Guha 2007: 103–110). A Constitution produced under such trying circumstances ought to minister to the triad of cognition, affection and conation, corresponding respectively to, thinking, feeling and willing of the people to paraphrase Immanuel Kant (Johnson and Cureton 2016). The process of willing is a deliberate and deliberative process at once. But the feeling component is what makes the Constitution publicly owned, that is, for the people. The Constitution of a country has to be an idea that is appreciated by the people and with which they identify because of which they are ready to follow consciously. This is once again a reflection of the Lincolnian dictum 'of the people, by the people, and for the people' in a more formal and philosophical language. A meta-political or meta-ethical understanding of the constitutional process is very essential. Here, the role of jurisprudence is paramount in guiding constitutional debates and situating the context of such debates. The Lincolnian dictum of democracy obligates the Legislature, the Executive and the Judiciary to foster a deliberative democracy however difficult it turns out to be. The aforementioned triad is a pithy expression of the requisite democratic thought process and ideas that would guide the polity, a feeling of democratization of social, political and economic processes that ought to pervade the popular imaginary, and the moral imperative to act according to the letter and spirit of the Constitution. So, in this sense, the Indian Constitution is a delicate balancing act and an audacious attempt all at once. The ground for a democratic polity in India was being prepared at multiple levels and on multiple fronts (Austin 2006: 1–2, 9–11).

Any Constitution is an attempt to achieve a reflective equilibrium between a general idea of the welfare or public good and needs of the people, on the one hand, and the ways and means of achieving them, on the other. So, in many ways, the formal guiding principles are always balanced with the substantive considerations. The substantive considerations could be social, economic, political, cultural and religious. One could discern an antinomic relationship between the formal procedural understanding and the substantive understanding based on a conception of good. Turner argues that the antinomic relation between liberalism and democracy, and the rule of law and policy act as a countervailing force to ideological liberalism, on the one hand, and ideology as such, on the other (Turner 2015). Ironically, such an understanding was known to the ancients in both formal and substantive sense. But the ideological juggernaut in the form of a liberal democracy or a modern republican polity that staked a claim to universality was not available to them. The separation of powers between various arms of the government, that is, the Executive, the Judiciary and the Legislature, is also a part of the process of mediation and channelization of the formal and substantive aspects of the Constitution. Lincoln's words seem to defy any form of codification which illustrates their interpenetrative nature. While 'of the people' and 'by the people' could denote both the Executive and the Legislature, generally, the Judiciary has the onerous responsibility of holding both the Executive and the Legislature accountable to the third part of Lincoln's dictum, 'for the people'.

DEMOCRACY: WHAT IT OUGHT AND OUGHT NOT TO BE

When the Constitution of India was being debated from the 1930s there were many ideological and theoretical claimants in moral, social, political, economic, religious and cultural spheres. But, increasingly, under the rubric of Gandhian thought, the left, the right and the centrists formed a panoramic view. Under the Gandhian umbrella, the social and religious conservatives, Marxists, liberals, republicans, spiritualists, atheists, Muslims, Christians, Jews, Buddhists, Jains, Sikhs and the depressed classes formed an amorphous but united front. When the idea of India was being chiselled into the Indian Constitution, the common concerns of all ordinary Indians were represented and discussed threadbare. The representation had its own politics, namely the politics of ideas and the politics of presence (Phillips 2000). When the question of individual rights, and the republican ideals of liberty, equality and fraternity were discussed, there was a general consensus (Austin 2006: 187–188). The major points of contention were with respect to the nature of the polity, the system of governance, universal suffrage, economy, protection to minorities, cultural rights, personal laws, the powers of the Executive, the Legislature and the Judiciary, and separation of powers (Austin 2006: 50–52). From the beginning, there was palpable tension between the advocates of stronger emphasis on due process and the will of the people. The objective of the Constitution was also equitable socio-economic development and preserving the political unity of India while also being cognizant of its cultural diversity (Austin 2006: XVII).

The Marxist critiques of Indian society and institutions are based on an assiduous historical reconstruction of various stages of the interplay between the capital and the labour. The class structure and its historical manifestation in India are the central themes in the Marxist analysis. But such an analysis, honed into an incisive critique of social, political, economic and cultural institutions, does not engage with the experience of the marginalized and hence neglects the most pernicious of institutions, the caste. To be fair, the Marxist critique views caste as an integral part of the socio-economic vector. This is where the essentialization of class as a grand narrative is oblivious to the Dalit experience (Nagaraj 2012). This is only a mild critique since the voice of the hitherto deprived classes could be heard but through the voice of the proletariat. But, does the Dalit voice speak for itself when it is subsumed under the category of class or does it become an idea sans presence? Many non-Congress leaders representing the backward and depressed classes were also waging struggles simultaneously, sometimes aligning with the British and opposing Congress Party or demanding more rights and representation. Ambedkar was the most famous of such leaders. There were innumerable people who were spearheading various struggles in the vernacular realm. Periyar E. V. Ramasamy Naicker was a strong proponent of Dravidastan. Muhammad Ali Jinnah, who was earlier a staunch Congressman, later turned against Congress to become the leader of the Muslims who wanted a separate Islamic Republic (More 2008: 21). The great Tamil poet Subramanya Bharathi was a nationalist who was a strong voice for women's liberation and anti-caste movements. Bharathi was initially a Tilak loyalist impatient with the Club culture of Congress. But later captivated by the Gandhian philosophy of *satya* and ahimsa he supported Congress. In every province, as Gandhi was constructing a pan-India movement, many of his loyal disciples were taking his social construction programmes to the rural, poor and under-nourished localities (Chokkalingam 2007).

As the head of the Constitution Drafting Committee, Ambedkar was able to utilize his deep theoretical and practical understanding of the alienating, exploitative and dehumanizing institution of the caste system to include safeguards to prevent discrimination against the deprived classes, down trodden, women, religious minorities and other marginalized groups (Austin 2006: 18–20). Ambedkar, unlike Nehru whose knowledge of India was mostly from the Western sources, had a deep knowledge of the Indian texts. Hence, even though his arguments in favour of modernizing economy, society, culture, politics and governance were influenced by his exposure to the prevalent models of republican and democratic systems of government, he was able to reconfigure various provisions in the Indian Constitution that would enable the people of India to aspire towards a secular, progressive, democratic republic (Austin 2006: 256–263). The Constitution of India is an imagining, a projection and an idea. Being an idea, it is also an abstraction, albeit from a concrete and contingent socio-historical lifeworld of India. In this process, positive and negative aspects of various institutions were evaluated. Those institutions and practices that are discriminatory violate the fundamental rights of the people and were jettisoned from the Constitution (Basu 2013: 90–95). Other socially empowering measures ensuring social justice through enabling mechanisms such as reservation for the deprived classes, universal suffrage, women's right to hereditary property, economic welfare, minority rights and cultural rights were institutionalized in the constitutional provisions. Ambedkar, while institutionalizing individual liberties, also institutionalized social responsibilities. Legal due process and democratic political representation have been amalgamated into the Indian Constitution. But it is much more substantive, that is, more comprehensive, to use the Rawlsian terminology, since unlike the American or the French political systems, the group rights, the rights of hitherto marginalized groups, were addressed with specific provisions (Austin 2006: 50). While the Indian Constitution has a formal character, which makes it conceptually accessible to all, in theory, the institutionalization of abstract ideas of justice, freedom, equality and happiness happens through the policy interventions of the executive, the legislative agenda of the upper house and the lower house of the Parliament, and the interpretive legal powers of the judiciary as the final arbiters of the law.

The relation between the formal Constitution and the political process that negotiates the ways and means of realizing the ideals enshrined in the Constitution is a hermeneutical relationship. But it could also be a conflictual relationship. As the political process yields more and more to the will of the people, that is, popular sovereignty, then it puts a tremendous strain on the sinews of the Constitution. Popular sovereignty gains momentum only as a demand for an immediate realization of the needs and desires of the people. Whatever social, political or economic measures needed in the eyes of the people immediately, that is, in the short term, could end up hampering the realization of long-term objectives, that is, the greater good (Austin 2006: 41–43). This is not to relegate the will of the people as a lesser requirement of a democratic or republican form of government. The Constitution provides sufficient leeway to recalibrate, strengthen or better the democratic process through protection of fundamental rights, good governance, enactment of better laws, devising beneficial policies and ensuring social justice. Hence, the public sentiment or will should be tempered with the public reason and public ethics (Wenar 2013). Here, the question of multiple public spheres crops up. Thus far, we have discussed the liberal-democratic and republican models of politics, where in the former individual rights are paramount, and in the latter, the will of the people, *la volonté generale*, to cite Rousseau (Rousseau 1923: 109–110). While in the Indian Constitution, the Constitution Drafting Committee headed by Ambedkar had special protections and enabling conditions for the least advantaged such as the Dalits, tribals, women, minorities, socially and economically backward groups, yet, traditionally discriminated groups seem to be invisible in the public sphere. To participate in the public sphere, to partake in the communicative activity, one needs linguistic and communicative competence to be a part of a communication community (Habermas 1987: 81–82). To a certain extent, in the current epoch, the rise of social media has created a more accessible and inclusive communication network which was inaccessible to hitherto marginalized groups. While Rawls disabuses excessive emphasis on the due process to the exclusion of realization of social good, there is a genuine reluctance to allow the executive or the legislature to intervene substantively to create an egalitarian social sphere lest individual rights are infringed upon. Here, political representation is also routed through democratic and legal due process with a strong emphasis on people expressing their preferences by voting for their choice of representatives. In the republican system of politics, the emphasis is not on the individual preferences but on a more robust or substantive understanding of what is public. For example, the concept of secularism evokes a strong moral and political reaction in France, where it is a defining value of the French republic (Padmanabhan 2013: 66–70). Hence, any perceived infringement of secularism touches an emotional chord of what constitutes the Frenchness, which is a part of the broader concept of the French nation. It is coeval with the birth of the French nation. In the French scenario, secularism is also connected with another aspect of the republican politics, which is the emphasis on direct democracy. The revolutionary impulse is triggered if the will of the people is not respected by the government.

CONCLUSION

The eminent Indian jurist Fali Nariman, recently in an interview, while discussing the archaic sedition laws of India, emphasized the need for constitutional morality. He also asserted that all the fundamental rights should be traced only to the Indian Constitution and not to any other institution. To paraphrase Nariman, the freedoms are not the gift of law to be taken away by law. The Founding Fathers of the American Constitution citing John Locke disabused any attempt to controvert the inviolability of freedom to pursue life, liberty, happiness and property. A sitting justice of the Supreme Court of India, Justice Bhagwati, during the enforcement of the infamous Maintenance of Internal Security Act (MISA), usually known only as the Emergency (1975–1977), waxed eloquent about individual liberty only to contrast it with the letter of the law while knowing fully well that his judgement contradicted the spirit of the law.[13] But Justice Bhagwati's judgement is a classic case of what Ronald Dworkin would call the lack of integrity in law (Dworkin 1986: 1–3). The first portion of Justice Bhagwati's judge-ment is decidedly liberal as it exhorts the insuperability of individual liberty and in the same breadth interprets the constitutional provisions

---

[13] Available at http://www.pucl.org/reports/National/2001/habeascorpus. htm. Bhagwati's opinion was delivered in the infamous ADM *Jabalpur Vs Shukla* case in 1976. Available at https://indiankanoon.org/doc/1735815/ (accessed on 7 March 2019).

in a literally conservative understanding. Dworkin's interpretation of 'Law as integrity' emphasizes the twin-pronged task of law to not only be procedurally fair but also advance social good such as equality. Dworkin argues that the judges cannot merely see laws as rules but as principles to be interpreted beyond mere procedural formalities and to establish a moral environment for just application of political power (Dworkin 1986: 87–89).

In the context of the ancient Greek thinkers, especially Plato and Aristotle, Plato was a trenchant critique of the Athenian democracy for being beholden to the opinion of the multitude (demos) and not to the formal/procedural ideas. The second part of Dworkin's argument that a system of justice should advance social good is what drives Plato's deduction of justice for individual from an idea of justice writ large in the polis. In Plato, there is no separation between the procedural and the substantive. The procedural determines the social good. Plato was an ultimate insider as a part of the Athenian aristocracy and for him the Athenian democracy was beyond redemption and ripe for tyranny. Aristotle was an outsider, a Macedonian, therefore not a citizen of Athens. While the formal also occupies a very important role in the Aristotelian scheme of things, it is not deduced from the universal or ideal but theorized from the particular. Constitution plays a major role in Aristotelian political schema. A strong social and political system is founded on a virtuous citizenry for Aristotle. The social, political and the ethical principles are contextual and hence dynamic. By improving the virtue of the citizens of a polis, Aristotle attempts to create an environment that is conducive for human flourishing. Both Plato and Aristotle, in a sense, are system builders. In the case of Aristotle, the system nourishes what is imbedded in human nature, of that of being rational, social and political. The Constitution is one such system (Aristotle 1885: 97–100; 1891). For Plato, in *Laws*, an ideal city ruled by god would be akin to a city ordered in obedience to reason. In such a city, regulations would be governed by reason which are to be known as laws (Bobonich and Meadows 2013). The citizens should follow the exemplars of virtues if they do not possess the requisite knowledge. Plato also introduces the notion of preludes which educate citizens to be persuaded by reason, what laws to follow, which laws are good and why laws are good in the first place. Prelude, interestingly, connects the formal laws to the substantive notion of good through a rational argumentation process (Bobonich and Meadows 2013). This has both an epistemic and ethical function and also connects them. This is absent in the *Republic*. Moreover, unlike the Socratic method in the *Republic*, the emphasis is on explaining the general ethical principles to the citizens and educating them about the value of laws. Here political becomes praxis whereas in the *Republic* it remains formal theory. So, in the *Laws*, for Plato, one perceives order through the laws and orients one's life accordingly. Interestingly, a state that follows laws is akin to a city ruled by the gods, citizens of which state would aspire to *eudaimonia* (Plato 1892: 273–276). Perhaps, this is what Nariman meant when he expounded the virtues of constitutional morality. Laws have a ring of concrete structure to them while the term Constitution appears to be a more hermeneutical framework.

Granville Austin never ceases to mention the contribution of the Constituent Assembly members to the delicate yet strenuous enterprise of designing a Constitution for India. While Fali Nariman emphasizes the foundations of constitutional morality in the contemporary epoch, Austin reiterates the emphasis on consensus, accommodative spirit, respect to diversity of not only opinions but also cultural perspectives, cooperative federalism, legal due process and representation of interests of the vast segments of Indian population that permeated the Constitution-imagining enterprise. Interestingly, Austin argues that the cultural and philosophical traditions of India—which has negotiated a tremendous amount of diversity over several millennia—played an important part in preparing the people of India for a transition from a colonial vassal state to a modern democracy (Austin 2006: 330). Thus, the Indian Constitution became the crucible of negotiation and contestation between antinomic interpretations of the Indian democratic experiment.

REFERENCES

Aristotle. 1885. *The Politics*, Vol. I. Translated by Benjamin Jowett. Oxford: Clarendon Press.

———. 1891. *Constitution of Athens*. Translated by Thomas J. Dymes. London: Seeley and Co.

Aristotle. 1893. *The Nicomachean Ethics*. Translated by F. H. Peters. London: Kegan Paul, Trench, Trueubner.

Austin, Granville. 2006. *The Indian Constitution: The Cornerstone of a Nation*. New Delhi: Oxford University Press.

Basu, D. D. 2013. *Introduction to the Constitution of India*. Lexis Nexis.

Berlin, I. 1958. *Two Concepts of Liberty*. Oxford: Clarendon Press.

Bobonich, Chris, and Katherine Meadows. 2013. 'Plato on Utopia'. In *The Stanford Encyclopedia of Philosophy* (Summer Edition), edited by Edward N. Zalta. Available at http://plato.stanford.edu/archives/sum2013/entries/plato-utopia/ (accessed on 7 March 2019).

Chokkalingam, T. S. 2007. *My First Meeting*. Tiruchirappalli: Bhanu Publishers.

Dworkin, Ronald. 1986. *Law's Empire*. Cambridge, MA: Harvard University Press.

Erikson, Erik. 1969. *Gandhi's Truth*. New York: Norton.

Farrar, Cynthia. 1992. 'Ancient Greek Political Theory as a Response to Democracy.' In *Democracy: The Unfinished Journey, 508 BC to AD 1993* (pp. 17–39), edited by John Dunn. Oxford: Oxford University Press.

Gandhi, M. K. 1947. *Mahatma Gandhi Collected Works 27 September 1947–5 December 1947*, Vol. 97. Available at http://www.gandhiashramsevagram.org/gandhi-literature/mahatma-gandhi-collected-works-volume-97.pdf (accessed on 7 March 2019).

———. 1955. *Ashram Observance in Action*. Translated by V. G. Desai. Ahmedabad: Navjivan Press.

———. 1962, 2009. *The Law and the Lawyers*, 82–117. Edited by S. B. Kher. Ahmedabad: Navajivan Publishing House. Refer to two important cases involving Gandhi. 1. Was it contempt of the Court? 2. The Great Trial.

Gibbon, Edward. 1906. *The History of the Decline and Fall of the Roman Empire*, Vol. 1. Edited by J. B. Bury. New York, NY: Fred de Fau.

Goldsworthy, Adrian. 2009. *How Rome Fell*. New Haven, CT: Yale University Press.

Guha, Ramachandra. 2007. *India After Gandhi: The History of the World's Largest Democracy*. London: Macmillan.

Habermas, Jürgen. 1987. 'The Theory of Communicative Action', Vol 2. *Lifeworld and System: A Critique of Functionalist Reason*. Translated by Thomas McCarthy. Boston, MA: Beacon Press.

———. 1999. *On the Pragmatics of Communication*. Translated by Maeve Cooke. Cambridge: Polity Press.

Johnson, Robert and Adam Cureton. 2016. 'Kant's Moral Philosophy'. In *The Stanford Encyclopedia of Philosophy* (Winter Edition), edited by Edward N. Zalta. Available at http://plato.stanford.edu/archives/win2016/entries/kant-moral/ (accessed on 7 March 2019).

Jowett, Benjamin. 1892. *The Dialogues of Plato*, Vol. III. Oxford: Oxford University Press.

Lane, Melissa. 2014. 'Ancient Political Philosophy'. In *The Stanford Encyclopedia of Philosophy* (Winter Edition), edited by Edward N. Zalta. Available at http://

plato.stanford.edu/archives/win2014/entries/ancient-political/ (accessed on 7 March 2019).

Lindley, Mark. 2006, July–December. 'Gandhi on Corresponding Duties/Rights'. *Anasakti Darshan* 2 (2). Available at http://www.mkgandhi.org/articles/mark. htm (accessed on 7 March 2019).

Machiavelli, Niccolo. 1882. *The Historical, Political and the Diplomatic Writings of Niccolo Machiavelli*, Vol. II. Translated by Christian Detmold. Boston, MA: James R. Osgood and Company.

Miller, Fred. 2012. 'Aristotle's Political Theory'. In *The Stanford Encyclopedia of Philosophy* (Fall Edition), edited by Edward N. Zalta. Available at http:// plato.stanford.edu/archives/fall2012/entries/aristotle-politics/ (accessed on 7 March 2019).

More, J.B.P. 2008. *Partition of India: Players and Partners*. Kannur: Irish.

Mouffe, C. 2000. *The Democratic Paradox*. London and New York: Verso.

Nagaraj, D. R. 2012. *The Flaming Feet and Other Essays. The Dalit Movement in India*. New Delhi: Orient BlackSwan.

Padmanabhan, S. 2013. 'Cultural Diversity and the European Union'. In *European Union in Changing World Order*, edited by Jayaraj Amin, 61–75. New Delhi: Kaveri Books.

Phillips, A. 2000. *Democracy and the Representation of Difference and the Politics of Presence: Problems and Developments*. Aalborg: Aalborg Universitet.

Pollock, Sheldon. 2009. *The Language of Gods in the World of Men*. New Delhi: Permanent Black.

Raghawan N. Iyer. *Means and Ends in Politics*. https://www.mkgandhi.org/g_relevance/chap28.htm

Rousseau, Jean-Jacques. 1923. *The Social Contract and Discourses*. Translated with an Introduction by G. D. H. Cole. London and Toronto: J. M. Dent and Sons.

Sen, Amartya. 1983, Spring. 'Evaluator Relativity and Consequential Evaluation'. *Philosophy & Public Affairs* 12 (2): 113–132. Available at http://www.jstor.org/ stable/2265309 (accessed on 15 March 2015).

Stewart, Frances. 2001. *Horizontal Inequality: A Neglected Dimension of Inequality*. UNU World Institute for Development Economics Research (UNU/ WIDER). Helsinki: UNU.

Turner, Stephen. 2018. 'The Method of Antinomies: Oakeshott and Others'. *Philosophy Faculty Publications*: 309. Available at https://scholarcommons.usf. edu/phi_facpub/309 (accessed 9 October 2019).

Vivekanandan, B., ed. 2002. *India Looks Ahead: Jayaprakash Narayan Memorial Lectures 1990–2001*. New Delhi: Lancers Books.

Wenar, Leif. 2013. 'John Rawls'. In *The Stanford Encyclopedia of Philosophy* (Winter Edition), edited by Edward N. Zalta. Available at http://plato.stanford.edu/ archives/win2013/entries/rawls/ (accessed on 7 March 2019).

Wiredu, Kwasi. 1996. *Cultural Universals and Particulars*. Bloomington, IN: Indiana University Press.

Chapter 2

Electoral Issues and the Constitution of India

N. L. Rajah

Of all experiments in government which have been attempted since the beginning of time, I believe that the Indian venture into parliamentary democracy is the most exciting. A vast sub-continent is attempting to apply to its tens and hundreds of millions a system of free democracy which has been slowly evolved over the centuries in this small Island, Great Britain. It is a brave thing to try to do so. The Indian venture is not a pale imitation of our practice at home, but a magnified and multiplied reproduction on a scale never dreamt of. If it succeeds its influence on Asia is incalculable for good. Whatever the outcome, we must honour those who attempt it.[1]

Sir Anthony Eden's observations above resonate with a resounding 'if' in the penultimate sentence—a sentiment shared by most world historians at that time. When India attained independence, eminent historians gave her democracy a decade of survival at best, given the

---

[1] Government of India. 1990. *Report of the Committee on Electoral Reforms.* https://adrindia.org/sites/default/files/Dinesh%20Goswami%20Report%20on%20Electoral%20Reforms.pdf (accessed 21 September 2019) (cited in Goswami 1990: 1–2).

geopolitical circumstances in which it had emerged. Ten years from 1947, democracy in India continued to flourish. Historians consoled themselves that it would survive in the subcontinent so long as Nehru—the ultimate democrat—existed, but not thereafter. Soon after Nehru's demise, *The Times* of London (Eden 1960) sent a reporter to cover the 1967 elections. Travelling through the country, he reported a mood of apathy among the people. He said that some Indians whom he met 'expressed a rejection of parliamentary democracy'. World historians must have smugly believed that their predictions were coming true. However, nothing changed in India for democracy. It bounced back with even more vigour after the Emergency, when it had been briefly eclipsed. The nation also achieved the notable distinction of eliminating the horrors of the Emergency—not by a violent revolution, but through a democratic electoral process. It was only after the 1980s that most historians grudgingly accepted that democracy was in India to stay.

The noted Indian historian, Dr Ramachandra Guha, in his book, *India after Gandhi: The History of the World's Largest Democracy* (BBC 2009), describes five social forces on which the establishment and progress of electoral democracy in the country has hinged. These are the complex elements of class, religion, language, caste and gender. To this list, I would add one more which, in the last six decades of Indian democracy, has developed into a sociopolitical force. That is dedicated political party affiliations.

Dr Guha's observations are undoubtedly true. They expose both the strengths and weaknesses of a parliamentary democracy kept alive by the combative forces in the electoral system. On the positive side, the significant influence of the five factors mentioned by Dr Guha have undeniably, and immeasurably, contributed to providing diversity of representation in Parliament which, in turn, acts as an invaluable check against any attempt at stifling the voice of the minorities, the downtrodden and women. On the negative side, the uncomfortable question that arises is whether it has done anything more than that. Have not the strengths that have contributed to the diversity and pluralism in Parliament also contributed to the fragmentation of interests and an apathetic indifference to the collective good of the nation? Paradoxically, only if an issue has no impact on the social forces pointed out by Dr Guha, and on political party affiliations, does it have any chance of smooth passage in Parliament.

It is a sad fact that electoral politics have failed to yield a large number of parliamentarians or legislators of the calibre of Edmund Burke. Admittedly, there are a few like him but the number is too small to make any significant impact. When he sought re-election to the British Parliament, he was confronted by his voters—all small traders—with his failure to address their interests in contrast to his penchant of concentrating only on what he referred to as 'national interest'. His reply is noteworthy. He said, 'I certainly have very warm good wishes for the place of my birth. But the sphere of my duties is my true country' (Guha 2007).

In this chapter, the link between electoral practices and their impact on the Constitution of India, or vice versa, and their collective impact on national interest will be examined.

ELECTORAL PRACTICES IN PRE-INDEPENDENT INDIA AND THEIR CONTINUATION

Elections in this country owe much of their origin to elections to the Provincial Councils of 1937, which were sanctioned by the provisions of the Government of India Act, 1935. Many of the practices in force during those elections continue to be observed even today. Much experience in organising these elections was acquired by the state machinery in pre-independence India, which included present-day Pakistan and Bangladesh.

It is not as if we did not have elections before that period. There were elections to the legislative councils of the presidencies and what we may today refer to as Urban Local Bodies. However, these need not detain our attention as they bore little resemblance to the electoral systems we observe today.

What impresses one in the first place about the 1937 elections is the manner in which the election campaigns were conducted to elect the four provincial governments. As Nehru famously described his own campaign:

In the course of about four months, I travelled about fifty thousand miles, using every kind of convenience for this purpose, and often going into remote rural areas where there are no means of transport. I travelled by airplane, railway, automobile, motor truck, horse carriages of various kinds. Bullock cart, bicycle, elephant, camel, horse, steamer, paddle boat, canoe and on foot. I carried about with me microphones and loud speakers and addressed a dozen meetings a day, apart from the impromptu gatherings by the roadside. (Shourie 2007)

It is interesting to note that, notwithstanding the surge in the print and electronic media, and the very many acts and rules regulating elections, this form of campaigning has continued to survive. The festive atmosphere which elections evoked earlier has, without doubt, been subdued to a great extent on account of rules and regulations against putting up posters and hoardings everywhere, using loudspeakers all through the day and night, and ceilings imposed on election expenditure, and so on and so forth, but the din and blare of democracy continue to operate in full force.

The limited franchise and separate electorates—the basis on which provincial elections were fought in 1937—were mercifully abandoned in favour of a bolder and more egalitarian concept of direct universal adult franchise. Freedom of press, as a common thread, existed even before the country attained independence and has continued into independent India. Fiercely protected by an independent judiciary, the freedom of the press has, by and large, been quite well preserved and protected, except for a few areas of concern like indiscriminate use of defamation laws by various state governments to muzzle free speech.

The legal system of pre-independent India continued its march into free India, strengthened by constitutional declarations that divided the Legislature, Judiciary and Executive. Rule of law reaches its pinnacle when it can aid the transfer of power without bloodshed or violence. It is in this sense that rule of law aided electoral laws to be applied in full force, albeit diminished in their vigour during emergency. Yet, it did rise again like the phoenix, through the electoral process, to shake away the angst created by an authoritarian regime.

The other noteworthy feature is that, in the Constituent Assembly debates, when provisions relating to elections in the Constitution were being debated, they were clearly being argued against the backdrop of the fundamental rights of freedom and expression, and with the clear understanding that fair and free elections in the country were not possible without concomitant access to free speech and expression.

The evolution of a separate chapter relating to elections in the Constitution is itself interesting. These are best expressed in the words of Dr Ambedkar himself in the Constituent Assembly debates:

In the very early stage in the proceedings of the Constituent Assembly, a Committee was appointed to deal with what are called Fundamental Rights. That Committee made a report that it should be recognised that the independence of the elections and the avoidance of any interference by the executive in the elections to the Legislature should be regarded as a fundamental right and provided for in the chapter dealing with Fundamental Rights. When the matter came up before the House, it was the wish of the House that while there was no objection to regard this matter as of fundamental importance, it should be provided for in some other part of the Constitution and not in the Chapter dealing with Fundamental Rights. But the House affirmed without any kind of dissent that in the interests of purity and freedom of elections to the legislative bodies, it was of the utmost importance that they should be freed from any kind of interference from the executive of the day. In pursuance of the decision of the House, the Drafting Committee removed this question from the category of Fundamental Rights and put it in a separate part containing articles 289, 290 and so on. Therefore, so far as the fundamental question is concerned that the election machinery should be outside the control of the executive Government, there has been no dispute. What article 289 does is to carry out that part of the decision of the Constituent Assembly. It transfers the superintendence, direction and control of the preparation of the electoral rolls and of all elections to Parliament and the Legislatures of States to a body outside the executive to be called the Election Commission. (Oldenburg)

One of the first laws passed under the provisions of the Government of India Act, 1935, was the Government of India (Provincial Elections) (Corrupt Practices and Election Petitions) Order, 1936. The power to enact such legislation flowed from Para 20. Schedule 5 of the Government of India Act, 1935, which authorised the Governor, exercising his individual judgement to make rules inter alia with respect to '(3) the conduct of elections' and '(5) corrupt practices and other offences at or in connection with elections'. This law also authorised the governor, on being presented with a petition complaining of corrupt electoral practices, to constitute a three-member tribunal to hear and adjudicate on the petition. The provisions for election disputes to be adjudicated by special tribunals continued after the Constitution of India came into effect with Art. 324(1) empowering the Election Commission of India (ECI) to appoint election tribunals. However, the power to adjudicate on election disputes was taken away from the ECI and vested with the high court following the enactment of the Constitution of India (Nineteenth) Amendment Act of 1966.

There is, however, no detailed study on how effective this change has been in stopping corrupt electoral practices. It is surprising that, till date, even the ECI has not commissioned a detailed study of this process.

One aspect is particularly noteworthy. The Indian legal system in general, with particular reference to election laws, has never been studied comprehensively. Most studies on this subject tend to focus quite disproportionally on the higher constitutional courts like the high courts and the Supreme Court. In the process, they have been remiss in not conducting an in-depth study of the lower courts, where the problems of the common man are submitted for determination. The local courts have had jurisdiction to deal with election petitions to set aside elections to local bodies. The high courts have possessed the powers to set aside elections to the state legislatures and the Parliament, while the Supreme Court has been vested with original jurisdiction to deal with election petitions relating to the election of the president and vice president of India.

Sadly, there has also been no serious study of how the courts have fared in exercising these powers. If such a study were instituted, it would provide a better picture of how effective the laws that seek to outlaw corrupt electoral practices are. Election petitions filed in courts have hardly had any significant effect in reducing these corrupt practices. In the first place, these cases do not get decided within five years of filing. After the 2009 Lok Sabha elections, close to 110 petitions were filed across the country in various high courts challenging various electoral practices. However, by the time the next round of elections in 2014 were announced, not a single one of these petitions had been decided. After the next round of elections, the petitions filed challenging the former elections are dismissed as infructuous. They cannot—and should not—be dismissed in this manner as a candidate could be disqualified for subsequent elections if he is found guilty. These petitions must, therefore, be taken to their logical conclusion.[2]

In spite of all the good work by the ECI, dark clouds continue to hover. As far back as 1998, in his address to the joint houses of Parliament, President K. R. Narayanan stressed the need for electoral reforms. He pointed out:

[O]ne of the causes of corruption and corrosion of values in our polity as well as criminalisation of politics stems from flaws in the electoral process. To ensure free fair and fearless elections and to prevent the use of money and muscle power, Government will introduce a comprehensive Electoral Reform Bill for which considerable ground work has already been done.[3]

Nineteen years down the line, one wonders what is holding back these reforms.

CONSTITUTIONALLY PERMISSIBLE RESERVATIONS IN POLITICAL INSTITUTIONS

Granville Austin, in his book, *The Indian Constitution: Cornerstone of a Nation*, has quite aptly noted that 'the Constitution is first and foremost

---

[2] Election Commission of India. Debate in Constituent Assembly on Part XIII Art. 289.

[3] For a more elaborate discussion, see Rajah (2014).

a social document'.[4] One of the tools with which it seeks to achieve social justice and equal opportunity is through reservations.

Historically, right from the time Indian legislative councils were established by the British Parliament, there has been clamour from various classes seeking reserved electoral seats in such councils. Capitulating to some of these demands, the Indian Councils Act of 1909, while giving effect to the Minto–Morley reforms, provided communal electorates for the Muslims. This was the first step in the British policy of divide and rule. The Congress had not expected this to happen. In the early days of the 20th century, the Muslim League had fared badly in the elections to legislative councils. For this reason, Congress felt that the British government would not be sympathetic to their cause. They reckoned wrong. At this point, Jinnah was exhorting Muslims to lend a helping hand to Britain's war effort while the Congress opposed it. This made Jinnah a safer bet for the British—and communal electorates for Muslims thus became a reality.

Subsequent governments in England did not favour communal electorates. The Montague–Chelmsford proposals, which preceded the Government of India Act, 1919, specifically denounced reserved electorates, stating:

> A minority which is given special representation owing to its weak and backward state is positively encouraged to settle down into a feeling of satisfied security; it is under no inducement to educate and qualify itself to make good the ground it has lost compared to its stronger majority….[5] (Austin 1999)

However, at Lucknow in 1916, the Indian National Congress and the All-India Muslim League had agreed to separate electorates for Muslims. Britain did not wish to rock the boat and hence communal electorates for Muslims continued.

---

[4] Address by Hon'ble President K. R. Narayanan at the beginning of the Budget Session in Parliament in March 1998.

[5] Government of Britain: India Office. Report on Indian Constitutional Reforms.

Following the demands made by the Muslims, other communities—the Sikhs, Anglo-Indians, Europeans, Indian Christians and non-Brahmins—also clamoured for special representation. Following the Montague–Chelmsford proposals, the British were not keen on ceding fresh territory. Reserved electorates for Muslims continued till the Constitution of India came into effect on 26 January 1950, but ceased thereafter since such a provision would offend Article 15(1) of the Constitution.

Reservation for the depressed classes received official attention for the first time before the Simon Commission. The report of the Commission elaborately set out the plight of the depressed classes which it perceived not as a problem of caste, but as an issue with distinct political overtones (Austin 1999).[6]

The First Round Table Conference, organised at London to consider the proposals of Simon Commission, was boycotted by Mahatma Gandhi. However, Dr Ambedkar attended the Conference and supported the proposal for reservation of constituencies for the depressed classes. The Conference itself was inconclusive. A second Conference, held eight months later, was attended by both Gandhi and Dr Ambedkar. Gandhi adamantly opposed separate electorates for the depressed classes, pleading that they should be included in the main body of Hindus and not be segregated. On account of the differing stand between different groups, this conference too was inconclusive.

Since the Conference failed to yield any consensus, Prime Minister Ramsay MacDonald, allegedly exercising powers as a mediator, proceeded to pass what came to be known as the Communal Award of 1932.[7] The award established separate electorates and reserved seats for minorities, including the depressed classes. Gandhi, languishing in the Yerawada prison at the time the award came into existence, reacted by declaring a hunger strike 'unto death' (Mandal 1999). On account of the widespread disapproval of the Award and Gandhi's fast-unto-death resolve, a fresh pact was reached on 24 September 1932. For the first

---

[6] Ibid.
[7] Office of Strategic Studies.

time, a specified number of seats for the provincial legislatures were taken from seats allotted to the general electorate and reserved for the depressed classes. Significantly, though the endeavour was to secure to depressed classes adequate political reservation, the pact also called for 'every endeavour' to give the depressed classes, 'fair representation', in public services.[8]

The reservation of seats for the depressed classes formed the backbone of the Poona Pact and was incorporated into the provisions of Government of India Act, 1935 (which went into force from 1937) and continued in some form or the other till they culminated in the constitutional provisions which we shall see presently.

The reservation for Anglo-Indians first found expression in the Cabinet Mission statement, issued on 16 May 1946 by the British government which set out a set of proposals to guide the framing of a new Constitution for India. This proposal, which included reservation of seats for Anglo-Indians ultimately found expression in Art. 331 and 332, but its indefinite continuance is sure to be questioned in the near future.

As far as reservation of seats for women is concerned, it has proceeded only to the extent of assuring them reserved seats in institutions of local self-government. In spite of vehement demands from many quarters, it is yet to become a reality in elections to Parliament and the state assemblies.

On account of the earlier concessions for various classes, the constitutional scheme with regard to reservations in elections to political institutions today is as follows:

- Seats for Schedule Castes and Schedule Tribes in the Lok Sabha—Art. 330;
- Seats for SC/ST to assembly constituencies—Art. 332;
- Seats for Anglo-Indians in Lok Sabha—Art. 331;
- Seats for Anglo-Indians in state assemblies—Art. 333;

---

[8] Text of the Pact is available at www.harijansevaksangh.org/Poona (accessed on 28 August 2019).

- Seats for SC/ST in Panchayats, including reservations in post of Chairpersons—Art. 243-D and
- Seats for SC/ST in municipalities, including for the post of Chairpersons—Art. 243-T.

Reservations for women, amounting to one-third of the seats within the categories mentioned in Arts. 243-D and 243-T are also provided for in these articles. In addition, Art. 243 also enables 50 per cent reservation of seats for women in all panchayats. Different states adopt different percentages of reservations for these seats. Amendments to Arts. 243-D and 243-T were brought in pursuant to the 73rd and 74th Constitutional Amendments, which attempted to raise panchayats and Urban Local Bodies to the status of constitutional bodies.

In addition, Arts. 243(D)(6) and 243(T)(6) provide an enabling provision for reserving seats for backward classes in panchayat and municipalities. The manner and modalities for achieving this are left to the various state governments.

Reservations for Schedule Castes and Schedule Tribes, and for Anglo-Indians, have been free of any major challenge on grounds of unconstitutionality. If at all issues reach the courts, they have revolved around the question as to whether a particular candidate could be classified as belonging to SC or ST. However, constitutional changes ushered in by Arts. 243-D and 243-T were challenged as being unconstitutional.

It was contended that some aspects of the reservation policy implied in elected institutions of local self-government, which enabled reservation in favour of backward classes, and those which contemplate reservation of chairpersons' positions in elected local self-government institutions, were in violation of principles such as equality and democracy, and thus offended the basic structure of the Constitution. In deciding these issues, the Supreme Court in *K. Krishnamurthy vs Union of India*[9] laid down certain important principles:

---

[9] (2010) 7 SCC 202.

(i) The nature and purpose of reservations in the context of local self-government is considerably different from that of higher education and public employment. In this sense, Article 243-D and Article 243-T form a distinct and independent constitutional basis for affirmative action and the principles that have been evolved in relation to the reservation policies enabled by Articles 15(4) and 16(4) cannot be readily applied in the context of local self-government. Even when made, they need not be for a period corresponding to the period of reservation for the purposes of Articles 15(4) and 16(4), but can be much shorter.

(ii) Article 243-D(6) and Article 243-T(6) are constitutionally valid since they are in the nature of provisions which merely enable the State Legislatures to reserve seats and chairperson posts in favour of backward classes. Concerns about disproportionate reservations should be raised by way of specific challenges against the State legislations.

(iii) We are not in a position to examine the claims about over breadth in the quantum of reservations provided for OBCs under the impugned State legislations since there is no contemporaneous empirical data. The onus is on the executive to conduct a rigorous investigation into the patterns of backwardness that act as barriers to political participation which are indeed quite different from the patterns of disadvantages in the matter of access to education and employment. As we have considered and decided only the constitutional validity of Articles 243-D(6) and 243-T(6), it will be open to the petitioners or any aggrieved party to challenge any State legislation enacted in pursuance of the said constitutional provisions before the High Court. We are of the view that the identification of 'backward classes' under Article 243-D(6) and Article 243-T(6) should be distinct from the identification of SEBCs for the purpose of Article 15(4) and that of backward classes for the purpose of Article 16(4).

(iv) The upper ceiling of 50% vertical reservations in favour of SCs/STs/OBCs should not be breached in the context of local self-government. Exceptions can only be made in order to safeguard the interests of the Scheduled Tribes in the matter of their representation in panchayats located in the Scheduled Areas.

(v) The reservation of chairperson posts in the manner contemplated by Articles 243-D(4) and 243-T(4) is constitutionally valid. These chairperson posts cannot be equated with solitary posts in the context of public employment.

Two further aspects are noteworthy. The concept of excluding the 'creamy layer' has no application to reservation of seats in political institutions. Secondly, Article 334, which originally provided that the system of reservations was to be in force for 10 years, has been periodically extended. As the law currently stands, these will continue to be applied till 2020. When reservation in educational institutions, and in employment, terminates constitutionally, it may be difficult to continue such reservations in political institutions.

ELECTIONS AND THE DOCTRINE OF BASIC STRUCTURE

The basic structure doctrine postulates that there are certain inviolable aspects of the Constitution that are immune to the amending power available to the Parliament.

Originally, the arguments of the petitioners before the Supreme Court in *Sankari Prasad vs Union of India*,[10] and *Sajjan Singh vs State of Rajasthan*,[11] were that Parliament and state legislatures are clearly prohibited from making laws that abridge fundamental rights in any manner. In both cases, the Supreme Court rejected this argument.

However, in 1967, while deciding *I. C. Golaknath vs State of Punjab*,[12] an 11-judge bench of the Supreme Court held that the amending powers of the Parliament are essentially the same as its legislative power. Parliament, therefore, did not have power through constitutional amendments to abrogate fundamental rights in any manner. The majority judgement invoked the principle of 'implied limitation on Parliament's power to amend the Constitution'.

'Basic structure' was argued for the first time by the renowned advocate M. K. Nambiar in the Golaknath case but the Supreme Court did not deem it fit to base its judgement on this doctrine.

The judgement in the Golaknath case was applied by the Supreme Court, inter alia, to strike down nationalisation of banks and to de-recognise erstwhile princes and take away their privy

---

[10] AIR 1951 SC (p. 458).
[11] AIR 1965 SC (p. 845).
[12] AIR 1967 SC (p. 1643).

purses. Two weeks after the Supreme Court delivered these judgements, Prime Minister Indira Gandhi dissolved Parliament and called for a snap poll.

For possibly, the first time in free India, the Constitution itself became an electoral issue. In the manifesto of the Congress party, 8 promises out of 10 related to amendments to the Constitution to restore the supremacy of the Parliament.

The Congress party was returned to power with two-thirds majority in 1971, and Indira Gandhi set about fulfilling her electoral promise of restoring parliamentary supremacy. A clutch of Constitutional amendments were passed. Through the 24th Amendment,[13] Parliament restored to itself the power to amend fundamental rights. The fundamental right of even the right to equality before the law and the equal protection of the laws was made subservient to Article 39 (b) and (c) relating to the Directive Principles of State Policy. Privy purses were abolished with the 25th Amendment,[14] and the 26th Amendment[15] placed an entire category of legislation dealing with land reforms in the Ninth Schedule, beyond the scope of judicial review.

The constitutional validity of these amendments came to be considered by the Supreme Court in the celebrated case of His Holiness *Keshavananda Bharati Sripadagalavaru vs State of Kerala and another.*[16] The judgement of the court was delivered through 11 separate judgements

---

[13] The Constitution (Twenty-fourth Amendment) Act, 1971, enabled the Constitution to dilute Fundamental Rights through Amendments. It came into force on 5 November 1971. The Supreme Court upheld its validity in the Keshavananda Bharathi case.

[14] The Constitution (Twenty-fifth Amendment) Act, 1971, passed to get over judgement of the Supreme Court in *Rustom Cavasjee Cooper vs Union of India*, popularly known as Bank Nationalisation Case. Sections 2(a) and 2(b) and the First Part of Sec. 3 of the 25th Amendment were upheld by the Keshavananda Bharathi judgement. However, the second part of Sec. 3, which prevented judicial review of any law that gives effect to the Directive Principles was declared unconstitutional.

[15] The Constitution (Twenty-sixth Amendment) Act, 1971. This amendment was passed to abolish the privy purses of former rulers of Indian states and their successors. It came into force on 29 December 1971.

[16] 1973 (4) SCC 225.

of the 11 judges who heard the case. The Supreme Court overruled Golaknath and held that an amendment to the Constitution was not the same as a law as understood by the provision of Article 13(2). The Court held that even fundamental rights could be amended. However, the limitation introduced through this judgement was that the basic structure of the Constitution could not be amended.

The Supreme Court, which had turned down M. K. Nambiar's plea in 1967 to apply the Doctrine of Basic Structure, willingly adopted and applied it in 1973 in the Keshavananda Bharathi case. Undoubtedly, the attempt of the Congress party to make the Constitution of India an electoral issue and promising far-reaching amendments to the Constitution in its election manifesto—and actually carrying out these promises, at least partially in 1971—must have played a significant role in bringing about this change of mind. The Court must have felt that some manner of safeguard was necessary to protect the core of the Constitution from interference by political forces. Thus emerged the Doctrine of Basic Structure.

The 1973 judgement did not exhaustively define what this basic structure was, but each judge gave a list of concepts which he held were part of the basic structure of the Constitution. Significantly, though many judges held that 'republican and democratic form of Government', 'democratic nature of the polity', etc., were part of the basic structure of the Constitution, not a single one of them explicitly held free and fair elections to be an integral part of the doctrine. That determination had to await another day. It did come up for the consideration of the Supreme Court in *Indira Nehru Gandhi vs Raj Narain,*[17] when the court was persuaded to apply the basic structure doctrine. Prime Minister Indira Gandhi's elections were called into question before the Allahabad High Court on the ground that electoral malpractices had been committed by her. This challenge was upheld. An appeal was filed before the Supreme Court when a conditional order of stay of the Allahabad High Court's judgement was granted by Justice V. R. Krishna Iyer. In the meantime, the Parliament passed the

---

[17] AIR 1975 SC 2299.

39th Amendment[18] to the Constitution; this took away the authority of the Supreme Court to adjudicate petitions regarding elections of the president, vice president, prime minister and speaker of the Lok Sabha. Instead, a body constituted by Parliament was empowered to decide such election disputes. Corresponding amendments were also made to The Representation of the People Act, 1951, and placed along with Election Laws (Amendment) Act, 1975, in order to save the prime minister from embarrassment in the event of the Supreme Court's rendering an unfavourable verdict. All this was done during the Supreme Court's summer recess and, when the matter was taken up for hearing, the Attorney General insisted that the court dismiss the appeals on account of the amendments to the Constitution and election laws.

Counsel for Raj Narain argued that the amendments were against the basic structure of the Constitution. Elaborate arguments were advanced by both sides but the court validated Indira Gandhi's election on the basis of the amendment to the Representation of Peoples Act, 1951, which had been brought into effect retrospectively. The 39th Amendment itself was upheld, but only after striking down that part which sought to restrict the power of judicial review where it interfered with the powers of the court to adjudicate election disputes. A split verdict of 4 to 1 was delivered with Justice A. N. Ray delivering a dissent in the judgement.

The judgement is noteworthy for making the concept of free and fair elections a part of the Doctrine of Basic Structure. Justice H. R. Khanna unequivocally held that democracy is a basic feature of the Constitution, and includes free and fair elections. (On the other hand, Chief Justice A. N. Ray, delivering the minority dissenting judgement, held that democracy was a basic feature of the Constitution, but not free and fair elections.) It is also worthwhile to note that in *People's Union for Civil Liberties (PUCL) and another vs Union of India and another*,[19] and *Kuldip Nayar and another vs Union of India & others*,[20]

---

[18] The Constitution (Thirty-ninth Amendment) Act, 1975, was passed to legitimise the election of Indira Gandhi in 1971. Art. 329A put the elections of the Prime Minister and Lok Sabha Speaker outside the power of judiciary.

[19] (2003) 4 SCC 399.

[20] (2006) 7 SCC 1.

the Supreme Court held that democracy, based on adult franchise, is part of the basic structure of the Constitution. It also proceeded to recall these principles in *Desiya Murpokku Dravida Kazhagam vs Election Commission of India*[21] when Chief Justice Altamas Kabir, speaking for a three-judge bench, held:

> There could, therefore be no doubt that democracy is a basic feature of the Constitution of India and democratic form of government depends on a free and fair election system.

The position that 'free and fair elections form a part of the basic structure of the Constitution' is here to stay and any Constitutional Amendment that would seek to whittle down this right in any manner would be protected by the Supreme Court in right earnest.

CONSTITUTIONAL MANDATES AND THE RIGHT TO INFORMATION IN ELECTIONS

Courts may protect free and fair elections, but it is challenging to exercise the constitutional liberty of free speech and expression (of which right to vote is an aspect) without access to related empowering information. What our founding fathers originally envisaged of fundamental rights has been expanded substantially by our constitutional courts. That is as it should be. As the Supreme Court observed in *P.U.C.L. vs Union of India*,[22] 'Fundamental rights themselves have no fixed contents, most of them are empty vessels into which each generation must pour its contents in the light of its experience.'

In its attempt to broaden the scope of the concept of freedom of speech and expression, the Supreme Court encompassed the right to know within the crucible of free speech. The first manifestation of that attempt by the Supreme Court resulted in the judgement in *R. P. Limited vs Indian Express Newspaper*.[23] The Court observed:

---

[21] (2011) 4 SCC 224.
[22] JT 2003(2) 520.
[23] AIR 1989 SC 190.

In view of transnational developments, when distances are shrinking, international communities are coming together for perspective in various fields including Human Rights, the expression; 'Liberty' must receive an expanded meaning.... It is wide enough to expand to full range of rights including right to hold a particular opinion and to sustain and nurture that opinion. For sustaining and nurturing that opinion it becomes necessary to receive information. Article 21 confers on all persons a right to know which include a right to receive information.

It must be noted that much before the Supreme Court recognised the right to know as being integral to the right to free speech and expression, the principle had already found acceptance in international treaties and conventions to which India was a signatory. Notably, Art. 19(1) and 19(2) of the International Covenant on Civil and Political Rights (ICCPR)[24] declares that everyone shall have the right to hold opinions without interference; everyone shall have the right of freedom of expression and this right shall include freedom to seek, receive and impart information and ideas of all kinds. Likewise, Art. 19 of the Universal Declaration of Human Rights, 1948,[25] provides that everyone has the right of freedom of opinion and expression, and this right includes freedom to hold opinion without interference and to seek, receive and impart information and ideas through any media, regardless of frontiers.

The principle that right to information is part of the constitutional right of free speech and expression came to be first applied by the

---

[24] The ICCPR is a multinational treaty adopted by the United Nations General Assembly on 16 December 1966 and is in force since 23 March 1976. India acceded to it on 10 April 1979. In *Vishaka & others vs State of Rajasthan*, the Supreme Court of India has held that the consideration of international covenants and norms is significant for the purpose of interpretation of guarantees provided under the Constitution.

[25] The Universal Declaration of Human Rights (UDHR) is a declaration adopted by the United Nations on 10 December 1948 at the Palais de Chillot, Paris. India is one of the 48 original signatories to the Declaration. While UDHR is not a treaty but a declaration, it is significant to note that it has been adopted with the object of defining the meaning of the words 'fundamental freedom' and 'human rights' appearing in the United Nations Charter and is binding on all member states.

Supreme Court in 2002 to election issues in a case which gave political parties cause for much concern.

The Delhi High Court, while allowing a petition by the Association for Democratic Reforms, directed the Election Commission to implement the recommendations made by the Law Commission in its 170th Report and make necessary changes in Rule 4 of the Conduct of Election Rules, 1961, to enable voters to gather at least certain primary information, that is, financial status, educational qualifications and criminal antecedents, if any, about candidates standing for elections.

The Union of India appealed against the judgement to the Supreme Court. *Union of India vs Association for Democratic Reforms and Another*[26] presented the Supreme Court with an opportunity to reinforce the concept that right to information is integral to free speech and expression. The Supreme Court, discussing various facets of the term 'election' and the width and amplitude of the Commission's power under, referred to various judgements including those in *Union of India vs Association for Democratic Reforms,*[27] *Mohinder Sing Gill and Anr vs The Chief Election Commissioner,*[28] *State of U.P. vs Raj Narain & Ors*[29] and *Chloro Controls (I) P. Ltd. vs Severn Trent Water Purification Inc. & Ors.*[30] Seven propositions were laid down, of which propositions No. 5 and No. 7 are significant to this chapter:

5. The right to get information in democracy is recognised all throughout and it is a natural right flowing from the concept of democracy. At this stage, we would refer to and of the International Covenant on Civil and Political Rights, which is as under: (1) Everyone shall have the right to hold opinions without interference. (2) Everyone shall have the right to freedom of expression; this right shall include freedom to seek, receive and impart information and ideas of all kinds, regardless

---

[26] *Union of India vs Association for Democratic Reforms* 5 (2002) SCC 294.

[27] *Mohinder Singh Gill and Anr vs The Chief Election Commissioner* AIR 1978 SC 851.

[28] *State of U.P. vs Raj Narain & Ors* (1975) 4 SCC 428.

[29] *Chloro Controls (I) P. Ltd. Vs Severn Trent Water Purification Inc. & Ors.* (1985) 1 SCC 641.

[30] (1985) 4 SCC 628.

of frontiers, either orally, in writing or in print, in the form of art, or through any other media of his choice.

The Supreme Court then went on to hold in para 7:

> 7. Under our Constitution, provides for freedom of speech and expression. Voter's speech or expression in case of election would include casting of votes, that is to say, voter speaks out or expresses by casting vote. For this purpose, information about the candidate to be selected is a must.

The earlier judgement of the Supreme Court was delivered on 2 May 2002. To sidestep the rigours of the Supreme Court judgement, a draft ordinance was prepared by the Union of India on the basis of political consensus at two all-party meetings of political parties held on 8 July and 2 August 2002. The ordinance route was deemed necessary as an earlier attempt to amend the law after parliamentary debate in July 2002 fell to the ground as Parliament had been rendered non-functional on account of frequent disruptions.

When the ordinance was sent to the President for his assent, then President A. P. J. Abdul Kalam, in an emphatic demonstration of the President's constitutional responsibilities and in exercise of powers under Art. 74(1) of the Constitution of India, returned the ordinance for reconsideration. The President felt that the ordinance was not in consonance with the Supreme Court's directives. Primarily, his discomfort arose from the fact that the ordinance stipulated such declaration to be made only by elected candidates and not by contesting candidates. He had also emphasised the fact that the ordinance made no provision on the court's directive that candidates be made to disclose their educational qualification.[31]

Political parties were not happy with the President's action, with Mulayam Singh Yadav going so far as to suggest that the President had returned the ordinance on the basis of the opinion of 'so-called intellectuals who have no understanding of the practical functioning

---

[31] For an elaborate summary of events, see Venkatesan (2002).

of Indian Politics'.[32] After the ordinance was returned by the Cabinet with no changes, the President reluctantly gave his consent.

The ordinance and its later avatars—the amendments brought in by Secs 33(b) and 33 (c) of the Act—were passed by the Parliament. These came to be challenged before the Supreme Court. A three-judge bench comprising M. B. Shah, P. Venkatarama Reddy and D. M. Dharmadhikari J. J. expressed separate but concurring opinions and declared the amended provision to be unconstitutional in *People's Union for Civil Liberties vs Union of India and Anr.*[33] Justice M. B. Shah (who, incidentally, was a member of the earlier bench too) observed:

> Merely because a citizen is a voter or has a right to elect his representative as per the Act, his fundamental rights could not be abridged, controlled or restricted by statutory provisions except as permissible under the Constitution. If any statutory provision abridges fundamental right, that statutory provision would be void.

Shah then held that that was enacted so as to eliminate the effect of the judgement in Association for Democratic Reforms,[34] and this could not have been done by the legislature.

Interestingly, Justice P. Venkatarama Reddy, one of the judges in the bench, noted that, in *Harpal Singh Bundel vs State of Madhya Pradesh*,[35] the Court had treated the right to elect as neither a fundamental right nor a common right, but as a pure and simple statutory right. Justice Reddy did not agree with this view and expressed his opinion thus:

> With great reverence to the eminent Judges, I would like to clarify that the right to vote, if not a fundamental right, is certainly a constitutional right.

---

[32] Ibid.
[33] (2003) 4 SCC 399.
[34] Ibid.
[35] (1982) 1 SCC 691 (PUCL).

The learned judge further underscored his opinion:

> Though the initial right cannot be placed on the pedestal of a funda-
> mental right, but, at the stage when the voter goes to the polling booth
> and casts his vote, his freedom to express arises. The casting of vote in
> favour of one or the other candidate tantamounts to expression of his
> opinion and preference and that final stage in the exercise of voting
> right marks the accomplishment of freedom of expression of the voter.
> That is where is attracted.

The judgement in the PUCL case did to constitutional perspective
regarding election law what the science of Eugenics attempts to do
to human genetics. It improved the very DNA of constitutional perspectives relating to election laws. In a subsequent judgement, the
principle that right to free speech and expression did not apply merely
to an exercise of that right in a positive manner in favour of a candidate alone, but applied with equal vigour to vote for the 'None of the
above' (NOTA) option, came to be recognised by the Supreme Court
in *PUCL vs UOI*.[36]

Inspiring as all these judgements undoubtedly are, we have to
recognise their limitations. There are two primary aspects relating to
candidates who stand for an election. The first relates to their personal
qualifications (or disqualifications), and the second, to their record of
public service. The second is as important—if not more—in determining the voters' choice of candidate. However, as the laws currently
stand, there is no facility to gather information regarding the second,
unless a candidate, impelled by a spirit of benign benevolence, decides
to favour the voting population with such information. This is largely
because there is still in progress, a raging debate to decide the question whether political parties are within the purview of the Right to
Information Act, 2005. The Chief Information Commissioner has
held that they are within the purview of the Act; political parties have
appealed the decision to the Supreme Court. If political parties are
brought within the ambit of the Act, it may be possible for the citizen to

---

[36] (2013) 10 SCC Page 1 (CIC).

demand that a record of public service of each candidate fielded by the party must be disclosed either proactively or on demand. The provisions of the Right to Information Act, with appropriate tweaking, may also be applied to all candidates who seek election to a public office so that these provisions are applied to independent candidates also.

Six decades and more after independence, we are still at the threshold of securing right to information that will enable the citizenry to select the best to govern them. The judgments of the Supreme Court giving expression to constitutional promises are just the beginning in that quest.

SOME RELATED RELEVANT ISSUES

An entire book would be necessary to cover the interplay of election laws, practices and the Constitution. Since the effort here is to highlight certain essential issues, an elaborate discussion has not been attempted. Nevertheless, at least a passing reference to certain other important election aspects and the Constitution would be in order.

The Constituent Assembly's attempts to maintain the independence of the Election Commission has been fortified by several judgements of various high courts and the apex court. The Supreme Court, in *Mohinder Singh Gill vs Chief Election Commissioner*,[37] held that the scope of the power of the Election Commission under Article 324 has to be construed widely and that it also operates in areas unoccupied by legislation.

Constitutional courts have not only restrained the executive from interfering with the electoral process, but have imposed admirable restraints upon themselves that inhibit even constitutional courts from interfering with the process once it has commenced until elections are completed and results announced. The rule of law laid down in *N. P. Ponnusamy vs Returning Officer*[38] has been repeatedly applied and respected by all courts:

---

[37] (1978) 1 SCC 405.
[38] 1952 SCR 218.

Any matter which has the effect on the election process should be brought up only at the appropriate stage in an appropriate manner before a special tribunal and should not be brought up at an intermediate stage before any court.

In *Hari Vishnu Kamath vs Syed Ahamed Ishaque*,[39] the Supreme Court pointed out that the word 'election' in Article 329(b) is used in a comprehensive sense as including the entire process of election commencing with the issue of a notification and terminating with the declaration of election of a candidate; an application under Article 226 challenging the validity of any one of these actions would thus be barred.

In *Nain Sukh Das vs State of U.P.*,[40] the Supreme Court declared beyond doubt that any law providing elections on the basis of separate electorates for members of different religious communities offends Article 15(1).

Since Article 102 (1)(a) disqualifies those holding office of profit under the government for elections to the houses of Parliament, the Supreme Court in *Guru Gobinda Basu vs Sankari Prasad Ghosal*[41] set out decisive factors and tests to determine what would constitute a disqualification under its provisions.

The Constitution makes the legislative power of Parliament, or of the legislature of a state, subject to Article 324. Supreme Court in *A. C. Jose vs Sivam Pillai*[42] clarified that no law made by Parliament under Article 327, or by the state legislature under Article 328, can take away or deprive the Election Commission of executive power in regard to the superintendence, direction and control of elections entrusted to it.

Though the healthy functioning of democracy depends as much on political parties as on anything else, it is intriguing that the word 'political party' first found mention in the Constitution only with the introduction of the Tenth Schedule to the Constitution through the

---

[39] AIR 1955 SC233.
[40] AIR 1953 SC384.
[41] AIR 1964 SC 254.
[42] AIR 1984 SC 921.

52nd Amendment Act, with effect from 1 March 1985. The Tenth Schedule to the Constitution was enacted to check the malaise of defections. Its validity was upheld by the Supreme Court in *Kihoto Hollohan vs Zachillhu.*[43]

In *Election Commission of India vs State Bank of India Staff Association,*[44] the Supreme Court held that, on a request by the Election Commission, the services of those Government servants who were appointed to public services and posts under the State or Central Government will have to be made available for the purpose of the conduct of elections. The attempts to make a single-member ECI into a multi-member panel and make the decision of the majority of the Election Commissioners the order of the Election Commission were challenged in *T. N. Seshan vs Chief Election Commissioner of India.*[45] The Supreme Court, however, rebutted these contentions, holding that the Election Commission is not the only multi-member body and that the acts of the government in making the ECI a multi-member body were constitutionally valid.

The Supreme Court's decision in *Common Cause vs Union of India,*[46] holding that the Election Commission has the power to issue directions requiring political parties to submit details of expenditure incurred or authorised by them, was a shot in the arm for the Commission in its attempts to regulate political parties.

In *Nain Sukh Das vs State of U.P,*[47] the Supreme Court held that the right to vote is not a fundamental right, but as we saw earlier, in *People's Union for Civil Liberties & another vs Union of India & another,*[48] this right was recognised as a constitutional right.

In *Arikala Narasa Reddy vs Venkataram Reddy Reddygari & another,*[49] the Supreme Court held that secrecy of ballot has always been treated as a sacrosanct and indispensable adjunct of free and fair election. It added that secrecy being a privilege in favour of the beneficiary, it is

---

[43] AIR 1993 SC 412.
[44] AIR 1995 SC 1078.
[45] (1995) 4 SCC 611.
[46] (1996) 2 SCC 752.
[47] AIR 1953 SC 384.
[48] (2003) 4 SCC 399.
[49] AIR 2014 SC 1296.

open to the beneficiary to waive it. The court also observed that this principle has diminished to some extent in view of the Rule of Whip as prescribed in the Tenth Schedule to the Constitution of India.

On a plea by Dr Subramanian Swamy to the Supreme Court that electronic voting machines or EVMs were not foolproof and were open to hacking, the Election Commission agreed to explore the possibility of incorporating a viable Voter Verifiable Paper Audit Trail (VVPAT) system as a part of the currently used EVMs to make the election system more transparent. Pursuant to directions issued by the court in *Subramanian Swamy vs ECI,*[50] the Commission filed a status report on the development of the VVPAT system. From the materials placed (where?) by both sides, Supreme Court recorded that it was satisfied that the 'paper trial' is an indispensable requirement of fair and free elections. However, it permitted the ECI to implement VVPAT in gradual stages or geographical area-wise, with necessary support from the Union of India.

CONCLUSION

India has one of the most enduring constitutions in the world. One may safely rely on the participation of the people, the authority of the Constitution and the involvement of the judiciary to keep elections in the country free and fair. As long as these aspects are adequately addressed and preserved, we may rest content that democracy in India will be in no peril.

REFERENCES

Austin, Granville. 1999. *The Indian Constitution: Cornerstone of a Nation.* Oxford: Oxford University Press.

BBC. 2009, 4 March. *India: Democracy's Dance.* http://news.bbc.co.uk/2/hi/south_asia/7914229.stm (accessed 21 September 2019).

Eden, Anthony. 1960. *Full Circle,* 246. Boston, MA: Houghton Mifflin Harcourt.

Guha, Ramachandra. 2007. *India after Gandhi: The History of the World's Largest Democracy.* London: Macmillan.

---

[50] (2013) 10 SCC 500.

Mandal, Jagdish Chandra. 1999. *Poona Pact and Depressed Classes*. Calcutta: Sujjan Publications.

Oldenburg, Philip. *India, Pakistan and Democracy: Solving the Puzzle of Divergent Paths*. Delhi: Manohar Publishers.

Rajah, N. L. 2014, 19 May. 'Don't Dismiss Those Election Petitions'. *The Hindu*.

Shourie, Arun. 2007. *The Parliamentary System: What We Have Made of It and What We Can Make of It*. New Delhi: Rupa publications (p. 239).

Venkatesan, V. 2002. 'Ordeal over an Ordinance'. *Frontline*. 36 (1996) 2 SCC 752vs.

Chapter 3

Voter Education
Importance and Impact

S. Y. Quraishi

The issues of poor voter turnout, under-participation of women and youth, and urban apathy have continued ever since democracy began in India in 1950. This clearly pointed to the need for voter education. It remained a matter of debate whether or not voters' education should be a mandate of the Election Commission of India (ECI). The general perception in the Commission was that 'we are umpires and our job is to set the rules of elections and enforce them rather than be concerned about voters' turnout'. 'Not our problem', some said. Some lamented the laziness of citizens for not making efforts for registration and voting, and advocated compulsory voting. However, I have always believed that voter education must be an integral part of electoral management. The reason is self-evident: since low turnouts lead to candidates with extremely low vote shares emerging as winners, they bring into question the successful candidates' legitimacy as representatives of the people.

CONTEXT AND PURPOSE OF VOTERS' EDUCATION

Citizens of India have, under the Constitution and the laws, rights and freedoms that ensure their ability to participate in the civil and political life of the state without discrimination or intimidation. These rights empower people to hold public authorities accountable on a regular basis, first and foremost through periodic elections.

Voter education is informing the public about their democratic rights, election procedures, political candidates and issues, and motivating them to participate fully in the process. It is necessary to ensure that all citizens understand their rights, where and how to register, how to check the voter lists and where, when and how to vote.

In India, voter turnout rates have mostly hovered between 55 and 60 per cent. This was the challenge the ECI faced in 2009–2010; in response, it established the Voter Education Division. Since then, there has been no looking back with every election, national or state, achieving record turnouts.

No democracy can grow or even survive without citizens' participation. This makes electoral literacy and civic engagement in public affairs essential. It is now a universally accepted principle that any democratic election requires informed participation. People's elected representatives should always be under pressure to perform and come up to their voters' expectations. However, it is important to remember that voters are not one homogeneous entity with some common expectations. There are several sub-categories such as young first-time voters, women voters, senior citizens, urban voters, rural voters and voters in difficult conditions; voters in each of these categories have differing needs, identities and access to information. Understanding the different segments of the target audiences is very important for addressing the specific needs of each segment.

It is not that the Election Commission did not engage with voter information activities before this initiative. For the elections to the Lok Sabha or state legislative assemblies, the Commission had generally sought to keep the voters informed about the details of the voting place and timing, kind of identification required, the registration process and how to vote using EVMs through standard notifications. But the efforts were sporadic and tame. The establishment in 2009 of the Voter Education Division with its flagship programme called SVEEP (Systematic Voters Education for Electoral Participation) sought to change things for ever.

A precursor of the movement was the 'Pappu campaign' in Delhi which was notorious for low voter turnouts. Based on a popular Hindi film song (*Pappu Can't Dance Saala!*), the campaign mainly targeted the reluctant non-voting so-called 'educated' elite and youth. The approach was to provoke voting action through chiding and shaming. The results were dramatic—voter turnout increased by 7.95 percentage points between the 2008 and 2013 elections to the Delhi Assembly, from 57.58 per cent in the former to 65.53 per cent in the latter. Later, in 2011, in West Bengal, the 'Anand Babu' voter facilitation and awareness helpline was a hit with callers who were able to obtain important information about elections. In Mumbai, *Jaago Re* (Wake Up), a private initiative aimed at improving voter registration, in the form of an advertisement by Tata Tea corporation in collaboration with an NGO, became very popular.

The SVEEP division realised that voter education is a dynamic and continuous process integrally linked to voter registration and turnout. It first took up the process of identifying the key gap areas in enrolment of women and youth, especially in the age group of 18 to 19 years. Low voter turnout of the youth and urban voters on poll day was the other glaring gap.

The Commission was already taking up a periodic health analysis of electoral rolls. An in-depth analysis of the electoral rolls was undertaken regularly to identify the gender ratio, elector–population ratio and number of electors in different age cohorts for each assembly constituency. These findings served as a reasonable basis for taking up some planned voters' education for filling the gaps in voter lists.

In a systematic approach, a new Division—Information, Education and Communication (IEC)—was set up in mid-2009. This division was renamed the Voters' Education and Electoral Participation (VEEP) Division before legislative assembly elections in Bihar in 2010. Later, the prefix 'Systematic' was added to it, to make the acronym SVEEP. The division immediately set about developing a sustainable policy, supportive framework, adequate programmes, necessary partnerships and requisite outreach activities.

Before developing communication strategies and materials, it was important to understand the reasons for voters' apathy and behaviour. Scientifically formulated Knowledge, Attitude, Behaviour and Practice (KABP) surveys were, therefore, conducted before coming up with voter education messages and methods, as a starting point. In the states which were shortly to have elections, baseline surveys were conducted well before the election process started. Such surveys help to analyse voting behaviour in the previous elections, to find out why people registered or did not register as voters, and voted or did not vote in the previous elections. It sought to identify the reasons for apathy towards voter registration; to understand the demographics of elector segments with lower enrolment and lower participation during polls; and to suggest measurable interventions for ensuring higher enrolment and higher voter turnouts.

The findings that emerged were used for formulating SVEEP interventions in the states/UTs. Some of the young people did not know that when they turned 18 years, they could enrol as voters. Many did not know the exact date of eligibility, that is, 1 January of every year. Most were unaware of the procedure involved. Importantly, general apathy about the importance of voting rights and indifference to politics of election was widespread. In many cases, the public showed contempt for politicians.

As for the low turnout of registered voters on the polling day, one was the erroneous impression that if they did not possess the voter card, they would not be allowed to exercise their franchise. A sustained campaign was launched to clear up this misconception and they were informed that other alternative documents which carried their photographs could be used if their Electoral Photo ID Card (EPIC) had not been issued to them. In some states, voters did not feel secure about casting their votes for fear of threats from militants like Maoists or intimidation by dominant castes. Accordingly, awareness campaigns were mounted to disseminate information on security arrangements as confidence-building measures.

While studying gender behaviour in Bihar and UP, the SVEEP Division found that women felt greater need for a safe and secure environment for voting as violence at the polling booths was a common occurrence. Targeted women-specific SVEEP campaigns highlighted the security and facilitation measures taken. The results were heart-warming. Women voters' turnout exceeded all expectations. They even outnumbered male voters, something unprecedented in the history of the two states. In Tamil Nadu, money power emerged as one of the factors used to influence electors. A sustained ethical voting campaign ensured that money power was curbed: many voters and civil society organisations (CSOs) report to ECI officials incidents of bribes and other inducements instead of pocketing these as had been their wont previously.

The timings of polling hours were not correctly understood by a number of respondents. They thought that at the stipulated time of closing of polls, they would be turned away and not allowed to vote even if they were still in the queue. A campaign was launched to dispel this misgiving, and voters were assured that anyone who reached the polling station even a minute before the closing time would be allowed to exercise his/her franchise. At the official closing time, slips are distributed to everyone in the queue, even if there are hundreds. To prevent misuse of this provision, the slips are issued backwards—from the last person in the queue to the head of the queue.

Once the attitudes and behaviours of the voters were identified, it was easy to develop communication messages which mainly revolved around three key messages:

- The right to vote is something to celebrate.
- It is important to go out to vote on the poll day without fail.
- The vote should be exercised voluntarily and ethically without any inducement or intimidation.

The SVEEP programme stands on three pillars of information, motivation and facilitation, the last one being based on the social marketing principle that information and communication is not enough: facilitation is equally important.

The next step was to explore all possible means of information communication and facilitation. The most important in the chain was the ECI's own frontline worker, the Booth Level Officer (BLO), who offered solutions to all the problems of voter registration, receipt of EPIC, etc. Most of the problems would be solved if the voters knew their BLO and approached him/her with their problems. A 'Know Your BLO' campaign was therefore launched to publicise the official's contact detail. To reach out to the young new voters who were mostly students, universities, colleges and even schools were made the new hubs of registration to ensure enrolment of students. Corporate houses were approached to reach out to their employees. Forms for voter registration were made available at all possible places of public access such as post offices, banks, fair price shops and educational institutions. Training camps were organised in schools/colleges to get the forms filled. NGOs and RWAs were engaged in urban areas and NYKS/ NSS (National Service Schemes) to reach youths and self-help groups in rural areas targeting women.

The Commission recognised that the success of SVEEP depends on the active support and involvement of other public agencies. To reach India's widespread and diverse population in every nook and corner, it was necessary to enlist cooperation of every conceivable agency in the field.... Partnerships for voters' education were pursued with government media organisations like All India Radio (AIR), Doordarshan, the Directorate of Advertising & Visual Publicity (DAVP) and the Song & Drama Division, Directorate of Field Publicity (DFP). Partnerships were also established with many CSOs through Memoranda of Understanding (MoUs). Several media organisations—print, electronic and social media—were approached to extend a helping hand, which they did with great results. Many voluntarily came forward.

Realising that youth are greatly influenced by their heroes, the Commission decided to approach iconic figures, such as former President A. P. J. Abdul Kalam, cricketer M. S. Dhoni and others. Buoyed by its great success, it then went on to involve regional and local icons too. This had an enormous impact.

In-process monitoring is extremely essential for necessary mid-course corrections. The campaign materials were, therefore, regularly monitored for relevance and impact and updated where necessary. Sharing success stories from states where elections were last held was encouraged, and the best practices were adopted by field formations for their own campaigns. CEOs were expected to coordinate among themselves for this kind of mutual exchange.... New material were constantly developed and circulated. Chief Electoral Officers were asked to come up with state-specific SVEEP plans and the district officers to prepare district plans keeping the local requirements, gap areas, culture, language and socio-economic realities in mind.

While the basic approach is common, every state has come up with its unique, innovative programmes. For example, Gujarat conveyed messages through traditional theatre called 'Bhavais', Maharashtra through 'Laavnis', Uttar Pradesh through 'Avadhi, Bhojpuri and Bundeli songs' and Delhi through pop 'Wake Up' campaigns. Extensive use was made of folk groups and street plays in states where these forms of entertainment are popular. Local festivals and cultural celebrations became the venues for electoral participation campaigns. In short, to cater to all target audience segments from youth to senior citizens, women or men, urban or rural voters, differently abled or illiterate, transsexuals or homeless, minorities, nomads, service voters or newly enfranchised NRIs, the ECI found a special strategy for reaching out to each one of them.

IMPACT

As the SVEEP activities gathered momentum, remarkable results started coming both in terms of large registrations and higher turnouts, especially of those segments that had been lagging behind like youth and women. Even the apathetic urban voters, for whom not voting was a fashion statement, were shamed into changing their attitude and participation. It started with Jharkhand, in the assembly election of 2010, where we had tested our strategy with a rudimentary application of the SVEEP programme. The state registered an increase of 11 percentage points over the parliamentary poll held just a year earlier. A few months later, Bihar showed an increase of 16 per cent. However, Assam and Puducherry showed modest increases. In 2012, Manipur had a turnout higher than that for the Lok Sabha elections in 2009 despite extraordinary regulation of voting in the wake of apprehensions about some bogus voting. Six states of West Bengal (84 per cent), Tamil Nadu (78 per cent), Uttar Pradesh (59 per cent), Uttarakhand (67 per cent), Goa (82 per cent) and Punjab (78 per cent) set records of voter turnouts in electoral history.... The participation turnaround in Uttar Pradesh whose turnout increased from 45.96 per cent in 2007 to 59.40 per cent in 2012, a rise of 29.24 percentage points, will remain a very special story for some time to come. The great finale came in 2014 Lok Sabha elections which too recorded the highest ever turnout in India's electoral history, namely 65.4 per cent.

The Commission observed 60 years, or Diamond Jubilee, of its formation on 25 January 2010 with year-long celebrations across the country. It used this opportunity and adopted the theme 'Greater Participation for a Stronger Democracy'. A range of activities taken up during the year-long celebrations included zonal symposia on sharing the best electoral practices, commemorative photo exhibitions depicting highlights of Indian elections from across the country, CSOs and academic institutions to assist in raising awareness among voters about their rights and duties.

NATIONAL VOTERS DAY

The most momentous activity for voter awareness generation, especially among the youth, was the creation of the National Voters Day (NVD). The electoral role analyses showed that a significant number of newly eligible voters (18+) were not getting enrolled, in spite of the annual revision exercise held at the grassroots levels. A nationwide campaign was undertaken to identify all eligible voters, who had or would attain the age of 18 years, as on 1 January 2011, enrol them and hand their EPICs at felicitation (including a pledge) organised in every polling station area. Though the main objective of the Commission for celebrating NVD was to increase enrolment of voters, the opportunity was used to create a sense of citizenship, empowerment, pride and participation to inspire them to exercise their franchise. The newly enrolled electors were, therefore, administered a pledge that they would always vote and vote without inducement. They were given a badge with the slogan 'Proud to Be a Voter—Ready to Vote' along with their EPICs.

The event is now being celebrated every year at the national, state and district levels in association with all stakeholders including political parties. Inspired by Indian experience, many other countries have also now adopted this model. NVD has proved to be the world's largest political empowerment of youth on a single day, as over 5 million freshly eligible and registered youth in the age group of 18–19 years were given their voter card on the very first NVD. There were, overall, 17 million electors who were given their EPICs on this day, belonging to all age groups. In succeeding years, the additional electors shot up to more than 38 million (2012), 28 million in 2013 and 37 million in 2014.

The range of activities could be mind boggling. All across the country, we organised marathons, processions, motorcycle and bicycle rallies, folk theatre, human chains, quiz competitions, talk shows and signature campaigns, pledge taking, essay writing, drawing and debate competitions in schools and colleges, street plays, besides the mass media.

NVD lectures by eminent scholars; functions by Mahila Mandals to focus on women registration; videos and audios aired on TV channels and FM channels; special facilitation centres involving the community and civil society members all contributed to making it a festival of democracy. A tableau of the ECI was presented in the Republic Day parade in New Delhi; this was on the theme of NVD. Similarly, in most states/UTs, such tableaux were displayed during Republic Day parades/functions.

Innovation became the name of the game.

THE LESSONS LEARNT

A campaign of gargantuan proportions cannot be expected to be entirely hiccup-free. SVEEP had its due share. The need for political neutrality being an absolute imperative, voters' education programmes had to be extremely careful, creating no impression that EC supported any party or candidate even implicitly. Unlike communication in health, education, rural development and other sectors, democratic participation campaigns can be strewn with landmines. Therefore, we encountered many tricky situations. In the West Bengal state assembly elections, a very enthusiastic campaign was planned involving Sourav Ganguly, former captain of the Indian cricket team and a true icon of Bengal and India, only after checking that he did not have any political affiliations, as the ECI does in all cases where icons are engaged for the SVEEP programme. But some political parties in West Bengal objected to this, raising instances of Ganguly's participation in certain political events. Not to leave scope for the slightest doubt, the Commission decided to drop the campaign with due apologies to the gracious gentleman. In another incident, a print media campaign with the famous quotation by Mahatma Gandhi 'Be the change you want to see', drew objections from the ruling party in Tamil Nadu, which alleged that it exhorted citizens to vote for a change in the government! The ECI ordered field staff to withdraw the message and even destroy the posters that had already been pasted in public places.

In mid–2011, the District Collector (also the District Election Officer) in Madurai district in Tamil Nadu was dragged to court for appealing to college students to participate in maximum numbers in the forthcoming legislative assembly elections. After an affidavit filed by the ECI that it was under its instructions that the collector had made his appeal, the court upheld the role being played by the Commission towards voters' education.

To prevent such possibilities in future, all the states have been given clear directives to get all their voter education messages and materials scrutinised by an expert committee especially formed for this purpose.

THE PARTICIPATION REVOLUTION

Citizens' energy for political participation through the method of representative democracy has been ignited. SVEEP has gained the momentum of a national movement. Many have called it a participation revolution. It is heartening to watch higher participation catching up even in campus elections and to see that the State Election Commissions want to adopt the SVEEP mantra to make people wake up to their responsibility in local polls.

There is a much bigger picture that has already attracted the notice of psephologists, political analysts and politicians. Is it possible that SVEEP has started impacting political outcomes and the formation of legislatures and executives? Once they are connected to the electoral process, they constitute an informed and motivated part of the electorate. These SVEEP voters, not taken into calculation by political parties, could provide the winning edge to candidates in constituency after constituency. The sooner these new voters are recognised, the better it will be for democracy.

Certainly, this will require a much more scientific analysis. But young voters, women voters and urban voters, who were clearly the missing link in elections earlier, are the most visible link today. Millions of these new voters are not yet entrenched in religion or caste or defined by any other label. It is important that they stay that way.

Chapter 4

Proportional Representation

Arvind Sivaramakrishnan and Chris Terry*

India and Britain are two of the world's most notable democracies. India is the world's most populous democracy, with over 800 million registered voters in the 2014 general elections. Britain is one of the oldest, and one which has exported its political model both to former colonies and beyond. The model in question, the Westminster model, is said to include an uncodified Constitution, a weak upper house, a strong unitary government, a clear distinction between opposition and government, dynamic, parliamentary (rather than presidential) democracy and the Simple Majority (SM) system leading to single-party majority government in its purest form (Lijphart 1999).

The Indian system differs from the classic Westminster model in several ways. India has a written Constitution and a specified quasi-federal structure in which state governments can have considerable influence on national policies. Nonetheless India retains the core feature of the Westminster system—an SM electoral system, known in the UK as First Past the Post.

*The authors particularly wish to state their appreciation of the part played in the preparation of this chapter by Katie Ghose, then CEO of the Electoral Reform Society, who welcomed the idea of the paper when Arvind Sivaramakrishnan suggested it to her and then made several valuable suggestions in the early drafting stages of it.

Britain and India have both begun to conform less to the archetypal Westminster model with time. The emergence of new political movements and parties has in part resulted from the decline of old identities such as social class. India has moved from the dominant-party system of the early years after independence to a multi-party democracy where majority governments are the exception, rather than the norm. Similarly, Britain has seen fragmentation, most notably resulting in Britain's first post-war coalition government in 2010, and has become something of an electoral system laboratory, with five separate electoral systems in use at various levels of government.

In both countries, politics is increasingly conducted with reference to the state (in India) or constituent country or region (of the UK). The quasi-federal nature of India and the emerging quasi-federal nature of the UK, where devolved regions are using their powers to an increasing extent, have major ramifications for the way electoral representation works in an SM system.

Yet the SM system's core feature is its disproportionality, which tends vastly to over-represent larger parties at the expense of smaller ones both nationally and within geographical areas of concentrated support. This is due to its use of single member constituencies, rewarding only the largest party in each constituency and disregarding the votes for opposition candidates. In the 2015 British election, the Conservative Party won 36.9 per cent of the vote, but 50.9 per cent of the 650 available seats, allowing it to form a governing majority of 12. The Labour Party won 30.4 per cent of votes and 35.7 per cent of seats. In 2017, the Conservative Party fell 12 short of a majority with 317 seats, but their 40.8 per cent vote share gave them 55 more seats than the second-placed Labour Party, which won 262 seats, or 40.3 per cent of seats, on a 40.0 per cent vote share. In India, in 2014, the Bharatiya Janata Party (BJP) won its outright majority of 11 seats on just under 31 per cent of the vote, or about 20.5 per cent of the total electorate. In India's 2019 general elections, the BJP won an outright majority of 31 seats, with 303 seats on 37.36 per cent of the votes; the record turnout of 67.11 per cent meant the BJP's win was achieved on 25.07 per cent of the total electorate. The second-placed party, the Indian National Congress, won 19.49 per cent of the vote, or

13.08 per cent of the total electorate, but its 52 seats amounted to only 9.58 per cent of the seats in the Lok Sabha.

There are three key aspects of SM systems in practice: fragmentation, geographical disproportionality and the existence of target or 'marginal' seats where election outcomes are effectively determined.

FRAGMENTATION OF VOTES

For several decades now, British voters have chosen to support a wider range of parties beyond Conservative and Labour, the traditional parties of government. The changes have been dramatic; the collapse of the Liberal Democrats, the growth in votes for the United Kingdom Independence Party (UKIP), and of votes and seats for the Scottish National Party (SNP) are illustrative of long-term changes in social and political identity, which in turn have created a more volatile electorate.

While the two major parties could once claim 96.8 per cent of the votes between them, this fell to 67.3 per cent in 2015, when 24.8 per cent of the electorate voted for a range of other parties, mainly UKIP, the SNP and the Green Party. In 2017, the two largest parties won 82.4 per cent of the vote share, which seems to be something of an exception to a long-term trend.

Fragmentation also leads to weakened mandates for both individual elected representatives and the government as a whole. Neither major party has won even 41 per cent of the votes at a general election since 2001, and in 2005 the Labour Party won a majority of 66 on 35.2 per cent of the votes. In 2010, the Conservatives won largest party status in a hung Parliament on 36.1 per cent and in 2015 they won a majority of 12 on 36.9 per cent, prompting opponents of the government to argue it has a weak mandate as a result.

For individual candidates, as SM only requires the person with the most votes to be elected, it is possible to be elected on less than half of the votes. In 2015, 331 of 650 British MPs were elected with less than half the votes of their constituents. Fifty were elected on less than 40 per cent and 8 were elected on less than 35 per cent. A new record was set for the lowest percentage vote for a winning candidate when the MP for Belfast South was elected on just 24.5 per cent of the turnout.

In India, the single-party dominance of the Congress Party effectively disappeared in the early 1990s, since when general elections have shown voting patterns which are fragmented in the case of certain parties and, in the case of other parties, almost totally determined by the respective parties' states. Elsewhere in the country, the Bahujan Samaj Party, a national party with a presence in several northern states, won nothing despite what was nationally the third-highest vote share of 4.1 per cent, and the Maharashtra-based Shiv Sena won 18 seats with a national percentage of 1.9 (*The Hindu 2014*).

DISPROPORTIONALITY: GEOGRAPHIC EFFECTS

Regional and national disproportionalities were prevalent in the UK 2015 results. The SNP won 50 per cent of the votes but 95 per cent of the Scottish seats at Westminster, leaving only three seats held by unionist parties who, together, won 46.7 per cent of the Scotland-based vote. Regions of England also demonstrated massive regional disproportionalities. In the South East England, the Conservatives won 50.8 per cent of the votes and 92.9 per cent of seats. In the North East, Labour won 46.9 per cent of the vote and 89.7 per cent of seats. In Northern Ireland, all 18 seats are held by groups local to Northern Ireland—whether unionist or nationalist.

These regional differences have sparked debate and increased the sense of a UK drifting apart politically. While it would be an exaggeration to lay the blame for increased UK tensions at the feet of the electoral system alone, the system exacerbates and exaggerates existing differences in the House of Commons. Having a region represented almost uniformly in a chamber can both help to create the impression that all voters in that region agree with that party, increasing the sense of difference between regions. Voters in a region poorly represented in a governing party may also not feel their concerns are listened to and understood.

Each nation of the UK is now ruled by a different party – the Conservatives in England, Labour in Wales andthe SNP in Scotland.

In Northern Ireland, the unity government formed by the Democratic Unionist Part and Sinn Féin and a Democratic Unionist Party and Sinn Féin-led unity government collapsed in January 2017, amid severe differences between the two governing parties, and at the time of writing (February 2019) the region has been without a government for over two years. This demonstrates the level of political change over the previous five decades, from a time when two major parties dominated the country with just a single government. The dominance of different parties in each constituent component of the UK creates the impression that these regions are monoliths of opinion. It also has an effect on the parties governing. In 2015, Labour won over 700,000 votes in Scotland, but in effect those 700,000 voters had to be represented by a single MP, who also had to be the voice of Scotland within the Labour Party. This MP must, furthermore, fill the position of Shadow Scottish Secretary, and is therefore tied to the Labour Party line through collective cabinet responsibility. After the arrival of two pandas at Edinburgh Zoo in 2011, a common joke was that Scotland had more pandas than Conservative MPs; the party had nevertheless won 16.7 per cent of the Scottish vote in 2010 and even at its lowest, in the 2011 Scottish parliamentary election, has won the support of 12.4 per cent of the Scottish electorate. There are now signs of party resurgence, as it won 22.9 per cent in the 2016 election to the Scottish Parliament, a result that may not have been possible without proportional representation. For the record, Labour won 7 Westminster seats from Scotland in the 2017 general elections, on 27.1 per cent of the turnout vote.

These figures also demonstrate the different effects of SM in the light of geographic vote spread. The SNP may have won fewer votes than either UKIP or the Liberal Democrats but those votes were concentrated into Scotland's 59 constituencies, when the UK had 650 in all.

In India, what is probably the SM system's outstanding feature, namely the disproportion between votes cast and seats won, has long been clear and recent elections at national and state level continue to exemplify the problem. In the 2014 general elections, the current ruling party at the time of writing, the BJP became the first party to win an outright majority in the Lok Sabha since the 1984 general elections; the scale of the victory was greater because the Indian National

Congress, which had led the previous two coalition governments, lost 162 seats to end with 44; indeed none of the parties at least nominally opposed to the BJP won enough seats even to form an official opposition. Government formation has been different in the UK, where First Past the Post has consistently led to single-party majority governments until 2010, when the first peacetime coalition government was formed since the 1930s.

In India in 2014, the Congress, which ended up with 8 per cent of Lok Sabha seats, gained 19.3 per cent of the vote (*The Hindu* 2014). By comparison, in the UK, Conservative party secured a majority on 36.7 per cent of votes cast—24 per cent of the electorate. Similar disproportionalities obtained in particular Indian states. In Tamil Nadu, the All India Anna Dravida Munnetra Kazhagam (AIADMK) won 37 of the state's 39 Lok Sabha seats on 44.3 per cent of votes cast in the state; its share of the national vote was 3.3 per cent.

The 2014 election differs from previous ones only in that some of the figures are even more strikingly disproportional. In the 2009 election, the Congress had emerged as the single largest party with 206 seats of its own in an alliance which totalled 262 or 48 per cent of seats, on 37.2 per cent of the vote; the BJP had 159 seats on 24.6 per cent, and the Left Front had 79 with 21.1 per cent (Wikipedia 2014). Even greater disparities can obtain in elections to state assemblies. In 2012, the Samajwadi Party (SP) won a crushing victory in the Uttar Pradesh state elections, taking 226 seats in the 403-seat assembly; its nearest rival, the Bahujan Samajwadi Party (BSP), won 80 seats, just under 40 per cent of the winners' tally. Yet the SP's win, amounting to 56 per cent of the assembly seats, came on 29.3 per cent of the vote, while the BSP had 20 per cent of the seats on a vote share of 25.9 per cent. The 3.4 per cent difference in vote share made a difference of 146 seats (Ramani 2012).

This disproportionality is an inherent feature of the SM system, which only increases as voting patterns fragment. In respect of India, however, caution is required over any general inferences about the scale or extent of it in every election, because pre-poll seat-sharing arrangements or similar deals are not as common in UP as they are, for example, in Tamil Nadu. In the latter case, a claim could be made that such deals facilitate some representation for social groups which might otherwise go unrepresented. A proportional system would provide a more accurate reflection of the range of voter preferences than the SM system does.

The 2012 UP results show another feature of Indian politics, which is that at state level most of the contests are effectively between two parties, with others at best a distant third, whether in general or state elections. In the 2014 general election, the AIADMK's main rival, the Dravida Munnetra Kazhagam, won no seats at all for its 27 per cent of the votes cast in parliamentary constituencies within Tamil Nadu, and the BJP won two seats with 18.5 per cent of the state-based vote. Indian general elections have even been described in terms which suggest that they amount to an agglomeration of two-party contests (Heath 2005: 148).

The consequences are, however, significant at national and state level, with the main third parties or third fronts substantially under-represented. In 2009, the Left Front's 79 seats were won on 21.1 per cent of the vote, an under-representation of 36 seats. In contrast, the winning Congress and the opposition BJP were over-represented by 60 and 25 seats, respectively. One result at both state and national level is that two parties decide the major policy issues or strategies, a matter which has been particularly significant in India; the Left Front's opposition to neoliberalism and to the nuclear deal with the USA was vocal but ultimately ineffective.

Another feature of the SM System is that small swings in voter support can mean that large numbers of seats are won and lost, while even slightly larger swings generate landslide victories. In the 2009 general elections, the BJP lost 3.4 percentage points in its voter support from the 2004 election, but the swing cost it 22 seats or 12 per cent of the 138 seats it had held in the 2004–2009 Parliament. Correspondingly, in 2014, the BJP's vote share rose by 12.5 percentage points, from 18.8 to 31.3, but the change brought the party no fewer than 166 more seats, and it finished with 282, or a gain of 120.2 per cent in seats won. In the UK, such effects can also occur, an issue examined in detail by

Professor John Curtice before the 2015 election (Curtice 2015). The most obvious example was the SNP's decimation of the Labour Party in Scotland to become the third largest party in the Commons on half the Scottish votes but a small UK-wide vote share. A relatively small shift in vote share, coupled with the geographical spread of its support, could have won the Labour Party many more seats.

TARGET SEATS

Thirdly, under SM systems, parties are shoehorned into tightly targeting relatively small groups of floating voters in marginal seats in order to win. Such seats do not exist for smaller newer parties, which is why in 2015 UKIP and the Greens won just one seat apiece for 12.9 per cent and 3.8 per cent of the vote, respectively. Similarly, the Liberal Democrats, having suffered the disproportionalities of the system for decades, had become experts in working around the system with tightly targeted, locally focused campaigning and tactical voting, although this was not enough to prevent major losses in 2015 from highly effective Conservative party targeting in the closest Lib-Dem Conservative marginal seats. UKIP, a much newer party, however, suffered from a geographically dispersed vote, securing one MP and coming second in 120 seats. The Greens' single seat is a testament to their creation of a base over many years in the city of Brighton. There are now 87 MPs from neither Labour nor the Conservatives, up from a mere 7 at the two-party system's height.

In India, the story is historically different. The post-independence period saw a dominant-party system with a single party capable of winning power but a highly fragmented opposition. India has continually had a significant number of seats held by parties beyond the two largest vote winners, an example of India's diversity even under the polarising aspects of the SM system. However the diverse nature of India means that from 1989 until 2009 no one party could win a majority, and parties cooperated in a variety of styles.

It has been argued that SM tends to lead to a two-party system, in a process known as Duverger's law. In reality, however, Duverger's law only tends to apply at the regional or constituency level, meaning

SM instead often creates a series of two-party systems as seen in both the UK and India. Of the major SM using democracies, only the USA has a true two-party system. A range of reasons accounts for these kinds of anomalies; in India they include pre-election arrangements whereby parties do not field candidates in particular constituencies or groups of constituencies, geographical concentrations of support as evidenced by the Tamil Nadu parties and the Shiv Sena in Maharashtra, and episodic falls in support, usually for incumbent parties; the latter is usually shown in reduced turnouts of voters who generally support the party or parties concerned. Therefore, campaigning is often targeted at relatively small groups of voters, often particular castes or communities. This narrows down the range of policies a party might offer, especially at local level; it also means mortgaging policy in advance, particularly over local or state-level issues, where candidates might have more say than they do over national matters. Targeted campaigning can, moreover, worsen caste and communal tensions; in the 2015 Bihar assembly election, a voter who declared his caste membership told a reporter on a national newspaper why he would vote for the BJP rather than any party or alliance connected with the former chief minister Lalu Prasad Yadav:

> I am a *baniya* and if Lalu comes to power he will never protect me. So I have to vote for Modi to keep myself safe from the Yadavs. (Cited in Thakur and Khanna 2015)

THE CONSTITUENCY LINK

One of the purported strengths of the SM system is the easily identifiable link between a constituency and its sole elected representative. When a representative in effect owes their seat to a particular group of voters, they are not representative of a whole constituency except formally; secondly, those who did not vote for the winner end up unrepresented, a matter of some moment either in a close two-party contest or in one where support is widely distributed among several parties.

Britain does not, on the whole, have campaigns targeted at narrow groups such as individual castes. Yet targeting remains an issue, owing to Britain's culture of safe seats, where even parties with reasonable support get nothing. Horsham, in southern England, was last represented by a MP from a party other than the Conservatives in 1880, and in May 2015 the incumbent MP won 57.3 per cent of the vote; UKIP came second with 14 per cent. Elections in the UK are effectively decided by results in a narrow series of 'marginal seats' which are genuinely competitive. In order to demonstrate this, before the 2015 general elections, the Electoral Reform Society predicted the winners of 368 out of 650 constituencies and despite the volatile election, all but five of these predictions turned out correctly. One of the effects on voters is the attention lavished on marginal seats at the expense of those who live in safe seats (the majority of the UK population). During the 2010 election, the amount spent on campaigning ranged from 14p per vote in the Labour safe seat of Bootle to £3.07 in the marginal seat of Luton South, targeted by the three largest parties. In the 50 seats with the closest gap between the two largest parties, on average they spent £1.31 per vote. In the 50 safest seats, they spent £0.50 on average (Terry 2013).

In India, voters are more likely to have contact with their state representative, the Member of the Legislative Assembly (MLA), or their local ward councillor than with their MP. What may amount to an attempt to enhance the link between MPs and MLAs, and their respective constituencies between elections has been made in India, in the form of the Members of Parliament Local Area Development Scheme (MPLADS), which was introduced in 1993 and has since been extended to MLAs. Under the MPLADS system, each MP is allocated ₹50 million a year of central government money for discretionary use in their own constituency. Although the Supreme Court confirmed the Scheme's constitutional validity in 2010, in the respective cases of Bhim Singh and Bondu Ramaswamy, the Scheme as a whole has been severely criticised for a range of reasons. One is that it blurs the distinction between the legislature and the executive and also undermines elected local bodies (K. C. Sivaramakrishnan 2010). Another is that it allocates funds to individual representatives but does not maintain sufficient oversight as to how the money is used. A third criticism is that the use of the money is arbitrary, erratic and mainly though not exclusively motivated by party-political considerations such as re-election campaigns (*Economic & Political Weekly* 2009; Pal and Das 2010).

As each constituency has only one representative at any given level, it remains open to an MP or an MLA to disburse Local Area Development Scheme (LADS) money only to supporters or other groups they favour or whose votes they may particularly need. In addition, funds are far more often spent on visible physical assets such as roads, bridges, walls and even places of worship rather than on, for example, ensuring that schools are properly staffed (Ramachandran 2005). This may well remain the case despite the fact that LADS spending is now more tightly monitored than it used to be (Kumar 2010).

RESERVED CONSTITUENCIES

In India, these amount to a specific attempt to ensure the representation of groups of voters who would otherwise be significantly disadvantaged by the severe inequalities and stratifications which obtain in Indian society; in India, the beneficiaries of reserved constituencies are those specified by the Constitution as Scheduled Castes and Scheduled Tribes, though under the principle of the universal franchise the entire electorate in any reserved constituency have the right to vote; electoral quotas of various kinds exist in over 100 countries (Jensenius 2015). Yet the Indian results have been at best mixed. India has one of the world's most extensive quota systems, but voters in reserved constituencies do not necessarily feel better represented, because their choice of candidates is limited to the group concerned, and because the candidates themselves are as bound to their respective parties as any other candidates. Furthermore, even in reserved constituencies the majority of the voters do not belong to Scheduled Castes, and turnouts of castes other than those for whom a constituency is reserved are often much lower than they are in unreserved seats; it is also the case that reservations have not brought about any enhancement in development outcomes (Jensenius 2012: 374, 380–381; 2015). One positive result, however, is that although having a Scheduled Caste representative has led to an increase in the number of public facilities in hamlets largely occupied by Scheduled Castes, there is no evidence that the elected representatives involved have specifically channelled public funds to their own caste groups (Jensenius 2015).

While the UK does not have anything as starkly defined as India's caste groups, it does have groups who are substantially under-represented in Parliament. The SM system is a contributing factor. One of the most noticeably under-represented groups, given that they account for slightly more than half the British population, is women. While 29.4 per cent of MPs in the House of Commons are now women, a record and a noticeable increase over the 22.0 per cent elected in 2010, it remains the case that women are noticeably under-represented in the UK compared to similar countries such as Germany (36.5% of whose lower house is made up of women), Sweden (43.6%) and Spain (41.1%). Indeed, the UK is ranked 39th out of 190 countries for gender representation in its lower house (International Parliamentary Union 2016).

Single-member constituencies and safe-seat culture are both problematic features of SM systems. Safe seats tend to keep incumbents in office, and in the UK this group is predominantly male. For instance, in the run-up to the 2015 election, 205 candidates stood who had been MPs since 2001 or earlier, spread across over 30 per cent of seats. Of this group only 14.6 per cent were women, with 175 male candidates being outgoing MPs who had won seats at the 2001 election or earlier (Mortimer and Terry 2015).

Single-member constituencies are common in SM systems and the UK voters elect one MP per constituency, with around 70,000–80,000 voters per constituency. In 'multi-member' constituencies, voters have more than one MP giving their constituency multiple representatives in Parliament. Gender and other types of diversity tend to increase as the number of seats in a constituency increases. When running multiple candidates parties therefore have a reason to run more diverse candidate slates, which would be reflective of the electorate they wish to represent. Frustrated with the current rate of progress, some parties have adopted temporary measures to open up the system to a more diverse candidature. For many years, the Labour Party has used all-women shortlists, allowing only women to stand in certain constituencies. This has led to an increase of the proportion of Labour female

MPs. However, all-women shortlists can attract controversy as they block men from even applying to be the chosen constituency candidate. Under SM, this is the only available tool to effectively guarantee women's representation and it is only because some of the use of such measures (alongside softer measures, such as mentoring and financial support) that the UK ranks where it does (highest among SM system users). One of the benefits of multi-seat constituencies is that it enables other forms of positive action, such as quotas that give voters candidates of both genders from which to choose.

Proportional systems with multi-member seats do not guarantee better representation, but they give parties a wider range of options with which to pursue such representation and also give parties an incentive to reach out to wider swathe of the community through more representative candidates.

The changing nature of voting patterns in both India and the UK—voter fragmentation and increasing regional disparities in results—has therefore created a similar series of issues. In India, a far larger country with multiple ethnic, linguistic and regional identities, the existence of party fragmentation, for example, as measured by the number of credible parties, and regional divergences is more established and clearly visible. Politics under the British electoral system have been affected by the same trends and effects and the UK is now experiencing greater political divergence within Scotland, Wales, Northern Ireland and England. We have seen therefore that SM causes great problems for a range of reasons. What kind of principles would underpin an alternative electoral system?

The history of electoral reform in Britain is long. The Electoral Reform Society was founded as far back as 1884, as the Proportional Representation Society. The First World War era all-party National Government launched a Speaker's Conference on aspects of electoral suffrage, registration and the electoral system; the Conference recommended a Single Transferable Vote (STV) system. This option was subsequently rejected by the Commons in a series of votes, at first by only seven votes. The subsequent collapse of the Liberals led to a dissipation of interest in electoral reform, but proportionality returned to the agenda after the Liberals regained strength from the 1970s onwards. The UK government initiated a commission on the electoral system, the Jenkins Commission, in 1998, but internal divisions kept the recommendation of a mixed system combining Alternative Vote (AV) with Mixed Member Proportional (Alternative Vote Plus) from proceeding further. The Labour government elected in 1997 did however initiate a variety of new electoral systems, particularly in the newly devolved assemblies and parliaments in Scotland and Wales.

The 2010 election saw the UK elect its first post-war coalition government. This resulted in a referendum on the AV system, a system which has several of the defects of SM, including disproportionality, but which was viewed as an improvement on SM by the majority of reformers. While AV was defeated in a referendum in 2011, just four years later the 2015 election provided major evidence of fragmentation and geographic polarisation, and therefore brought the issue back into public debate. While electoral reform is unlikely to be achieved in this legislative term, given the UK government's commitment to retain First Past the Post, interest in alternatives continues to grow among political parties and the public.

In India, proportional systems have been discussed occasionally. In 1928, the Motilal Nehru Committee strongly favoured a Proportional Representation (PR) system (Jensenius 2014). The colonial government rejected PR with the racist excuse that it was too complicated for Indians; PR was also rejected in 1949, for being 'too complicated for India' (Jensenius 2014). In 2015, the Law Commission published a detailed report on a range of electoral issues, including electoral systems, but concluded in favour of an additional member system (AMS) and recommended that the Government of India examine the Commission's own report of 1999 with a view to make that report's provisions workable. One of the Commission's concerns was that a PR or an AMsystem would result in an excessively enlarged national Parliament or one with a plethora of parties, and another concern was that even a 5 per cent threshold would exclude many significant parties whose support was mainly state-based (Law Commission 2015: 87).

Given the failings of SM systems to reflect modern voters' views in both India and the UK in a multi-party era of the kind outlined earlier, we propose the following principles for the basis of a new electoral system for India and the UK. A new electoral system should:

Be proportional: The political diversity of voters' views are not properly represented by the SM system and this creates issues of misrepresentation nationally and locally. Therefore, any new system should produce an outcome in terms of seats relatively in line with the way people vote, both nationally and within different regions.

Be representative: SM systems block the ability of parties to help achieve institutions that reflect diversity among society, including the range of political attitudes among the electorate.

Maximise voter choice: Modern voters are politically diverse and evidence suggests they increasingly wish to elect both party candidates and candidates without a party badge and to see a broadly reflective group of representatives in national parliaments.

Produce strong and equal mandates for individual members: One advantage cited for SM systems is that every representative has a clear and equal mandate from the electorate. There is no competition between different types of representative as can occur in systems where representatives are divided into list or constituency candidates (as happens in Mixed Member Proportional or AMSs).

Allow for identifiable constituencies and representatives: The UK and India are geographically as well as demographically diverse. Voters should have a clear relationship to their representatives and feel their representatives are accountable to them; SM is said to possess those virtues more strongly than other systems. While SM recognises this, it does not recognise the differences within regions. A single MP cannot represent the nuances and complexity of views across a constituency. An electoral system should allow voters to feel a connection with their representatives through representation of clearly identifiable areas, but should also deliver representatives who can more fully represent the whole population of an area.

Since 1997, Britain has been something of an electoral system laboratory. While, before that point, Britain used SM systems in all elections, the election of the 1997 Labour government under Tony Blair led to devolution settlements and with these new political bodies a proliferation of new electoral systems. From 1999, Britain's representatives to the European Parliament were also elected by a new system: the closed party list.[1] The newly devolved Scottish Parliament was elected by the AMS, similar to the system used in Germany and New Zealand. Variants of this system were also used for the Welsh and London Assemblies, created in 1999 and 2000, respectively. Directly elected mayors, most notably that of London, would be elected by the Supplementary Vote system, a variant of the Contingent Vote system also used in Sri Lankan presidential elections. This system was also adopted from 2012 for elections for Britain's new directly elected Police and Crime Commissioners. Northern Ireland's new Assembly was to be elected via the STV.[2] For its part, the Scottish Parliament changed the electoral system for Scottish local government elections to STV, starting with the 2007 elections.

The closed party list system used for the election of Great Britain's Members of the European Parliament is perhaps the most easily comparable to SM in that it is the only system used by every citizen across the UK. This system splits the UK into 12 regions, with the 11 regions of Great Britain using a closed–list system.[3]

The system retains simplicity for the voter, who need only cast a single cross against the party of their choice, a process similar to voting in a SM election. However, closed lists are critiqued for producing Members of the European Parliament (MEPs) who are distant from and anonymous to their electors and for giving parties too much control as voters are forced to choose or reject the whole list of candidates. Opinion polling regularly finds low recognition levels for Britain's MEPs. A May 2014 poll, just two weeks before European Parliament

---

[1] Excepting Northern Ireland, which uses an STV system.

[2] Local government has also been elected by STV in Northern Ireland since 1973.

[3] In essence, a voter puts a cross against their party of choice and parties receive a proportional allocation of seats based on the D'Hondt formula. The seats are allocated to parties depending on their order in the party's 'list', submitted before the election. If a party wins three seats, then the top three candidates on their list are elected.

elections, found that only 11 per cent of respondents felt confident they could name one of their MEPs compared to 52 per cent who felt they could name an MP. A system, such as an open-list or STV system, that allowed voters some say in who their MEPs are from among the party candidates, would allow for a greater sense of connection between voters and MEPs. This is backed up by evidence comparing other European countries (Hix and Hagemann 2009). Closed-list systems hence fail on our final principle of a clear connection between voters and identifiable representatives representing discrete areas.

The devolved legislatures of Scotland and Wales, as well as the London Assembly, are all elected by the AMS. In the British variant, voters have two ballots, one for a constituency representative and one for a party list. A majority of seats are elected by SM. These SM seats are then grouped into regions in Scotland and Wales with 7 and 4 representatives elected, respectively. In London, there is a single London-wide grouping. Seats are then handed out to parties in these regions on the basis of a calculation using the D'Hondt formula. This means that the list seats 'compensate' for proportionality by 'topping-up' parties to a proportionate allocation. However, due to small differences such as number of list seats in each region, and the relative numbers of SM seats to list seats, the implementation of AMSs actually differs quite noticeably in terms of proportionality.

The system may be seen as combining defects of both SM and list systems. For instance, safe seats still occur, and the closed-list nature of the proportionally elected seats can still make representatives seem distant. The two types of mandate have also caused issues with the two types of representatives being seen differently by voters. In Wales, this led to a change in the electoral law to ban candidates from standing on both the list and in a constituency, argued as being a way to stop 'second-best' constituency candidates winning on the list. Nevertheless, AMS can produce broadly proportional results and thus alleviate significant defects of the SM system. It has also enabled parties to sustain their presence in diverse areas, rather than face crushing defeats and subsequent challenge of rebuilding from a tiny base, common under SM systems.

PROPOSED ALTERNATIVE: SINGLE TRANSFERABLE METHOD OF PROPORTIONAL REPRESENTATION

The STV is a form of proportional representation with multi-member constituencies. Voters rank candidates in order of preference, by placing a 1 against the name of the candidate they prefer most, a 2 against the candidate who is their second preference, etc. Voters are free to decide how many candidates they rank.

Candidates must reach a quota to be elected and the percentage of the vote needed to win a seat is either stipulated under electoral law or calculated by a formula, one version of which is:

$$Q = \frac{\text{Total valid ballot papers received}}{\text{Number of seats} + 1}$$

(Electoral Reform Society 2011)

Q is the minimum quota a candidate must achieve in order to be elected, and every candidate who reaches the quota on first preferences wins a seat; the quota can be under 10 per cent depending on the turnout. If not enough candidates reach the quota to fill the available seats, the count continues with second preferences.

If a candidate gets more votes than the quota on first preferences, their second preference votes can be distributed appropriately to the other candidates, in a 'top-up' procedure; a weighting can be given to these distributed votes. Counting stops when all the seats are filled (Electoral Reform Society 2011).

STV is used for indirect elections to India's Upper House, to the Northern Ireland Assembly and for Northern Irish and Scottish local elections as well as in the Republic of Ireland, Malta and the Australian Senate. The Northern Irish political scene differs vastly from Great Britain, featuring as it does a totally different party system and a society riven by long-standing ethno–nationalist conflict. The choice of STV was made so as to guarantee PR for all parties and communities, and to minimise wasted votes. STV guarantees representation on community lines as unionists and nationalists can cast preferences for the party of their choice, with the knowledge that their vote cannot be 'wasted' and will travel to other parties in their community if they so wish. Finally, it was hoped that STV would result in voters casting preferences across their community boundaries, over time helping to break down religious divisions.

Scotland before 2007 had councils which were in effect one-party assemblies. Glasgow, Scotland's largest city, had a council where 89.9 per cent of seats were held by the Labour Party on 47.6 per cent of the vote. Midlothian's small 18 member council had only seen one opposition member elected in 1999. While 12 of Scotland's 32 councils were under No Overall Control (with no absolute majority), others lacked clear lines of accountability and opposition to hold them to account, a problem that continues to exist in England, where, for instance, after the 2015 local election five local authorities had no opposition representatives whatsoever.[4]

The introduction of STV in Scottish local government also eliminated uncontested seats—seats where only one candidate stands. There were 61 such in 2003, and none in 2007 or 2012. Councils have become much more politically diverse and former one-party councils have developed strong oppositions, becoming genuinely competitive. Candidates report reaching out to make contact with potential voters in areas they previously would not have spent time in (Electoral Reform Society 2013).

The multi-member STV wards mean voters have councillors from multiple parties giving more voters a representative closer to their views. There is some evidence that voters encourage their representatives to compete on constituency service, a welcome phenomenon which arguably keeps constituency service aspect of the link between resident and representative strong. The system has also showed itself durable in different electoral situations: from the partisan urban politics

---

[4] Knowsley, Manchester, Newham, East Hertfordshire (though one councillor has since left the ruling party and become an independent) and Mid Sussex.

of Glasgow to the island politics of Shetland, where independent rather than party candidates stand. As STV is candidate- rather than party-centric, such partisan and non-partisan elections work broadly similarly. In addition, against accusations that STV is too difficult for voters, people have also proved sophisticated in their use of their preferences.

Although STV has not brought about a rise in gender balance or a clear rise in turnout, it has vastly improved the quality of electoral accountability in Scotland, in contrast with persistent problems of one-party councils and uncontested seats that continue to dog England and Wales. A 2015 report for the Electoral Reform Society from the University of Cambridge looking at public procurement data found £2.6 bn of overspending linked to this poor electoral accountability (Fazekas 2015).

THE ADVANTAGES OF SINGLE TRANSFERABLE VOTE
Wider Choice for Voters

Parties can field more than one candidate, and independent candidates can also stand. STV gives voters more options than any other electoral system, and parties also have an incentive to field a range of candidates in order to maximise the number of second and third preferences. This reduces the temptation to select candidates mainly or solely on the grounds of their gender, caste or faith; secondly, candidates cannot risk alienating their own supporters with attacks on other candidates, because their own supporters may vote for the others as second or third preferences. This could also reduce the need for targeted campaigning. Furthermore, a personally unpopular candidate is unlikely to obtain second- or lower preference votes, and voters do not need to vote tactically so as to keep a candidate out, because the range of successful candidates is by definition wider than it is under the SM system.

Fixed Constituency Boundaries

When adopting STV, there is no need to redraw constituency boundaries so as to maintain roughly the same number of voters in each one. This allows for constituencies that more accurately represent constituency boundaries, by covering, say, a city or an English county. The number of representatives per constituency can be varied according to demographic changes, and the risk of gerrymandering can be weaker.

Assemblies Represent the Range of Voter Preferences

The elected assembly gives a much more accurate representation of the range of support among voters, and in particular gives significant third and fourth parties due weight. Two Indian examples support this point strongly. In the 2004–2009 Lok Sabha, PR would have given the winning Congress (on its own) 146 seats rather than 206, the BJP 134 and not 159, and the Left Front 115 instead of 79. Quite apart from the fact that 148 seats would have gone to other parties, the implications for parliamentary scrutiny of the executive—for example in respect of the composition of parliamentary committees—and for debate on draft legislation are obvious.

In certain state elections, the adoption of PR would have even more striking results. The SP, which won 226 of 403 assembly seats on under 30 per cent of the vote in the 2012 landslide, would have won only 117 seats and would have been 105 short of a majority; the second-placed BSP would have won 104 seats.

In India, a possible problem for a PR system is that post-election negotiations might well replace the current, already complicated and sometimes fragile, pre-poll alliances and seat-sharing agreements. Such deals often involve several parties. Pre-election agreements under the SM system, however, reduce the range of options available to voters at the ballot box, and the relevant decisions are taken not by the voters but by the party leaderships concerned. A PR system would give some of the relevant power of decision back to voters.

Far Fewer 'Wasted' Votes

Under STV, far fewer votes are cast for losing candidates or unnecessarily cast for the winner, and most voters can identify a representative whom they personally helped to elect. This can enhance the voters' sense of the link to their representatives.

Choice of Representatives between Elections

After an election, voters have a choice of representatives to approach, and can compare the representatives' responses. This can provide a more nuanced link between voters and their representatives than SM does. A possible advantage of STV for India is that successful candidates will generally not know whose votes have got them in, because they may have needed second- and third-preference votes in order to reach the quota.

No Safe Seats

Parties need to campaign everywhere, not just in marginal seats, and representatives cannot be complacent after being elected; they need to pay closer attention to their constituencies between elections. Politicians do not always like this; in the Republic of Ireland, where STV is used for all assemblies, they have twice tried to scrap STV, but the public defeated both attempts in the ensuing referenda (Electoral Reform Society n.d.). When the electoral system was discussed by the Republic's Constitutional Convention[5] in 2013, change was once again rejected.

A Possible End to Reserved Constituencies

A PR system using STV could end the need for reserved constituencies in India, as it would enable the election of assemblies which represent many more sections of society than they do at present; it would also, very probably, enlarge turnouts.

STV Is Not Difficult for Voters to Understand

On the evidence, voters grasp STV quickly, and generally use several preferences with care. In the 2012 Scottish local government elections, for which STV had first been used in 2007, over 65 per cent of

---

[5] Made up of 66 randomly selected citizens and 33 politicians.

voters in constituencies with 11 or more candidates used three or more preferences (Baston 2007; Curtice 2012: 13–14).

CONCLUSIONS

The increasing fragmentation, regionally and nationally, seen in both India and the UK, makes reform imperative. A country whose politics fail to properly represent all points of view, whether electoral or demographic, can only create disenchantment with the political process. It can mean government based on sectional interest. Any system also requires competition to create accountability. SM systems fail on these scores.

To its supporters, SM's failings are a feature, not a bug. But, in fact, SM has failed to function as its supporters claim. Neither India nor the UK is a two-party system. In India, the 2014 single-party majority was an aberration to the recent trend, not a usual occurrence. While the UK has had only one term without single-party majority government in recent decades, all evidence suggests that hung parliaments are to become more likely with time, and even the most recent election confirmed long-running trends of fragmentation and regional polarisation, while also electing a majority government on less than 37 per cent of the vote.

The simple reality is that neither Indian nor British voters conform to the expectations of the system, thus the SM system does not bear out even its supporters' justifications for it.

The principles we set out to evaluate electoral systems are principles designed for the modern age. While no electoral system is perfect, the electoral evidence shows that the STV is the system which best matches these principles.

Electoral systems cannot be considered in isolation from several wider issues, such as the nature and function of elected assemblies. The Indian Law Commission has noted a tension between the effectiveness of an assembly clearly ruled by a majority party and one in which several parties form a coalition government (Law Commission

2015: 83–84). This tension between the effectiveness of an assembly and its representative character has also been noted by Raymond Plant (Plant 1993). However, academia has never shown an empirical link between single-party majority government and governing effectiveness (Lijphart 1999). Outside academia, diverse groups now acknowledge the struggles of a two-party system in multi-party era, ranging from unionists keen to keep UK intact to those on left and right who feel in this context too much attention is drawn to centrist politics without expression or influence of pluralist views. The evidence we have adduced here, however, suggests that the SM electoral system itself, by generally favouring two larger parties above all others and by producing highly disproportionate majorities, contributes to the difficulties currently manifest in assemblies elected under it. By focusing primarily on electoral systems, we have tried to show here that a proportional electoral system could provide a solution to many of the problems the SM system generates, precisely because it would produce assemblies which represent the range of voters' preferences far more accurately than the SM system can do, because it provides voters access to a range of their own representatives, and because it reshapes the link between representatives and their respective constituencies.

REFERENCES

Baston, Lewis. 2007. *Local Authority Elections in Scotland*. Electoral Reform Society. Available at http://www.electoral-reform.org.uk/downloads/Scottishlocalgovernmentreport.pdf (accessed on 3 April 2008).

Curtice, John. 2012. *2012 Scottish Local Government Elections*. Electoral Reform Society. Available at http://www.electoral-teform.org.uk/images/dynamicImages/file512f4e5ae047f.pdf (accessed on 20 October 2012).

———. 2015. *The Lottery Election*. Electoral Reform Society. Available at http://www.electoral-reform.org.uk/sites/default/files/files/publication/the-lottery-election.pdf (accessed on 10 June 2016).

Economic & Political Weekly. 2009. 'Abuse of Privilege'. Editorial. *Economic & Political Weekly* 44 (26–27).

Electoral Reform Society. 2011 *What Is STV?* Available at http://www.electoral-reform.org.uk/publications/ (accessed on 28 February 2014).

Electoral Reform Society. N.d. 'Does Ireland Use Proportional Representation?' https://www.electoral-reform.org.uk/does-ireland-use-proportional-representation/ (accessed 21 September 2019).

Electoral Reform Society. 2013. *An Ordinary Election—STV in Edinburgh*. Available at https://www.youtube.com/watch?v=KflPqrMbBl0 (accessed on 4 April 2016).

Fazekas, Mihaly. 2015. *The Cost of One-Party Councils: Lack of Electoral Accountability and Public Procurement Corruption*. London: Electoral Reform Society.

Heath, Oliver. 2005. 'Party Systems, Political Cleavages and Electoral Volatility in India: A State-wise Analysis, 1998–1999'. *Electoral Studies* 24 (2): 177–199.

Hix, Simon, and Sara Hagemann. 2009. *Could Changing the Electoral Rules Fix European Parliament Elections?* Available at https://www.cairn.info/revue-politique-europeenne–2009–2-page–37.htm (accessed on 10 June 2016).

International Parliamentary Union (IPU). 2016. *Women in National Parliaments*. Available at http://www.ipu.org/wmn-e/classif.htm (accessed on 10 June 2016).

Jensenius, Francesca Refsum. 2012. 'Political Quotas in India: Perceptions of Political Representation'. *Asian Survey* 52 (2): 373–394.

———. 2014. 'Caught between Design and Expectations: The Path-Dependent History of Political Quotas in India.' *Journal of Asian Studies* 3.

———. 2015. 'Development from Representation? A Study of Quotas for Scheduled Castes in India'. *American Economic Journal* 7 (3): 196–220.

Kumar, Mohinder. 2010. 'On the So-called Fund Misutilisation under MP-LADS'. *Economic & Political Weekly* 45 (25): 102–104.

Law Commission of India. 2015. *Electoral Reforms*. Law Commission Report No. 255. New Delhi: Government of India.

Lijphart, Arend. 1999. *Patterns of Democracy*. London: Yale University Press.

Mortimer, Josiah, and Chis Terry. 2015. *Women in Westminster: Predicting the Number of Female MPs*. Available at http://www.electoral-reform.org.uk/sites/default/files/files/publication/women-in-westminster.pdf (accessed on 10 June 2016).

Pal, Rupayan, and Aparajita Das. 2010. 'A Scrutiny of the MP-LADS in India: Who Is It For?' *Economic & Political Weekly* 45 (10): 63–68.

Plant, Raymond. 1993. *Report of the Working Party on Electoral Systems*. London: Labour Party.

Ramachandran, V. 2005. 'A Chronic Aberration'. *Economic & Political Weekly* 40 (19): 1965–1967.

Ramani, Srinivasan. 2012. 'A Flawed Democracy—The Case for Proportional Representation in India'. Available at http://kafila.org/2012/03/15/a-flawed-democracy-the-case-for-proportional-representation-in-india-srinivasan-ramani/ (accessed on 9 February 2014).

The *Hindu*. 2014, 27 May. 'Issues in Electoral Arithmetic'. Editorial. Available at http://www.thehindu.com/opinion/editorial/issues-in-electoral-arithmetic/article6050328.ece (accessed on 12 September 2014).

Terry, Chris. *Penny for Your Vote?: Counting the Costs of an Unfair Electoral System*. Available at http://www.electoral-reform.org.uk/sites/default/files/Penny-for-your-vote-costs-of-fptp.pdf (accessed on 10 June 2016).

Thakur, Meenal, and Pretika Khanna. 2015, 9 October. 'BJP Takes on History, Nitish Kumar in Bihar Elections'. *Livemint*. Available at http://www.livemint. com/Politics/nikKVHg8HbjB98k98Am3vM/BJP-takes-on-history-Nitish-Kumar-in-Bihar-elections.html (accessed on 13 December 2015).

Wikipedia. 2014, 26 February. *Indian General Election, 2009*. Available at http:// en.wikipedia.org/wiki/Indian_general_election,_2009 (accessed on 28 February 2014).

PART II

Political Processes

Chapter 5

The Election Commission of India and General Elections

N. Gopalaswami

INTRODUCTION

India attained independence from British rule in 1947 and became a republic by adopting a Constitution on 26 January 1950; the new Constitution made India a sovereign democratic republic, and the 42nd Amendment, passed in 1976, made the country a sovereign secular socialist democratic republic. In 1950, India was a largely agrarian country with a population whose literacy rate was about 15 per cent with female literacy at an abysmally low 7 per cent. The lawmakers were however not deterred, but intuitively placing their faith in the democratic spirit of the people, they both adopted a democratic model of governance and underlined their faith in the citizens of India by opting for universal adult franchise. People have repaid that trust in ample measure by participating enthusiastically in exercising their franchise in all 17 general elections to date and more than 350 elections to the state assemblies. At independence, India adopted the single member Simple Majority or First Past the Post (FPTP) system, which was already used by the colonial power, the United Kingdom. The Election Commission of India (ECI) was empowered as a constitutional authority, with plenary powers incorporated in Part XV of the Constitution in Articles 324 to 329. The ECI was constituted on 25 January 1950, one day before the country became a Republic.

THE EARLY YEARS

The first Chief Election Commissioner (CEC) had a daunting task in planning the entire procedure for the holding of the first countrywide elections. Keeping in view the low literacy levels, he decided on having one separate box and a symbol for each contesting candidate to enable the voter to easily identify the candidate of his/her choice. The first general election was held over a period of 7 months, despite the political executive being unhappy with such a long-drawn-out election, as the staff had to be trained in understanding the election law and in implementing it correctly. Further preparation of voters list and printing of ballot papers were all time-consuming efforts. By the time of the third general election in 1962, individual candidate boxes were replaced by one single box for all candidates and a single ballot paper was introduced carrying names of all candidates with their symbols printed alongside; the earlier pencil marking procedure gave way to rubber stamps with the attendant problems of smudging and impressions over the name of other candidates than the one chosen by the voter; modified rubber stamps with a circular arrow mark instead of 'x' mark were introduced to recapitulate a few changes. In addition, problems of enrolment in the voters list, preventing 'bogus' entries in the electoral roll, preventing malpractices during election time were some of the issues that the ECI tackled over these years with varying degree of success.

Notwithstanding these problems, the ECI, through many innovations and with its commitment to delivering a free and fair election, has earned respect and reputation, within and outside the country, for well-organised elections, though the sheer size of its operation has been mind-boggling. Part of the credit for this achievement should go to the political leadership and political parties for having given the ECI and its decisions due respect and acceptance. Another contributory factor is the neutral bureaucracy in which the Constitution-makers placed their faith to run the administrative machinery of the country.

INDIAN ELECTIONS GO ELECTRONIC—THE INTRODUCTION OF ELECTRONIC VOTING MACHINES

The ECI found problems with the use of ballot papers as the electorate size kept rising in tune with the rapid increase in population. The electorate, which was 173.2 million in 1951, was at 356.2 million in 1980. The printing, the logistics for checking and transportation, the handling of ballot papers of increasing size with the steady increase in the number of contesting candidates and, not the least, the counting of large number of ballots that used to take the best part of a day—all these problems made the ECI explore alternatives to ballot papers. By 1981, the ECI was ready with an electronic voting machine (EVM), largely shaped to mimic the ballot paper, which it put to use from 1982 onwards but in small steps, only to be stopped in its tracks by the Supreme Court (SC), which embargoed EVMs in 1984, on the ground of lack of legal provision. It was a decade before the Parliament passed the required law, and a parliamentary committee aided by the advice of an Expert Technical Committee set up for the purpose recommended the use of EVMs. Inexplicably, the ECI started using the machines only in 1998; it hastened slowly, so to speak, by gradually increasing the number of machines used, until finally, it started using EVMs in the whole of one state election after another from 2001 onwards and then extended the practice nationwide for the first time in the 14th general elections to the Lower House of Parliament—Lok Sabha (LS)—in 2004. Since then, the EVMs have come to stay, having got the approval of the electorate for the ease of operation at the polling booth, totally eliminating the category of 'invalid' votes, and, more importantly, for making counting of votes so quick as to make results available within 8 hours as against the earlier day-long operation.

But the EVMs' phenomenal success led to some unforeseen problems. Defeated candidates made it a habit to voice doubts about results claiming 'fixing' of the machines by the winning candidates aided and abetted by the government in office. The ECI's response was to strengthen transparency by introducing two-step randomisation in allotting a machine to a polling station, sharing the machine's identity number to enable party representatives at the polling booths to check it and finally a two-step mock poll—one before the machines were despatched from the storage facility and the second at the polling station, before the commencement of the poll. Notwithstanding all these measures, when challenges were mounted in the SC citing lack of a Voter Verifiable Paper Audit Trail (VVPT), the ECI agreed to introduce the latter but over a period of time, in the light of costs and logistics of manufacturing over 1.5 million VVPATs.

Since the 2014 General Elections to the Parliament, EVMs with VVPT have been introduced, though selectively. Costs have come down drastically over this period with design modifications and other cost reduction measures, with the result that EVMs and VVPATs are now about $250–300 (₹17,000–20,000) per piece.

The Indian EVM is a simple machine that keeps adding the number of hits a button gets, stores the data and displays it when the 'result' button is pressed at the counting table. It is a stand-alone machine that is not connected to any network and therefore cannot be accessed from outside through any wireless signal. A unique feature of the EVM is the addition of a button 'NOTA' (2014): short form for 'None of the Above'. This button can be pressed by a voter when he/she decides that none of the contesting candidates is good enough to receive his/her vote. Though at present NOTA can merely provide psychological satisfaction to a dissatisfied voter, this feature has the potential to send a signal to parties and candidates if there is general dissatisfaction over candidate selection by political parties. According to a study done by the ECI, use of EVMs in place of ballot papers saves 8,000 tonnes of paper in one election, and 16,000 tonnes every 5 years as there is one general election to the Parliament and one general election to every state assembly during that period, an unintended but very welcome benefit.

CONDUCTING ELECTIONS—CHALLENGES AND RESPONSES

Corruption and hypocrisy ought not to be inevitable products of democracy as they undoubtedly are, today.

—Mahatma Gandhi (Vol. 3, p.301, *Collected Works*)

Politics is often acknowledged as a means to the pursuit of power, and in a democracy levers of power are accessed through the medium of elections. Periodic elections held in a free and fair manner are the very basis of a democracy and hence its importance. 'Eternal vigil is the price of democracy' may be a cliché but that exercise of keeping the vigil starts from the first step, namely the holding of periodic elections to let the citizen choose representatives to exercise power on their behalf for a defined period of time. The ECI has had a fine track record in competently conducting elections to the Parliament and state assemblies, but the process has not always been a smooth one. As the initial euphoria of achieving independence and status as a republic abated, slowly and surely mere pursuit of power became the goal and electoral malpractices reared their head.

Manipulating the electoral rolls, booth capturing, bogus voting were some of the malpractices that became rampant in some parts of the country. As the elections were managed by state government officials, manipulating the staff was also another tactic used by the politicians. Poll-eve transfers of officials in charge of elections, bringing in officials, especially police personnel, perceived to be sympathetic to the ruling dispensation were some of the actions that put a question mark on the neutrality of the election machinery and the fairness of election process.

It is in this scenario that T. N. Seshan, a retired senior bureaucrat, took charge as CEC in 1990, and in the next few years he embarked on a clean-up by merely effectively exercising the powers vested in the ECI by law. First, governments were made to accept that ECI was in charge of all civil and police officials of the administration involved in election work and for the entire duration of the election have to abide by the orders of the ECI; that ECI can ask for transfer officials whose neutrality was suspect in its opinion and the governments have to comply with the request; that the state was bound to provide assistance of additional police forces as sought by the ECI and their deployment would be within the competence of the ECI. Two very important steps taken by the ECI under Mr Seshan were: (a) that every voter will be given a photo identity card (ID) by the ECI officials to prevent impersonation at the polling booth and the states should provide enough funds to enable issue of photo IDs; (b) the government of the day in no way can disturb the level playing field and should adhere to the Model Code of Conduct (MCC) scrupulously failing which the ECI can take both administrative and legal actions to secure compliance. Thus, the ECI regained the moral high ground and secured the premier role that the Constitution gave it in the conduct of election.

THE MODEL CODE OF CONDUCT

One of the issues that agitates all political parties during the run-up to elections is the potential of ruling parties misusing powers over government machinery for political gain. Much discussion in the Constituent Assembly debates centred around possible manipulation of electoral rolls by ruling parties. But the ambit of the suspicion grew much wider after independence as governments in office controlled considerable funds and could favour some constituency or the other and such favours peaked in the period immediately before the elections. Administration in Kerala state (1960) took the initiative to prepare a draft code of conduct for political parties and candidates, discussed with political parties and arrived at a consensus on the dos and don'ts during electioneering. Since incumbent governments had the best advantage, the code of conduct had much that was envisaged to neutralise it. Not using government servants directly or indirectly in campaigning or influencing voters; not appropriating all public venues for electioneering by the ruling party; not using government facilities like guest houses, vehicles by government ministers for party or election related work; not luring voters by announcing new schemes after elections are called; not appealing for votes on religious or caste lines affecting relations between communities and castes; and avoiding personal criticism during campaign speeches were some of the restrictions proposed. This unique document even had an all-party committee headed by the chief minister of the state for overseeing its implementation. Subsequently it was adopted in many other states as well with the responsibility for implementation being cast in the ECI, which further refined it and from 1990 onwards, has been implementing it rigorously. This unique document voluntarily accepted by political parties themselves has by and large been adhered to by them though it is not legally enforceable and so mere violation of the MCC does not make it a prosecutable offence. It is more a self-disciplining 'moral' code put together in a true democratic spirit by the stakeholders. It has contributed immensely to keep the political discourse sane during election season.

CURRENT CHALLENGES
Muscle Power

India may be one country united by many national institutions but it has diverse cultures, languages and customs. With varying levels of education, economic prosperity and other social indicators, it is no wonder that in terms of political culture there is tremendous variation from area to area and state to state. If there are many states where elections are orderly and peaceful, there are also states/areas where raw muscle power and money power are on display. Use of muscle power to win by booth-capturing or intimidation especially of the poor and downtrodden sections of society was widely reported from certain areas but in the last decades strong measures by the ECI have almost totally eliminated booth-capturing and have largely curbed voter intimidation. This has, however, been achieved by the ECI deploying heavy police contingents which effectively silenced the guns of the goons. Intimidation, often of lower caste voters, by intermediate and upper caste muscle-men, has been largely neutralised by preventive arrests of potential troublemakers prior to poll day and by providing special police escorts to voters. Another step has been to provide separate polling stations for the vulnerable sections of society in relaxation of the general rule that one village generally should have only one polling station for a voter strength of 1,000–1,200 voters.

Money Power—Buying Votes

While Indian elections have not been free from candidates indulging voters with gifts which mainly took the form of liquor and food for those attending public meetings, new forms of voter 'capture' came into vogue post-economic liberalisation in the mid-1990s. With increasing economic activity, more state spending in major projects and more privatisation of services, there was more at stake for the politician aiming to capture the levers of power and this resulted in heavy expenditure in elections by the candidates, much in excess of the ceiling prescribed. Since there was no ceiling on party expenditure, that loophole was exploited to conceal candidate expenditure. Increasing penetration of visual media and communication facilities meant TV advertisements and mobile phones' SMS added to conventional public meetings and street-corner speeches pushing up expenditure. With sizeable increase in youth voters comfortable with technology, it was inevitable that candidates and parties extensively used Facebook, Twitter, etc., employing an army of people for constant updation of information adding to expenditures. Yet most candidates filed expenditure statements that were lower than even the permitted expenditure though it was common knowledge that actual expenditures were far in excess of the prescribed ceilings. But the uglier part of the story is the distribution of hard cash for votes in states such as Tamil Nadu and Andhra Pradesh. A parallel development was the buying of favours from the media, both print and visual. Despite elaborate arrangements to stop illegal cash flows and excessive expenditure in elections, the ECI did not succeed in that mission.

Paid News

An equally pernicious practice that developed was buying favours from media, both print and visual, by paying for it which in the first instance was initiated by corrupt elements in the media itself, the chief culprit allegedly being the vernacular press. The ECI makes elaborate arrangements through its expenditure observers posted to track candidates' expenditure, videotaping their public meetings and cross-checking their expenditure bills and statements. Notwithstanding all that there has been so for only one case of disqualification for false reporting of election expenditure of a member of Legislative Assembly of Uttar Pradesh state (Press Information Bureau, Government of India 2011). Another case of a former Chief Minister of Maharashtra state, where an investigating journalist unearthed 'paid news'—an arrangement where the candidate pays the media for putting out news about him/her—and the defeated candidate sought action, is pending in the SC of India.

The rampant use of money by candidates and parties in elections has been a cause for concern as most of it involves 'black' money or unaccounted and tax-evaded income. It is not unusual for many commentators to criticise elections for spawning 'black money,' little realising and refusing to acknowledge, that runaway election expenditure is not the cause but merely the manifestation of the 'black' money in the economy.

'Criminals' in Legislatures

An inevitable fallout of increasing use of muscle power and choice of contestants based on a 'Winnability' formula employed by the political parties has been the steady increase in candidates with criminal cases pending against them; more disturbingly, those accused of serious offences like murder, rape, dacoity, robbery and the like often contest and win election. If initially parties merely used muscle-men to improve their chances to win, later muscle-men saw their chance to attain legitimacy by themselves seeking party nominations to enter legislatures. All parties have their share of such candidates/legislators and over the years their numbers have been growing. Civil society organisations have demanded a legal bar on contestants charged with 'heinous' offences, but citing possible political vendetta, if mere charge sheet was to be a bar to contest elections and not conviction for an offence, successive parliamentary committees have rejected this demand though Law Commissions headed by eminent judges have recommended the measure. According to a study by a non-governmental organisation (NGO), the Association for Democratic Reforms (ADR), the current (16th) LS has 34 per cent of MPs with criminal cases pending against them (up from 30% in 2009) of whom 21 per cent have serious charges against them (up from 15% in 2009) (Association for Democratic Reforms 2014: 47).

Conducting Elections in Left-Wing Extremism Affected Areas

India has been affected by extremist group activities in different parts of the country, some even before independence. While in the north-eastern states of the country secessionist groups had been widely active earlier, now such groups are confined to one or two states only. Local administrations have been successful in containing them during the elections; local parties have at times colluded with them or have co-opted them but these movements have not seriously disrupted the election process.

However, the insurgency led by the Left-wing extremist groups in the tribal areas of the country affecting a considerable part of as many as five states—Bihar, Jharkhand, Odisha, Chhattisgarh, Madhya Pradesh and Maharashtra—does pose serious challenges during elections. So the scale of deployment of armed police forces of the Union in these areas has been high and successfully conducting the poll has been quite a task. There have been instances in which polling stations have been relocated for fear of attacks, including attacks on security staff and civilians, who chose to vote despite calls for boycotts. There have also been instances when polling never took place in the first instance at the announced location because the staff was too scared and this when discovered later had led to fresh polls, with more police personnel to provide cover, or at less vulnerable new locations. All in all, election after election this challenge has persisted.

First Past the Post Electoral System

India, like the UK, adopted the FPTP or Simple Majority system to decide the results in each constituency. The full import of the negative aspects of this system became evident only after the first few elections, as in the early years there was an overwhelming dominance of one party almost throughout India. Later, however, as the electorate became less inclined towards one party, and divided as it was by caste and community and other such factors, more and more winners came to be decided by a minority of the votes cast. With turnout never crossing the 60 per cent mark in most elections, both to the Parliament and the State Assemblies, the winners typically came to represent not more than 30 to 40 per cent of the voters and 20 to 25 per cent of the electorate. The situation is acute in the economically backward states of UP and Bihar. Taking all 29 states into consideration, only two states, Kerala and Gujarat, had a better record with a larger proportion of the winning candidates scoring 50 per cent or more of votes polled in their respective constituencies because of the emergence of only two parties having state-wide appeal. An alternative suggested is to prescribe a minimum of 50 per cent plus one vote for the winner and going for a run-off election between the winner and first runner-up if the first round fails to throw up a decisive winner. The introduction of a Proportional Representation (PR) system, or its variants, such as a hybrid system, has been suggested as another alternative (Law Commission of India 2015).

High Number of Parties and Contestants

With an electorate that is influenced heavily by considerations of caste and community, the inevitable fallout has been the proliferation of parties vying for the votes of specific sections of the population. With parties selecting 'winnable' candidates based on caste and community affiliations, from election to election the average number of contesting candidates has been going up. The all-India average stood at 15 candidates per constituency in the 2014 general elections, causing further division of votes and lowering the threshold for victory (Election Commission of India 2017: 55). The scene has been complicated by a legal lacuna as the ECI has powers to register new political parties but does not to de-register even those ones that show neither any visible political activity nor contest elections.

Political Parties—Lack of Transparency and Inner Party Democracy

The Indian Constitution did not have any mention of political parties till a 1989 reference in an anti-defection law. But from the beginning elections were fought on party lines with the ECI notifying a symbols order that governed allotment of symbols to ECI-recognised state or national party and free symbols for unrecognised parties and independent candidates. Though the conditions of registration provide, inter alia, for periodical inner party elections, most parties appoint office-bearers by selection rather than election, a sad lack of inner party democracy. While all parties adhere to the requirement to submit audited annual accounts, they are rather opaque on sources of their incomes. Parties have steadfastly refused to have their accounts audited by the government auditor as suggested by the ECI. Demands by civil society groups and ECI's proposal for a law to regulate the political parties have not found traction with successive governments.

Voter Apathy

The ECI is the prime mover for voter registration and it proactively undertakes this work every year starting from September for the voter list that will be published on 1 January of the following year. Though complaints of missing names surface from time to time, problems arise mainly because with elections held once in 5 years, voters generally bestir themselves to register only in the period before the election year. Further, with uneven economic growth and rapid urbanisation, there is large-scale intrastate and interstate movement of people and capturing the changes, in the absence of a unique ID, has become difficult and problem of missing names and duplications has persisted. The attempt of the ECI to integrate the voter ID card with the pan-India unique ID (Aadhaar), which is based on iris and finger print data, has run into problems with the SC embargoing its use, as of now, on privacy concerns.

While polling has been, barring exceptions, below 60 per cent in most elections, the worrying factor has been the poor polling in urban areas and more particularly the reluctance of the better educated to exercise their franchise. The trend changed for the better in 2013 and in the 2014 general elections in part because of the voter education campaign of the ECI and partly because of vigorous voter mobilisation by political parties.

Women's Representation

Even though women voters form half the electorate, women's representation in legislative bodies has mostly been below 10 per cent. Women's groups have been agitating for reserving 33 per cent of seats. Though successive governments in the last two decades have expressed their sympathy for this cause and have tried to move a legislation, consensus has eluded the political class on this issue.

Notwithstanding that on many of the issues satisfactory resolution through legislative action, a prerogative of the Parliament, has not come about, civil society groups have been raising the issue of electoral reforms in many fora and have mounted challenges in the courts. The ECI has also been taking these issues up periodically by itself and before bodies such as the Law Commission, the Commission to review the Constitution and the like. But the response of the political establishment has been lukewarm. This, however, has not in any way diminished the quality of elections conducted by the ECI which has distinguished itself by delivering elections in the last six decades that have won praise all round.

THE COURTS, ECI AND ELECTION LAW

The ECI as a constitutional body has its responsibilities spelt out in the Constitution with election commissioners treated as equivalent to the judges of the SC in status, exercising quasi-judicial powers to decide matters coming up before them. However, their decisions are subject to judicial review. Over the years the higher judiciary, be it the high courts (HCs) or SC, has generally supported the actions of the ECI if the actions concerned are integral to the conduct of free and fair elections. The higher judiciary has also supported civil society efforts to empower voters.

Courts Not to Interfere during the Course of Elections

The Indian Constitution bars the courts from entertaining any plea against steps initiated by the ECI while elections are under way (Article 329). Courts have therefore refused to interfere when (a) nominations are rejected, (b) elections are rescheduled or countermanded, (c) polling or counting is under way, (d) election results are declared or (e) staff including police personnel are deployed. Courts have interpreted the constitutional provisions broadly to cover every activity related to the conduct of elections. This, however, does not mean permanent injunctions. The courts have taken up such issues after elections in order to ensure that there has been no miscarriage of justice and that the ECI has strictly adhered to the provisions of law and has not in any manner compromised with the mandate to conduct a free and fair poll.

While the courts have upheld the pre-eminent position enjoyed by the ECI in the conduct of elections, the following landmark judgements will show how the courts have supported ECI action and also empowered the voters.

1. *Mohinder Singh Gill and another vs Chief Election Commissioner* (Civil Appeal 12 97 or 1977)

   During the 1977 general elections, the CEC ordered the cancellation of an entire poll when there was disturbance during counting and the SC upheld order of the HC in not entertaining the contestant's petition to cancel CEC's order, holding that during the pendency of poll process courts cannot interfere.

2. *Election Commission of India vs State of Haryana* (Civil Appeal No. 2182 of 1984)

   The ECI had notified a by-election despite the state government's view that the law and order situation was not conducive to the holding of the poll. The HC upheld the contention of the state government but the SC reversed that decision, holding that the timing of an election was the prerogative of the ECI.

3. *Lakshmi Charan Sen and Others vs Election Commission and Others* (Civil Appeals 739 to 741 and 742 of 1982)

   The SC observed that the HC should not entertain any petition that would have the effect of postponing elections indefinitely so as to create a situation where a government of a state cannot be carried on as per the Constitution.

4. *Indrajit Baria and Others vs Election Commission of India* (Case No. 364 to 382 of 1984)

   The SC declared that defects in a finalised Electoral Roll cannot be the ground in election petitions to challenge a duly held election.

5. *Kanhaiya Lal Omar vs CEC and Others* (Writ Petition No. 11738 of 1985)

   A symbols order was challenged on the ground that as such an order is legislative in character, the ECI was not competent to make it. The SC held that the ECI drew its strength from the plenary powers vested in it by Article 324(1) of the Constitution.

6. *Union of India vs Association of Democratic Reforms (ADR) and Peoples' Union for Civil Liberties (PUCL)* (Writ Petition (C) No. 294 of 2001)

   The SC agreed with the contention of the two NGO bodies, ADR and PUCL, that contesting candidates should be obliged to file, along with the nomination, two sworn affidavits—one, giving details of their assets and liabilities; and the second, giving details of criminal cases pending against them.

   This was a landmark judgement that sought to empower the elector citizen with better information about the candidates enabling him/her to make an informed decision in exercising their franchise.

7. *Lily Thomas vs Union of India & Ors, Lok Prahari vs Union of India & Ors* (Writ Petition (Civil) No. 490 of 2005 and 231 of 2005)

   This judgement, made on 10 July 2013, had far-reaching consequences. The petitioners, a lawyer and an NGO, respectively, had questioned the legality of the provision in Sec.8(4) of Representation of the People Act, 1951, which protected from disqualification sitting legislators convicted of an offence if they appealed against that order in a competent higher court within 3 months. By agreeing with the contention of the petitioners and striking down the provision, the SC struck a blow for cleaner legislators.

8. *PUCL and Another vs Union of India and Another* (Writ Petition (Civil) No. 161 of 2004; decided on 27 September 2013)

The SC allowed a plea by two NGO bodies that there should be a separate button saying 'NOTA' on EVMs to provide an opportunity to a voter to express his/her disapproval if none of the candidates was found fit to receive his/her vote. The judgement was especially commendable for the way it overcame the objection of the government to the invoking of writ jurisdiction, applicable only to a constitutional right, whereas the right to vote was merely a statutory right. SC distinguished the right to vote, a statutory right and the citizen's act of voting at the booth, a manifestation of the constitutionally guaranteed fundamental right to freedom of speech and expression.

CONCLUSION

India chose the path of democracy with full adult franchise. Grass-roots level democratic institutions have come up at village and town level with local body elections to choose their representatives. In these 65 years, democracy has taken deep roots with people participating in elections voluntarily and enthusiastically. This is a tribute to the ordinary men and women on the street who have placed great faith in the institutions of democracy. That is one reason why despite many privations and inequities, the country has not gone the 'dictatorial' or 'military rule' path though countries in the neighbourhood have struggled to remain on the path of democracy. It is also a tribute to the founding fathers and the political class of the country. That reforms are needed to make politicians in power more accountable and responsive is an unexceptionable and widely held opinion but as things stand today, every Indian can be justifiably proud of being a citizen of the largest democracy in the world.

REFERENCES

Association for Democratic Reforms. 2014. *Lok Sabha Election Watch 2014*. Available at https://adrindia.org/research-and-reports/documents-publications (accessed on 7 March 2019).

Election Commission of India. 2017. *Electoral Statistics Pocket Book*. New Delhi: Election Commission of India.

Law Commission of India. 2015. *Electoral Reforms*. Law Commission Report No. 255. New Delhi: Government of India. Available at http://lawcommissionofindia.nic.in/reports/Report255.pdf (accessed on 16 February 2019).

Press Information Bureau, Government of India. 2011, 21 October. *Disqualification of Smt. Umlesh Yadav, MLA from Uttar Pradesh for Filing Incorrect Account of Election Expenditure—Suppression of Expenditure Incurred on 'Paid News'*. Available at http://pib.nic.in/newsite/PrintRelease.aspx?relid=76804 (accessed on 7 March 2019).

Chapter 6

India's Democracy
Lost and Regained

M. G. Devasahayam

THE BACKDROP

Long years ago, we made a tryst with destiny, and now the time comes when we shall redeem our pledge, not wholly or in full measure, but very substantially. At the stroke of the midnight hour, when the world sleeps, India will awake to life and freedom.

These historic words were spoken by India's first Prime Minister Jawaharlal Nehru in the Constituent Assembly to which power was to be transferred from the colonial regime. This heralded democracy in the ancient land of India ravaged by conquerors and plunderers for centuries, and this happened at midnight on 14–15 August 1947. Democracy for India should have been ushered in at mid-day! But it happened at midnight, perhaps a bad omen.

Jawaharlal Nehru probably had some premonition. So, he entered a strong caveat:

We rejoice in that freedom, even though clouds surround us, and many of our people are sorrow-stricken and difficult problems encompass us....We shall never allow that torch of freedom to be blown out, however high the wind or stormy the tempest.

This freedom was to give opportunity to the common man, to the peasants and workers of India; to fight and end poverty and ignorance and disease; to build up a prosperous, democratic and progressive nation, and to create social, economic and political institutions which will ensure justice and fullness of life to every man and woman. It is to them that Nehru said the future beckoned! Little did he realise that about a quarter of a century later his own daughter would blow out that 'torch of freedom'!

'IDEA OF INDIA'

The future Nehru talked about was to be built on the idea of independent India. 'Objectives Resolution' moved by Nehru himself in 1946 seeking a Republic 'wherein all power and authority of the Sovereign Independent India, its constituent parts and organs of government, are derived from the people' (Nehru 1946). As early as 1922, Gandhiji had described *Swaraj* as merely a 'courteous ratification of the declared wish of the people of India' (Gandhi 1922). Visions of these two top Founding Fathers envisaged people-centred democracy with a bottom-up decision-making process that would give the common man, the peasants and workers of India a place in the sun.

Structurally, India's democracy was to rise storey by storey from the foundation comprising of self-governing, self-sufficient, agro-industrial, urbo-rural local communities. These self-governing entities will control and regulate the use of natural resources for the good of the community and the nation. The highest political institution of the local community is the *gram sabha*, of which all the adults are considered members. The next storey was the *panchayat samiti* and then the *zilla parishad* (district council) which was to be formed by the integration of the *panchayat samiti*s of the district. All the district councils of a state would come together to create the state assembly. The state assemblies, in like manner, would bring into being the Lok Sabha. Thus, the political institution at each level is an integration of all the institutions at the lower level. In this bottom-up structure, there is no place for political parties (Narayan 1959).

Development would not follow the Western pattern of mega industrialisation, urbanisation and individuation. India's economy would be a people's economy, one that would chart out a distinct course in economic development. India would pursue need-based, human-scale, balanced development while conserving nature and livelihoods. God-given resources—land, water, jungle and minerals—belong to the people and would be managed at grass-roots level.

These ideas of India built into the Preamble of the Constitution (1950) became the 'Philosophy of the Republic'. Unfortunately, the earlier ideas and the philosophy were not reflected in the form of government built into the Constitution. Instead it was a top-down system and structure, a near replica of what was in the Government of India Act, 1935, enacted during British Raj–an all-powerful Parliament and central government, with limited powers for the State Legislatures and governments, respectively, and no powers for Panchayats and Urban Local Bodies. There was no trace of *Swaraj*.

Even this contrived and highly centralised structure is presided over by leaders from political parties that practice very little democracy or accountability. These entities function as, so to speak, loose cannons without constitutional mandate and legislative rigour, in a virtual free-for-all. Over a period of time, the Legislature and Executive became tools for the powers-that-be to rule rather than an instrument for the people of India to govern themselves with genuine accountability. The higher judiciary—the Supreme Court and the respective high courts—by their very structure were far removed from the people in terms of distance, cost and procedures accessible only to the government agencies and the well-heeled. Since the appointment of superior court judges is through a spoils system where political favouritism plays a large part, most of them were pro-government. Their commitment to fundamental rights and civil liberties was very thin. People were rendered as mere 'voting machines' deprived of voice and choice when it came to life, liberty and livelihood!

The biggest political favour in the appointment to higher judiciary was the elevation of Justice A. N. Ray as Chief Justice of Supreme Court by the then Prime Minister Indira Gandhi regime, superseding three senior judges of the top court—Justices Jaishanker Manilal Shelat, A. N. Grover and K. S. Hegde.

The appointment was made on 25 April 1973, a day after the SC's judgement in the Kesavananda Bharati case, where a 13-judge Constitution bench, by a 7–6 verdict, had outlined the 'basic structure' doctrine of the Constitution and had prohibited its amendment by the Parliament. This had greatly disturbed the autocratic ambitions of Indira Gandhi. While Justice A. N. Ray was among the six dissenting judges in the case (supporting amendment of basic structure), Justices Shelat, Hegde and Grover, whom he had superseded, were on the side of the majority prohibiting amendment (Press Trust of India 2018).

This had been viewed as an attack on the independence of the judiciary and resulted in a major political controversy and was a key issue in the JP Movement that followed. During Emergency when Supreme Court upheld the election of Indira Gandhi by setting aside the Allahabad High Court verdict JP was of the opinion that this was a dishonest judgement because Chief Justice A. N. Ray was under great personal obligation to Indira for appointing him as Chief Justice of India, superseding other judges. As such, he could not be expected to be impartial. This was a big blow to the integrity of the highest court of law in the country (Devasahayam 2011).

ABANDONING THE 'IDEA OF INDIA'

As Independent India's first Prime Minister who enjoyed uninterrupted power for 17 years (1947–1964), Jawaharlal Nehru was expected to create a political, administrative and economic bulwark based on the 'idea of India', on which the future was to be built. Politically, it should have been a strong grass-roots democracy based on *panchayat raj* institutions. Administratively, there should have been a paradigm change from a colonial–command system to a democratic-participatory framework of governance. The model of economic development should have been people-centred, with 'production by the masses' instead of 'mass production' (Hoda n.d.). With value-added agriculture as the root, appropriate technology and infrastructure as the trunk, manufacturing small/medium industries as branches and widespread service sector as canopy, Nehru could have raised India's polity and its economy as a strong tree with deep roots.

But Nehru took a different path. Simultaneously he pursued communism and capitalism and called it mixed economy. Torn between these opposing 'ideologies', Nehru wanted to create a balance between the rural and the urban as well as agricultural and industrial sectors in his economic policies. He saw no contradiction between these and stated that they could go hand in hand. Nehru hailed Western-style large and heavy industries as 'temples of modern India' and big dams to be the very symbol of India's collective growth and source of energy. For Nehru, 'industrial engineering and agriculture met on a common platform'. So, farming, which should have been the growth catalyst for the vast mass of people, lost out.

Nehru's brand of mixed economy attempted to bring together disparate elements—command and control colonial structure; highly centralised state-owned Soviet communism and the relatively decentralised private-owned industrial capitalism—under one roof. Communists and capitalists were tied together and asked to march towards prosperity and progress under the tutelage of colonial institutions! Though Nehru dreamt of achieving the best of these systems, India ended up suffering the worst of all these. With democracy sans grass roots and its economy on shaky grounds, the 'idea of India' stood abandoned. The natural corollary was economic stagnation, widespread poverty, unemployment and deep-set iniquity.

Soon Nehru's daughter Indira Gandhi assumed the mantle of the prime ministership. She made a political virtue of the poverty (*garibi*) inherited from her father, coined the slogan of '*garibi hatao*' (banish poverty) and won a massive electoral victory in 1971. When this orchestrated hype flopped, public anger surfaced. The democratic structure Founding Fathers had put together did not have strong safety valves to absorb this anger. The poor and chaotic economy bequeathed by Nehru was flogged to the full by Indira Gandhi. As for institutional framework, at the time of Nehru's death it was still 'work-in-progress'. Anger among the youth crystallised in the form of JP Movement against corruption, unemployment and price rise.

The ground was ripe for Indira Gandhi to fully exploit the economic distress and public unrest and portray democracy and its institutions as hurdles for economic growth and poverty alleviation. She was willing to resort to political dictatorship to implement her autocratic agenda and was only waiting for the right moment to strike. The moment came as the JP Movement gathered speed. This was the premonition Nehru had and it came true 28 years later, again stealthily, at midnight on 25–26 June 1975.

JP AND HIS MOVEMENT

During the freedom struggle, Jayaprakash Narayan (JP) was the front-line foot soldier of Mahatma Gandhi. He never sought power and did not enjoy it even for a day. Well before Indira was anywhere near politics, JP had been offered the posts of Union cabinet minister and deputy prime minister and he turned them down. Though considered the natural successor to Nehru as prime minister, JP chose to withdraw from power politics, to engage in the more enduring struggle against poverty, social evils and violence.

The Quit India Movement launched by Mahatma Gandhi on 8 August 1942 was only making halting progress in the initial months. On 8 November, the night of Diwali that year, JP made a daring escape from the high security Hazaribagh Jail and the British regime launched a massive manhunt to capture him 'dead or alive'. This inflamed the nation and hastened the path towards independence. A. P. Sinha, a friend of his whom JP tried to persuade to join the escapade, stated his inability and instead said: 'I would not be able to give you the help you need. Let me cover your getaway. You have got the passion that can make people's spirits soar. You can inspire them to self-sacrifices, to accept sufferings. You are a great national leader' (Scarfe and Scarfe 1998: 81).

As he matured into public life, JP wanted to overhaul the entire Indian society. For him, the political system had to be responsive to the aspirations of the poorest of the poor; the glaring inequalities that our economic system breeds had to end; the educational system should be geared to the needs of the nation; the canker of corruption in India's political and administrative system had to be eradicated; the various social ills that afflict our country had to end.

For JP, freedom transcended politics and included freedom from hunger, poverty and ignorance. This conviction was the hallmark of JP's struggle throughout his life before and after independence. On the attainment of independence, when people scrambled for loaves of office, JP stood apart, concentrating his efforts on leading the Congress Party towards the socialist path. He decided to dedicate himself totally to Mahatma Gandhi's ideal of *Sampoorna Swaraj* and pursue his efforts towards 'people's participatory governance' and corruption-free, value-based public life. In his eventful political career, JP always served as a carrier of expectations, a catalyst of mighty happenings and moulder of such events.

True to his idealism and passion, JP, at the ripe age of 72, responded to the call of the students to lead them in their struggle against corruption, unemployment and high inflation which was threatening to turn violent and go beyond control. In the face of terror and repression unleashed on the students by the governments of Bihar and Gujarat, JP took charge and thus was born the 'JP Movement' that shook corrupt and authoritarian governments to their very foundation. On 5 June 1974, at the Gandhi Maidan in Patna, JP addressed a gathering of about 1 million people, perhaps the largest public rally in India since Independence. In his two-hour speech, the ailing JP called for 'total revolution', the transformation of Indian society along essentially Gandhian lines.

A well-researched paper on the JP Movement has this to say:

> The JP Movement was a coalition of organisations and individuals with very diverse beliefs, preoccupations, life circumstances and objectives. Nevertheless it can be said that central to the concerns of JP and many

other participants was the issue of making Indian democracy work better, particularly so that it might more fully meet the needs of the vast numbers of poor and marginalised Indians who were ill-served by the status quo.

As JP expressed it at the 5 June rally:

> The people are groaning under the hardships they have had to undergo during these twenty-eight years of Swaraj [self-rule]. There is hunger. There are high prices and corruption. One cannot get anything done without paying a bribe ... Even the educational institutions are becoming corrupt. The future of millions of youth is uncertain and dark ... The number of the unemployed among the poor and the uneducated is increasing day by day. Poverty has continued to increase in the last few years in spite of vociferous repetitions of the slogan 'Abolish Poverty'. Various laws have been legislated, including the law imposing ceiling on land-holdings for eradicating landlessness, etc. But today there are more landless agricultural workers than ever before. The land has been snatched away from poor farmers. ... [T]he villages ... are already divided into the exploiter and the exploited, the rich and the poor. The main task is not simply one of doing away with these differences in a superficial manner but of establishing social and economic equality. (Salter 2000: 2)

As could be seen, strengthening of India's democracy and making it work better for the people was the central concern of the JP Movement. As the Movement was progressing and spreading fast, on 12 June 1975, the Allahabad High Court held Prime Minister Indira Gandhi guilty on charge of corrupt practices in the election. JP briefly changed focus and advised Mrs Gandhi to resign on moral grounds until her name was cleared by the Supreme Court. Instead, she clamped.the Emergency on the nation.

EMERGENCY COMMENCES—DEMOCRACY LOST

On the midnight of 25–26 June 1975, Fakhruddin Ali Ahmed, President of India, signed a crisp three-line proclamation:

In exercise of the powers conferred by clause (1) of Article 352 of the Constitution, I, Fakhruddin Ali Ahmed, President of India, by this Proclamation declare that a grave emergency exists whereby the security of India is threatened by internal disturbances.

The Emergency that followed extinguished freedom and democracy, suspended fundamental rights of citizens, fettered freedom of the press and resorted to illegal detention and abuse of citizens.

Files on Emergency maintained by Union Home Ministry revealed the following:

1. Proclamation of Emergency was not preceded by a comprehensive assessment of the 'grave emergency that threatened the security of India' as mentioned in the promulgation. There was no assessment or report on the files. There is no report of any 'internal disturbance' or major threat to law and order. In fact, the first assessment of the alleged threat of internal disturbance was made more than a fortnight after the imposition of Emergency. It was in the form of a Report on the situation before and after 25 June 1975 from the Intelligence Bureau, submitted on 11 July.

2. This gives the lie to Prime Minister Indira Gandhi's letter to the President on 25 June 1975 night saying that information had reached her that 'there is an imminent danger to the security of India being threatened by internal disturbance'. Furthermore, this recommendation to impose Emergency did not have the approval of the Union Cabinet which is mandatory. This meant that Emergency was declared and a functioning democracy was turned into a personal autocracy on the basis of lie and falsehood by the Head of Government to Head of State.

3. No constitutional or civil authority at the centre or any State Government was involved in the decision to promulgate Emergency. It was the decision of a small coterie.

4. The President was cowed down by a mere telephone call from the Prime Minister. There was no application of mind on his part.

5. Arrests of senior leaders, including JP, were made even before the President signed the proclamation.

6. There was no whimper of protest by the Union Cabinet, senior bureaucracy and parliamentarians belonging to the ruling Congress Party.

The Union Cabinet met at 6 a.m. on 26 June and meekly gave ex post facto approval to the 'promulgation of the Emergency'. On the same evening, the Cabinet met again and gave approval for 'imposing press censorship'. On 28 June, the Cabinet approved amendment to the Defence of India Act and Rules. On 29 June, the Cabinet met again to approve the Maintenance of Internal Security (Amendment) Ordinance, 1975. The senior bureaucracy just caved in without even a mild protest. All they did was to formalise the 'extinction of democracy' by issuing directions and instructions under the 'Union War Book' to maintain internal security and Notifications under Article 359 depriving citizens of the right to move the courts under Articles 14, 21 and 22 of the Constitution. Documents brought under the scrutiny of the Shah Commission, the one-man Commission appointed to enquire into the Emergency excesses, confirm all these.

According to official sources, 32,690 preventive arrests were made during the Emergency period. But Shah Commission puts the figure at 110,806. After most of the arrests were made, the Intelligence Bureau prepared a 'Top Secret' Report on 11 July 1975, justifying promulgation of the Emergency and upholding Indira Gandhi's contention that she was only putting 'democracy back on the rails'. Most of the content of this report was reproduced in a booklet titled *Why Emergency*[1] brought out in July 1975 and placed in Parliament in the third week of July and the resolution was bulldozed through.

A compilation of activities of the President, Parliament and Executive during the Emergency would reveal as to how Freedom and Liberty in India was being extinguished. Having by and large reduced the legislature and executive to impotency, courts were the primary targets during the 'Emergency Session' of Parliament held in July and August 1975. With the proclamation of Emergency, the President had already suspended enforcement of Fundamental Rights under Article 14 (Equality before Law), Article 21 (Protection of Life and

---

[1] Booklet titled *Why Emergency* was laid on the table of Parliament when the Resolution to approve the proclamation of Emergency was moved on 21 July 1975. Available at http://www.scribd.com/doc/138076777/Shah-Commission-of-Inquiry–3rd-Final-Report (accessed on 30 August 2019).

Personal Liberty) and several clauses of Article 22 (Protection Against Detentions). Veteran BJP leader Mr L. K. Advani, who spent the entire period of Emergency in jail, has listed the draconian measures taken by the Emergency minions:

1. Courts were barred from pronouncing on the validity of a proclamation of Emergency or President's Rule or an ordinance;
2. Maintenance of Internal Security Act (MISA) was amended to prevent courts from giving relief to detainees even by virtue of common law or natural law;
3. The Election Law was amended to bar courts from adjudicating matters regarding the date of appointment, resignation, dismissal, etc., of a government employee;
4. The judgement of Allahabad High Court unseating Mrs Gandhi was declared null and void by constitutional amendment;
5. Courts were stripped of their authority to deal with disputes relating to the election of President, Vice-President, Speaker and Prime Minister;
6. Representation of the People Act and MISA were included in the Ninth Schedule and thereby made immune to judicial review.
7. MISA was amended so as to provide that those detained during the Emergency need not be furnished the grounds of detention. They could be indefinitely kept in prison without an idea as to why they had been jailed.

The *Why Emergency* document opens with these gems of words, which can rival those of Joseph Goebbels of Nazi Germany:

> The declaration of Emergency and the various actions taken by the Government to restore discipline, order and stability in the country have been welcomed by people from various strata of Indian society. The Prime Minister has said that the attempt of the Government is to put democracy 'back on the rails' and to ensure that the activities of an organised anti-democratic minority did not lead to the end of the very institutions of representative Government which the nation had evolved over the years. (Devasahayam 2006: 32–33)

The document portrayed democratic activities like the student protests in Gujarat in early 1974, the Bihar agitation that followed Gujarat and the concerted efforts by certain opposition parties under the inspiration and leadership of JP to spread the movement to other parts of the country and the plans and programmes of the National Coordination Committee of People's Struggle as deliberate attempts aimed at undermining the Constitution and destroying the very institutions through whose instrumentality democracy can flourish. These activities were described as deep and widespread conspiracy, which had been brewing against the Prime Minister and the Government led by her. It claimed that in the name of democracy, it had been sought to negate the very functioning of democracy. Public protests—an essential democratic activity—were branded as negation of democracy. A strange and convoluted logic indeed!

The document concludes:

> A situation has arisen where these Opposition parties have forgotten basic precepts and democratic functioning. If they are allowed to go on, the result will be sapping the confidence of the nation in its cherished institutions; and instead of 'democracy' we will have chaos and anarchy. No Government worth the name could stand by all this and allow the country's security, stability and economy to be imperiled. The nation's interests demanded firm and decisive action.

Proclaiming Emergency was the 'firm and decisive action' that extinguished democracy. Media response was poignant. *Times of India* in its 'obituary reference' wrote: 'O'Cracy D. E. M., beloved husband of T. Ruth, loving father of L. I. Bertie, F. R. E. Dom and Justicia expired on 26th June, 1975'.

EMERGENCY DISSECTED

What was the purpose of performing such a draconian act of 'extinguishing' India's nascent democracy? There are many contentions and the most bizarre of them all comes from Mrs Gandhi herself. Soon after the proclamation of Emergency, when Pupul Jayakar, the cultural czarina and close personal friend of Mrs Gandhi asked the latter, 'How can you, the daughter of Jawaharlal Nehru, do this?' Mrs Gandhi retorted:

> You do not know the gravity of what was happening. You do not know the plots against me. Jayaprakash and Morarjibhai always hated me. They were determined to see that I was destroyed.... Jayaprakash's wife Prabha was very close to my mother but with her death relationships have altered. Jayaprakash has always resented my being Prime Minister...He has never discovered his true role. Does he want to be a saint or a martyr? Why does he refuse to accept that he has never ceased to be a politician and desires to be the Prime Minister?

Mrs Gandhi had trivialised the 'murder of Indian democracy' and made it all look like a personal feud for power between JP and herself and the old man's jealousy in not becoming the Prime Minister! But the fact as we have seen is that JP had turned down each of the top positions including prime ministership offered to him. Regarding the charge of personal animosity, nothing could be farther from truth. The chemistry of JP is incapable of harbouring 'personal animosity' towards any one, least of all Indira Gandhi. After all, she was 'Kamala Nehru's child who grew up on Prabha's [JP's wife] laps'.

There are several versions of the imposition of Emergency and its fallout. The most authentic inside version is that of Professor P. N. Dhar, one of Mrs Gandhi's most loyal and closest advisors and a long-time Principal Secretary to the Prime Minister. According to him, declaring Emergency was a severe setback in the political evolution of India.

> Under the new dispensation the rule of law was drastically abridged; citizens were deprived of their fundamental rights; freedom of the press was curbed through strict censorship; political dissent was suppressed through arrests and harsh police measures; and officialdom assumed arbitrary powers, which it exercised without being accountable. In sum, these events changed the basic relationship between the citizen and the state and indeed threatened to change the character of the state itself.

Despite this admission, Dhar tries to rationalise by suggesting that 'Indian democracy' had already broken down before Indira Gandhi suspended it. In support, he quotes B. R. Ambedkar's view expressed in the Constituent Assembly: 'Democracy in India is only a top dressing on Indian soil, which is essentially undemocratic'. Dhar does not go as far as Ambedkar and pronounce India unsuited to democracy. But he builds up a formidable case for his view that in the months preceding the proclamation of Emergency, India had become democratically ungovernable. This is a fallacy. In actual fact, being a nascent democracy, its institutions and instruments were taking roots and as usual were facing teething troubles.

It was not the breakdown of democracy or law and order that led to the proclamation of Emergency. It was the failure of Mrs Gandhi to govern. The economy was collapsing due to the combined onslaught of Bangladesh refugees, termination of US aid, decline in agricultural production, sharp increase in oil prices and the unprecedented bout of inflation—23 per cent in 1973 which escalated to 30 per cent by middle of 1974. Despite massive electoral mandate from the people in the Parliament (1971) and State Assembly (1972) elections, Mrs Gandhi miserably faltered in responding to this crisis. No worthwhile economic policies or strategies were devised to counter these economic maladies and no purposeful governance given to the country to overcome this turmoil. Whatever steps taken were patchwork and half-hearted. Economic policies hovered between past political commitments and new economic compulsions and meeting the demands of radical ideologues on the one hand and a pragmatic response to the realities on the other. It was this ideological and administrative incoherence that marked economic governance in the early 1970s. This naturally led to public unrest and student agitations.

Dhar nevertheless admits:

The unchallenged leadership of Indira Gandhi (after the Bangladesh war) gave her an exaggerated sense of power. She now began to feel that she could make the Congress party an instrument of her own will. Having suffered at the hands of powerful bosses in the states earlier, she wanted party leaders in the States to be people entirely of her own choice ... nominated Chief Ministers who owed their ascension to the wishes of her high command rather than to their own strength in the State legislative party. This had a demoralising effect on the party.

The sequence that followed the Allahabad High Court judgement is well enough etched in India's political memory. But Dhar has added close-quarters view of, not distant speculations about, the reasons and compulsions, which shaped Indira Gandhi's mind. She did not accept the 'conditional stay' because in her view it 'diminished her authority' to deal with what she saw as dangerous turmoil all around her. Indira Gandhi showed 'more faith in the repression of political opponents and dissidents in her party than in her own ability to engage them constructively or to fight them politically'. Platitudes and explanations apart, it is the corrosion of Mrs Gandhi's faith in herself, her party, the people and democracy that led her to the Emergency (Dhar 2001).

JP, the 'villain and victim' of Emergency, has his own perception on the background and causes that led to the imposition of Emergency. He is of the view that the working of Mrs Gandhi is characterised by drift and she acted in the manner she has done since she felt 'her position as PM was threatened'. But this was only a matter of timing and JP was positive that the disguised communists in the party, the CPI and, behind the scene, Soviet agents must have prepared a detailed plan for substituting a totalitarian system for the democratic one that India had until 25 June. To all the three of them—the PM, the communist stooges in the Congress and the CPI—democracy was anathema and they were planning for long years the steps from which their goal could be achieved: first 'social democracy' and then naked communist party rule under carefully disguised Russian tutelage.

Justice J. C. Shah, the one-man Commission, has this to say:

> Mrs Gandhi in her anxiety to continue in power brought about a situation which directly contributed to her continuance in power and also generated forces which sacrificed the interests of many to serve the ambitions of the few. Thousands were detained and a series of totally illegal and unwarranted actions followed involving untold human misery and suffering.

Repudiating the spurious theory of 'grave threat to national security', Justice Shah was emphatic that

> there was no evidence of breakdown of law and order in any part of the country, nor of any apprehension on that behalf. The economic condition was also well under control and had in no way deteriorated. There was not even a report of an apprehension of any serious breakdown of the law and order situation or deterioration of economic condition from any public functionary. The public records of that time, both secret and public, and newspapers spoke with unanimity that there was no unusual event or even a tendency in that direction to justify the imposition of Emergency.

As the Civil Rights stalwart Rajni Kothari puts it:

> It was a state off-limits, a government that hijacked the whole edifice of the state, a ruling party and leader who in effect treated the state as their personal estate. It was the imposition of a highly concentrated apparatus of power on a fundamentally federal society and the turning over of this centralized apparatus for personal survival and family aggrandizement. It was one big swoop overtaking the whole country spreading a psychosis of fear and terror with the new upstarts (Sanjay and all) storming away through whatever came their way, pulling it all down and calling boo to it all. And it happened in this country after 28 years of democratic functioning.

As a palliative to the fatal blow dealt on democracy, on 1 July Mrs Gandhi announced a 20-Point programme promising to liquidate the existing debts of landless labourers, small farmers and rural artisans. The programme planned to extend alternate credit to them, abolish bonded labour and implement the existing agricultural land ceiling laws. It provided house sites to landless labourers and weaker sections and it revised upwards minimum wages of agricultural labour. The programme also provided special help to the handloom industry by bringing down the prices, preventing tax evasion and smuggling, increasing production and streamlining distribution of essential commodities. It increased the limit of income tax exemption up to ₹8,000, and liberalised investment procedures. But these did not work as later events would unravel.

EMERGENCY ENDS—DEMOCRACY REGAINED

Emboldened by 'intelligence reports' of her popularity and 'success' and the perception that opposition to her rule was crumbling and JP, the only mass leader, was sick and demoralised, Indira Gandhi decided to end Emergency in January 1977 and called for the sixth General Election to Lok Sabha. The eyeball-to-eyeball confrontation between the autocrat and the democrat began with the latter swinging into action to redeem his pledge to return India to democracy.

In his inimitable style, without wasting any time, JP put into effect the political blueprint he had worked out while in detention and refined later. Due largely to his untiring efforts, immediately after coming out of jails, the Opposition leaders announced the merger of Congress (O), Jan Sangh, Bharatiya Lok Dal and the Socialist Party into the new Janata Party. The Congress was dealt a blow by the sudden defection of Jagjivan Ram, H. N. Bahuguna and Nandini Satpathy who formed the Congress for Democracy. Along with the DMK, the Akali Dal and the CPM, it forged a common front with the Janata Party in order to give a straight fight to the Congress and its allies, the CPI and the AIADMK in the elections in March 1977.

The Opposition made the Emergency and its excesses and the restriction on civil liberties major issues for its election campaign. The people also treated the elections as a referendum on the Emergency. JP created a public upsurge by touring the country intensively and addressing mammoth gatherings. This he did despite being tied down to dialysis twice a week. At many places, large crowds intently listened to JP's appeal through pre-recorded tapes:

Free India—Defeat the Dictators

In the name of all those who struggled for our country's freedom, I appeal to each one of you. Free India, defeat the dictators. This is the last chance. If you falter, 19 months of tyranny shall become 19 years of terror. Our goal is progress with justice. (Jai 1998: 27–29)

JP was clear that freedom and accountability went together, and that this would mean a free public discourse; the horrors of the previous

19 months, of arbitrary arrest and torture, of the mass destruction of homes, and more, were the signs of dictatorship, not democracy.

Yet, as JP forcefully reminded his audience and all India, those who imposed the Emergency now had to offer their apologies and take account of the people. JP added here that for India's minorities fundamental rights and a 'free open society' were even more important than they were for the minority; he pledged that the Janata Party would create a civil rights commission specifically to protect the rights of minorities, and that it would make the right to work a fundamental right. Warning people against those who would hoodwink them, he called on the citizens of India to vote for the Janata Party in the then-imminent general election, and concluded thus:

> Defeat the dictators. We can then build a free and Gandhian India.
> (Jai 1998: 27–29)

This powerful and passionate message reached the hearts of most of the electorate and led to a deluge. The Janata Party and its allies were victorious with 330 out of 542 seats. Congress and its allies got 182 seats, the rest going to miscellaneous groups. Winning just 2 out of the 234 northern seats, the Congress Party was virtually wiped out in the seven northern States. Both Indira and Sanjay Gandhi were defeated. Only South India saved the party, largely because the region did not feel the rigours of the Emergency to the same extent and because JP's voice could not reach many parts.

In the assembly elections held in June 1977, Janata and its allies came out victorious in most of the States. Control over both the Parliament and the State assemblies enabled the Janata Party to elect unopposed its own candidate, N. Sanjeeva Reddy, as the President of India in July 1977.

The Janata government took immediate steps to dismantle the authoritarian features of the Emergency regime and to restore liberal democracy. It reinstated fundamental rights and full civil liberties to the press, political parties and individuals. Through the 44th Constitutional

Amendment, it also modified the 42nd amendment, passed during the Emergency, repealing those of its provisions which had distorted the Constitution. The powers of the Supreme Court and the high courts to decide on the validity of Central and State legislation were also restored. Democracy was back on the rails.

BLUEPRINT FOR TRUE DEMOCRACY

JP, who led the battle to regain India's lost democracy, had a blueprint for it as early as 1959. Even today, every word of it rings true and relevant. Core of this blueprint was that our political institutions should be based on the principles that had been enunciated and practised in the ancient Indian polity because (a) it would be in line with the natural course of social evolution and (b) those principles are more valid from the point of view of social science than any others. Western polity is based upon an atomised society, the state being made up of an inorganic sum of individuals. This is both against the social nature of man and the scientific organisation of society.

No kind of democracy can exist without the democratic freedoms—freedom of conscience, of association, of expression—and the rule of law. Where these freedoms do not exist, nor the rule of law, there can be no democracy. If our present political institutions are to be soundly based, if they are to draw sustenance from Indian soil and, in turn, are to sustain, revive and strengthen the whole fabric of Indian society, they must be related to the social genius of India, and their texture must be woven again with an organically self-determining, self-developing communal life in which occupations, professions and functions are integrated with the community (sui generis). This is not only a question of constitutional forms or political systems. It is a creative question in the widest sense of the term. It is a question of an ancient country finding its lost soul again.

Due to the colonial onslaught, the old village communities have survived in nothing else than their physical existence. They are no longer living communities acting jointly for the solution of individual or communal problems and for the development of their moral and material life. It was a result of the deliberate policy of an alien government that neither understood the character of a communitarian polity nor felt secure in the presence of such strong traditions of self-government and self-help. Nevertheless, the very fact that the villages do exist physically provides us with a readymade foundation to build upon.

A word that figures boldly on the ancient signpost is dharma. Indian polity held that the state was subject to the rule of dharma, which it was its duty to uphold and protect. The concept of dharma was of great importance in ancient India and it was rooted in community life and the social ethics of the community exercised a powerful influence over the state.

With community having been badly shattered, the roots of dharma have no soil from which to draw sustenance. Dharma has therefore declined and ceased to exercise any influence not only upon the present polity, which is a wholly foreign implantation and has no roots in the Indian soil, but upon all social activities such as commerce, education, labour, administration and priesthood. Unless life in India is again organised on the basis of self-determining and mutually coordinating and integrating communities, that organic self-regulation of society, which the concept of dharma represented, will not be possible. To that extent, democracy will remain distantly removed from the life of the people.

A decade after the unveiling of this blueprint things were getting from bad to worse with power and authority getting more and more centralised. So JP burst out at a New Delhi conference of voluntary agencies in 1969: 'I say with a due sense of responsibility that, if convinced that there is no deliverance for the people except through violence, JP will take to violence'. But in his heart JP was one with Mahatma Gandhi on the view that democracy or the Swaraj of masses can never come through untruthful and violent means. In their notion of democracy, 'the weakest should have the same opportunity as the strongest', and that can 'never happen except through non-violence'.

For JP, The foundation of India's polity and economy should be based on the 'Idea of Independent India' which alone can sustain a country of such vast multitudes. To make this happen, JP advocated 'participatory party-less democracy'. Loss of faith in political parties, governments and grand political projects has led people to turn more to grass roots and specific-issue politics and to the use of new tactics. Though its ideological underpinnings—in India and elsewhere—are vague and incomplete. India's Constitution and Representation of People's Act provide for party-less democracy by not recognising political parties as legal entities.

Political parties and governments formed by them are failing dismally. What is the alternative? It is in response to this persistent query that JP supported an essentially Gandhian model of party-less democracy in which there would be multiple levels of governance, with each electing the one above and each practising consensual decision-making, and a distribution of power that sees most power located in self-reliant and semi-autonomous villages and decreasing amounts as one went up the levels.

JP's philosophy of 'participatory democracy' was contraposed to electoral or 'representative democracy'. He was not just asking for electoral reforms, as frequently suggested, but arguing against what he considered a basically flawed system. This is what he had to say:

> The fundamental defect...is that this form of democracy is based on the vote of the individual ...the system is based on a false premise; the state cannot be an arithmetical sum of individuals. The people, the nation, the community can never be equated with the sum of individual voters.

How true? Individual voters can be easily targeted and corrupted by offering bribes and freebies by mafia politicians and political parties. This is precisely what is happening in many parts of India destroying the integrity of elections and sanctity of democracy.

According to JP, party rivalries give birth to demagoguery, depress political ethics and put a premium on unscrupulousness and aptitude for manipulation and intrigue. Parties create dissensions where unity is called for, exaggerate differences where they should be minimised. Parties often put party interests over the national interests because centralisation of power prevents the citizen from participating in government; the parties, that is to say, small caucuses of politicians, rule in the name of the people and create the illusion of democracy and self-government.

Hence the call for 'participatory, party-less democracy'. On this tenet was based JP's 'Total Revolution' of 1974 which culminated in the installation of the first-ever non-Congress government in 1977. Because of its shaky existence, Janata Government could not do anything in furtherance of this tenet. It was only in 1992 that 73rd and 74th Constitutional Amendment Acts were enacted devolving power to the Panchayat Raj Institutions and Urban Local Bodies. But even now true decentralised, participatory and party-less democracy remains a distant dream.

REFERENCES

Devasahayam, M. G. 2006. *JP in Jail—An Uncensored Account*. New Delhi: Roli Books.

———. 2011. *JP Movement—Emergency and India's Second Freedom*. New Delhi: Vitasta.

Dhar, D. P. 2001. *Indira Gandhi, the 'Emergency' and Indian Democracy*. New Delhi: Oxford University Press.

Gandhi, Mohandas Karamchand. 1922, 5 January. 'Independence'. *Young India*. Available at https://archive.org/details/in.ernet.dli.2015.211536/page/n949 (accessed on 30 January 2019).

Hoda, Surur. n.d. *Schumacher on Gandhi*. Available at https://www.mkgandhi.org/articles/Schumacher-on-Gandhi.html (accessed on 4 March 2019).

Jai, Janak Raj. 1998. *Voter's Dilemma: Indian Political Scene*. New Delhi: Regency Publications.

Narayan, Jayaprakash. 1959. *A Plea for Reconstruction of Indian Polity*. Kashi: Akhil Bharat Seva Sangh Prakashan.

Nehru, Jawaharlal. 1946, 13 December. *Objectives Resolution*. Constituent Assembly Debates. Available at https://cadindia.clpr.org.in/constitution_assembly_debates/volume/1/1946–12–13 (accessed on 6 February 2019).

Press Trust of India. 2018, 7 July. 'Two Hours Given to Justice A N Ray to Decide on CJI Post?' *India Today*. Available at https://www.indiatoday.in/pti-feed/story/two-hours-given-to-justice-a-n-ray-to-decide-on-cji-post–1286810–2018–07–16 (accessed on 5 March 2019).

Salter, Robert Graeme. 2000. *Swaraj and Sweepers: The JP Movement and the Future of Transformational Politics*. PhD Dissertation. Melbourne: Victoria University of Technology.

Scarfe, Allan, and Wendy Scarfe. 1998. *JP: His Biography*. Hyderabad: Orient BlackSwan.

Mitta, Manoj. 2010, 10 December. 'Emergency Papers Found, Minus Indira Signature'. *Times of India*. Available at https://timesofindia.indiatimes.com/india/Emergency-papers-found-minus-Indira-signature/articleshow/7074117.cms (accessed on 30 August 2019).

Chapter 7

Reforming Politics and Elections through Legal Changes

Jagdeep Chhokar

Electoral reforms have been the topic of a lot of discussion for a very long period of time.

Despite this discussion, hardly any significant reforms have been initiated by any government over the years. There have been very few changes in the electoral and political systems and it would not be incorrect to say that whatever changes of significance have come about have happened through the judiciary.

The most fundamental provision of law governing elections is Article 324 of the Constitution of India which says:

> 324. (1) The superintendence, direction and control of the preparation of the electoral rolls for, and the conduct of, all elections to Parliament and to the Legislature of every State and of elections to the offices of President and Vice-President held under this Constitution shall be vested in a Commission (referred to in this Constitution as the Election Commission).

The phrase "superintendence, direction and control of the preparation of the electoral rolls for, and the conduct of, all elections...shall be vested in a Commission" gives the ECI plenary power in all matters related to the elections to the Parliament and State Assemblies. This plenary power has been operationalized in the Representation of the People Act (RP Act), 1950, and the RP Act, 1951. The details of the processes have been laid down in the Conduct of Election Rules, 1961.

Notwithstanding the existence of the earlier laws, the first government appointed committee, the Goswami Committee, had this to say about state of elections and electoral reforms in 1990:

> Leaving now our laurels alone, it becomes imperative to take stock of the present state of affairs which causes concern and anxiety because of the existence of the looming danger threatening to cut at the very roots of free and fair elections.

> The role of money and muscle powers at elections deflecting seriously the well accepted democratic values and ethos and corrupting the process; rapid criminalisation of politics greatly encouraging evils of booth capturing, rigging, violence etc.; misuse of official machinery, i.e. official media and ministerial; increasing menace of participation of non-serious candidates; form the core of our electoral problems. Urgent corrective measures are the need of the hour lest the system itself should collapse.

> Electoral reforms are correctly understood to be a continuous process. But attempts so far made in this area did not touch even the fringe of the problem. They appeared to be abortive. Some of the recent measures like reduction of voting age and anti-defection law are no doubt laudable and the basic principles underlying those measures should be appreciated. But there are other vital and important areas in election field completely neglected and left high and dry.

It will be obvious that this description has a contemporary ring to it. Two observations, "attempts so far made in this area did not touch even the fringe of the problem" and "other vital and important areas in election field completely neglected and left high and dry," are particularly evocative.

Though the Conduct of Election Rules came into force in 1961, the Goswami Committee went on to say, "All these four decades, especially after 1967, the demand for electoral reforms has been mounting up." This means that the need for electoral reforms had started to be felt just within six years of the rules coming into effect.

The judiciary commented on the situation prevailing in the political and electoral arenas while adjudicating election petitions which are almost always filed by losing candidates. Most of these judgments pertained to the specific legal issue agitated by the petitioner against the respondent. All these were therefore individual cases.

With the legislatures, controlled by political parties, not doing anything worthwhile and judiciary's response being limited to election petitions filed by individuals, no significant improvements happened in the electoral and political systems. In effect, there were no systemic reforms. This is when civil society stepped in, in the late 1990s.

THE BEGINNING: THE DISCLOSURE OF CANDIDATE ANTECEDENTS' JUDGMENTS

Possibly the first public interest litigation (PIL) for electoral reforms was filed by the Association for Democratic Reforms[1] (ADR) in December 1999. The petition was prompted by (a) media reports that a large number of persons with criminal cases pending against them were contesting elections, and getting elected, and (b) the 170th Report of the Law Commission of India titled "Reforms of the Electoral Laws." Some research into the existing legal provisions revealed a lacuna in law.

While Section 8 of the RP Act, 1951, disqualified a person, who had been convicted for imprisonment of two years or more of certain criminal offences, from contesting elections for six years, there was nothing in the law about those persons who had criminal cases *pending* against them. Such persons, with criminal cases pending against them, were the ones who were contesting elections, and often getting elected. Since cases could be pending anywhere in the country and not necessarily in the constituency from where the person was contesting,

---

[1] accessed on December 4, 2015.

there was no way for voters to know about pending criminal cases against candidates.

The Law Commission of India had recommended in its 170th report that "it is also necessary for a candidate seeking to contest election for furnish details regarding criminal case, if any, pending against him, including a copy of the FIR/complaint and any order made by the concerned court" (Para 6.3.2).

In keeping with the earlier recommendation of the Law Commission of India, ADR filed a PIL in Delhi High Court requesting that every candidate contesting elections to the Parliament and State Assembly be asked to disclose criminal cases pending against him/her while filing their nomination. The Delhi High Court announced its judgment[2] on November 2, 2000, upholding the request made in the PIL, and

> directed that the Election Commission shall secure to the voters the following information pertaining to each of the candidates standing for election to the Parliament and to the State Legislatures and the parties they represent:
>
> 1. Whether the candidate is accused of any offence(s) punishable with imprisonment? If so, the details thereof
> 2. Assets possessed by a candidate, his or her spouse and dependent relations.
> 3. Facts giving insight to candidate's competence, capacity and suitability for acting as parliamentarian or legislator including details of his/her educational qualifications.
> 4. Information which the election commission considers necessary for judging the capacity and capability of the political party fielding the candidate for election to Parliament or the State Legislature.

The high court concluded the judgment saying, "The norms and modalities to carry out and give effect to the aforesaid directions should be drawn up by the Election Commission within four months."

---

[2] accessed on December 7, 2015.

The Empire Strikes

Before the four months allowed by the high court to the ECI to draw up "The norms and modalities to carry out and give effect to the aforesaid directions" were over, the Union of India filed a Special Leave Petition (SLP) in the Supreme Court (SC) of India challenging the decision of the high court with the plea that matters pertaining to elections were a legislative issue and the judiciary had no role in that at all and should not, and could not, interfere. Several political parties filed intervention applications asking to be made "interveners to the petition" so that they could also express their view to the court.

Not surprisingly, all political parties supported the contention of the appellant, the Union of India. It seemed clear that the entire political establishment did not want the information about the criminality of candidates to be revealed to the voters. Arguments on behalf of the Union of India in the hearings in the SC were led by the Attorney General and the Solicitor General of India. The political parties were represented by senior advocates, one of whom was then a member of the Rajya Sabha.

After several hearings, the SC upheld the decision of the Delhi High Court on May 2, 2002.[3] The SC agreed with the contention that it was a legislative matter but stated that it was a settled law that if (a) there was a "gap in legislation," and (b) public interest was suffering, and (c) the Legislature had not found time or inclination to fill the "gap in legislation," then the judiciary had a right, even a duty, to fill the "gap in legislation" till such time that the Legislature decided to act on it. The SC made the directions of the high court more specific, holding as follows:

> In this view of the matter, it cannot be said that the directions issued by the High Court are unjustified or beyond its jurisdiction. However, considering the submissions made by the learned counsel for the parties at the time of hearing of this matter the said directions are modified as stated below.

---

[3] accessed on December 7, 2015.

The Election Commission is directed to call for information on affidavit by issuing necessary order in exercise of its power under Article 324 of the Constitution of India from each candidate seeking election to Parliament or State Legislature as a necessary part of his nomination paper, furnishing therein, information on the following aspects in relation to his/her candidature:

1. Whether the candidate is convicted/acquitted/discharged of any criminal offence in the past—if any, whether he is punished with imprisonment or fine?
2. Prior to six months of filing of nomination, whether the candidate is accused in any pending case, of any offence punishable with imprisonment for two years or more, and in which charge is framed or cognizance is taken by the Court of law. If so, the details thereof.
3. The assets (immovable, movable, bank balances, etc.) of a candidate and of his/her spouse and that of dependants.
4. Liabilities, if any, particularly whether there are any over dues of any public financial institution or Government dues.
5. The educational qualifications of the candidate.

The court concluded by laying down a time frame: "Hence, the norms and modalities to carry out and give effect to the aforesaid directions should be drawn up properly by the Election Commission as early as possible and in any case within two months."

The ECI wrote to the Government of India that the most efficacious way of implementing the judgment was to amend the Conduct of Election Rules. The government responded to the ECI saying this matter required developing a political consensus which will take longer than two months and that the ECI should seek more time from the SC. The ECI responded to the government saying they (the ECI) did not need more time and if the government needed more time, they (the government) should approach the SC. Just before the two months were to be over, the ECI issued a detailed order implementing the SC judgment.

The Second Strike

The ECI's order of June 28, 2002, turned out to be almost like setting a cat among the pigeons. An all-party meeting was held on July 8, 2002.

It was attended by representatives of 21 political parties. It was *unanimously* decided that implementation of the decision of the Delhi High Court of May 2, 2002, will not be allowed and, if it was necessary to amend the RP Act, 1951, for this purpose, this Act shall be amended in that very session of the Parliament.

A draft bill to amend the RP Act was thus prepared and circulated to all political parties on July 15, 2002. This bill could not be introduced in the Parliament as it was adjourned due to disruptions over what came to be called the Petrol Pump Scam.[4] Since the bill to amend the RP Act could not be processed in the Parliament as the Parliament was no longer in session, the government contemplated issuing an Ordinance for amending the RP Act in accordance with the proposed draft bill. As the news of the proposed Ordinance was known, 33 persons representing civil society organizations from all over the country met the newly elected president, A. P. J. Abdul Kalam, and apprised him of circumstances leading to the possibility of the Ordinance being sent to him. This group also informed the President that the proposed Ordinance has a section (Section 33B) which said that no one could ask any candidate contesting elections anything other than what was listed in the draft bill. This action of prohibiting questions to be asked violated citizens' fundamental right to freedom of speech and expression, guaranteed under Article 19(1)(a) of the Constitution of India.

The Cabinet did send the Ordinance to the President on August 23, 2002. The President returned the Ordinance without signing it. The Cabinet, however, sent it back to the President in exactly the same form on August 24, 2002, and following a well-established convention, the President signed the Ordinance,[5] and it, thus, became the law of the land.

The Ordinance and the subsequent Act were challenged in the SC in three separate petitions which questioned the constitutionality of the amendment of the RP Act. After several hearings, the SC, in a

---

[4] Available at http://www.rediff.com/news/2002/aug/09par.htm (accessed on December 7, 2015).

[5] The Ordinance was subsequently passed unanimously by the Parliament in the form of the Representation of the People (Amendment) Act.

historic judgment[6] delivered on March 13, 2003, declared the amendment of the RP Act "unconstitutional" and "null & void," saying "The judgment rendered by this Court in Association for Democratic Reforms (supra) has attained finality, therefore, there is no question of interpreting constitutional provision which calls for reference under Article 145(3)."

Following the SC judgment, the ECI issued an order on March 27, 2003, implementing the judgment of May 2, 2002.

Thus ended the first attempt to reform politics and elections, taking four years.

THE LILY THOMAS/LOK PRAHARI CASE

As the decision in the ADR case came to be implemented, the presence of people with criminal cases pending against them being present in the Parliament and various State Legislative Assemblies came into sharper focus in the public eye, resulting in greater public interest in and scrutiny of this phenomenon. This increased scrutiny revealed a legal lacuna or loophole which had hitherto escaped public attention. This was a subsection 4 (of Section 8) of the RP Act, introduced in 1989. The amended Section 8(4) read as follows:

(4) Notwithstanding anything in sub-section (1), sub-section (2) or sub-section (3), a disqualification under either subsection shall not, in the case of a person who on the date of the conviction is a member of Parliament or the Legislature of a State, take effect until three months have elapsed from that date or, if within that period an appeal or application for revision is brought in respect of the conviction or the sentence, until that appeal or application is disposed of by the court.

Subsection 4 of Section 8 has to be understood in the context of the preceding subsection 3 of the same Section 8. Section 8(3) says:

(3) A person convicted of any offence and sentenced to imprisonment for not less than two years...shall be disqualified (from contesting

---

[6] accessed on December 7, 2015.

elections) from the date of such conviction and shall continue to be disqualified for a further period of six years since his release.

What subsections 3 and 4, read together, mean in plain English is the following:

- If a person is "convicted of any offence and sentenced to imprisonment" of two years or more, he/she cannot contest elections during the period of the imprisonment and six years after the release from imprisonment.
- But, and this is the key, the person so convicted, happens to be a sitting MP or an MLA on the date of conviction, then this MP or MLA gets a reprieve of three months during which he/she can file an appeal to a higher court against the conviction, and even if the appeal is admitted for hearing (NOT decided in the convicted person's favor), this person can continue to be an MP or MLA and can even contest elections in future till the appeal is finally decided by the higher court. This "higher court" in practice turned out to be the SC. As is the common experience, it can take anywhere between 10 and 15 years for a criminal case to be decided in a lower court, particularly if the accused happens to be an influential person and is actively trying to delay the proceedings. Even if the person is convicted by the lower court, he/she appeals to the high court where again it can take 10 to 15 years. If the conviction of the lower court is upheld by the high court, the person appeals to the SC where again it can take 10 to 15 years.
- The above scenario often resulted in a situation that a person who is an MLA or MP, and who may have, in fact, committed a heinous crime can and did continue to be an elected representative and contest in one election after another, for something like 30 years till the case was *finally* disposed of by the SC. This period of 30 years would often cover the entire working period of a politician-cum-criminal.
- On the other hand, an ordinary citizen who gets convicted by even a lower court cannot contest any election till he/she is exonerated by a higher court, thus giving an unfair advantage to a sitting MP or MLA.

It is this provision of Section 8(4) of the RP Act that was challenged in two PILs filed in 2005, one by a SC lawyer, Lily Thomas, and the other by a civil society organization by the name Lok Prahari. The petitions filed in 2005 came up for hearing in 2012–2013, presumably due to the usual backlog in the judiciary. The matter was argued vigorously in court with Fali Nariman appearing for Lily Thomas and the General Secretary of Lok Prahari, S. N. Shukla, representing Lok Prahari. Assistant Solicitor Generals Siddharth Luthra and Paras Kuhad appeared for the Union of India. Data gathered by ADR during the intervening years regarding candidates with criminal cases pending against them, who got elected as MPs and MLAs, was relied upon by Fali Nariman during the arguments.

After hearing the arguments over several days, the SC pronounced its judgment[7] on July 10, 2013. It held that subsection 4 of Section 8 of the RP Act was unconstitutional, saying, in Para 20 of the judgment:

> Parliament, therefore, has exceeded its powers conferred by the Constitution in enacting sub-section (4) of Section 8 of the Act and accordingly sub-section (4) of Section 8 of the Act is *ultra vires* the Constitution.

Attempts to Undo the Judgment

Just as had happened in the ADR case, the government of the day tried to undo this judgment too, but for politically partisan reasons. It had to do with what had come to be known as the Fodder Scam.[8] With the trials in 44 out of 53 cases having been completed in May 2013,[9] judgments in some of these cases were expected any time. The leader of the Rashtriya Janata Dal (RJD), and the former Chief Minister of Bihar, Lalu Prasad Yadav, who was a Member of Parliament at the time the judgment came, was one of the prime accused in the Fodder Scam. As the RJD was supporting the government of the day in the Parliament, which itself was running low on support, it tried to undo the judgment.

[7] accessed on December 25, 2015.
[8] accessed on December 25, 2015.
[9] accessed on December 25, 2015.

The first step was to file a review petition in the SC against the judgment. As there was some apprehension about the review petition being successful, the government also introduced a bill to amend the RP Act on August 8, 2013, to say that representatives should not be disqualified immediately after conviction and given some time to appeal.

The SC rejected the review petition on September 4, 2013, and the Rajya Sabha, in its wisdom, decided to refer the bill to a Standing Committee for detailed consideration and making a recommendation to the House.

It was at this stage, with the Fodder Scam judgment expected any time which, according to popular expectation, would convict Lalu Prasad Yadav and unseat him from the Parliament if the Lily Thomas judgment stood, that the Cabinet decided to recommend to the President that an Ordinance be promulgated to make the same bill that was with a Standing Committee to the Rajya Sabha into law. This was against all canons of constitutional propriety because the Bill was now a property of the Parliament, the Legislature. Therefore, the government, the Executive, had no constitutional right to interfere with the legislative process, which is already underway with the Bill being with the Standing Committee of Rajya Sabha. While these attempts were still on, the Vice-President of the ruling party publically expressed his disagreement with the proposal for an Ordinance. The proposal for the Ordinance was thus dropped and the judgment remained valid.

On October 1, 2013, Rasheed Masood became the first MP to lose his membership of Parliament under the new guidelines, when he was sentenced to four years' imprisonment for cheating, forgery and corruption in September 2013 in what had come to be known as the MBBS seats scam.

Subsequently, Lalu Prasad Yadav was convicted to imprisonment of five years in the Fodder Scam and was disqualified from the Parliament on October 22, 2013.[10] Another Lok Sabha MP from the JD(U), Jagdish Sharma, was also disqualified along with Lalu Prasad Yadav.

---

[10] accessed on December 25, 2015.

Since then, one more MP and five MLAs, including the then Chief Minister of Tamil Nadu, J. Jayalalithaa, have been disqualified.[11] The Lily Thomas/Lok Prahari judgment has thus become settled law.

THE NOTA JUDGMENT

This judgment came for a PIL filed by the People's Union for Civil Liberties (PUCL) in 2004, though the judgment[12] finally came on September 27, 2013.

The source of the PIL lay in Rule 49-O of the Conduct of Election Rules,[13] 1961, which provides for an "Elector deciding not to vote" and reads as follows:

> If an elector, after his electoral roll number has been duly entered in the register of voters in Form 17A and has put his signature or thumb impression thereon as required under sub-rule (1) of rule 49L, decided not to record his vote, a remark to this effect shall be made against the said entry in Form 17A by the presiding officer and the signature or thumb impression of the elector shall be obtained against such remark.

Why would a voter who decides "not to vote" even go to the polling station? The reason lies in the uncomfortable fact that if a registered voter does not cast his/her vote, there remains a possibility, however small, of an imposter casting a vote in place of the registered voter in connivance with the polling booth staff. This means that the vote of the voter has been misused or that the voter has "allowed" his/her vote to be misused. Rule 49-O provided the registered voter an option to avoid such a situation.

The rule, as formulated, suffered from one infirmity, however. This was the requirement that "a remark to this effect shall be made against" his/her name by the presiding officer and "the signature or thumb impression of the elector shall be obtained against such remark" has

---

[11] accessed on December 25, 2015.

[12] accessed on December 26, 2015.

[13] accessed on December 26, 2015.

the effect of violating the secrecy of the voter's decision not to vote for any of the candidates on the ballot. This is because the "register of voters in Form 17A" can be accessed after the election, by any interested person, particularly the candidates who contested that election, now even under the Right to Information Act (RTI Act). And once that is accessible, while the names of the voters who voted become known without the knowledge of which candidate did they vote for, the names of those who did not vote of any candidate become known specifically. This raises the possibility of vendetta against those who did not vote for any of the candidates.

It was to counter against this possible violation of the secrecy of the voter's decision that the PUCL filed a PIL in 2004.

The operative part of the judgment reads as follows:

> In view of our conclusion, we direct the Election Commission to provide necessary provision in the ballot papers/EVMs and another button called "None of the Above" (NOTA) may be provided in EVMs so that the voters, who come to the polling booth and decide not to vote for any of the candidates in the fray, are able to exercise their right not to vote while maintaining their right of secrecy. Inasmuch as the Election Commission itself is in favour of the provision for NOTA in EVMs, we direct the Election Commission to implement the same either in a phased manner or at a time with the assistance of the Government of India. We also direct the Government of India to provide necessary help for implementation of the above direction. Besides, we also direct the Election Commission to undertake awareness programmes to educate the masses. (Para 61)

Implementation and Aftermath of the Judgment

After the judgment, the ECI decided to provide a NOTA button in all its EVMs. This button has also been used in various elections to varying degrees. Some citizens' groups have also campaigned for its use. Its use has however not had the desired results, at least not yet. What desired results can be expected from the use of the NOTA button?

In this context, it is worth reproducing a paragraph from the judgment:

> Giving right to a voter not to vote for any candidate while protecting his right of secrecy is extremely important in a democracy. Such an option gives the voter the right to express his disapproval with the kind of candidates that are being put up by the political parties. When the political parties will realize that a large number of people are expressing their disapproval with the candidates being put up by them, gradually there will be a systemic change and the *political parties will be forced to* accept the will of the people and *field candidates who are known for their integrity*. (Para 55; italics added)

The highlighted part "political parties will be forced to…field candidates who are known for their integrity" is the key here. Merely providing a NOTA button and recording the number of votes cast for that button does not really work toward achieving the purpose that the SC seems to have had in mind.

The lacuna that remains and due to which it may not be out of place to mention that the ECI has only fulfilled the letter of the SC judgment and has not gone by the spirit of the judgment is that according to the existing rules, even if all except one voters in a constituency vote for NOTA, and that one remaining voter votes for a candidate, that candidate will be declared elected.

It has been brought to the notice of the ECI and has been written in the media that the following needs to be done to satisfy the spirit of the SC judgment:

- In case the NOTA button gets more votes than any of the candidates, none of the candidates should be declared elected and a fresh election should be held in which none of the candidates in the first round are allowed to contest.
- In the fresh election, with fresh candidates and with a NOTA button, only that candidate should be declared elected who gets at least 50 percent + 1 of the votes cast; if even in this round the "none of the above" option gets the highest number of votes cast, or if none of the candidates gets at least 50 percent + 1 of the votes cast, then there should be a runoff between the top two candidates.

This may appear to be somewhat complicated, but the Law Commission of India recommended this as far back as 1999 in its 170th report. It was also prescient enough to say that the whole process will become much easier "if electronic voting machines are introduced throughout the country."

An important issue related to NOTA came up in the recently concluded local body elections in Gujarat. The State Election Commission (SEC) had initially declined to provide a NOTA button on the ground that the SC judgment had directed the ECI to provide a NOTA button and had not directed the SECs to do so which were independent constitutional authorities. A PIL was filed in the Gujarat High Court asking for directions to be issued to the Gujarat SEC and the high court did ask the SEC to provide the NOTA button.

The issue became more complex when it was alleged by some people that there was collusion between candidates and between political parties in some constituencies where all but one candidates withdrew from the contest, resulting in what were labelled "uncontested winners."

Though this was not accepted by the high court, the issue remains valid as described further:

> Based on the above, it should be clear that with NOTA having been mandatory, the concept of an uncontested election does not survive. As a matter of fact, a so-called unanimous election could even be the outcome of malpractices such as horse-trading and collusion among candidates or even political parties. In such situations it could even be the very anti-thesis and negation of democracy as it would deprive the citizen of the most fundamental choice which, according to the judgment "Democracy is all about." Rather than insisting on not providing NOTA in the so-called uncontested elections, the State Election Commission should "undertake awareness programmes to educate the masses" as directed by the Supreme Court.

NOTA, implemented in the right spirit, has the potential to change for the better the way elections happen in the country. The hope is that the law on NOTA will evolve with time.

APPLYING THE RTI ACT TO POLITICAL PARTIES

This is an issue which started off as a quasi-judicial one but has ended up in the SC where it is still under litigation at the time of writing.

The Background

Experience gained through getting the ADR 2002 and 2003 judgments on the disclosure of criminal, financial, and educational antecedents candidates led to the realization that there were limits to what focusing on individual candidates can achieve by way of improving the electoral and political systems in the country. The most important and critical participant in the entire electoral and political processes in the country are the political parties. It is perhaps more accurate to think of political parties as the controllers of the electoral and political processes rather than mere participants in these processes. While the control of political parties on these processes is more like a stranglehold, two manifestations should suffice.

The first is the myth that voters have a free choice. When people in general in India are asked where does the government come from, an overwhelming proportion responds by saying "We elect the government." While this is reassuring as an indication of the depth to which the concept of democracy has seeped into the public psyche in India, a little reflection shows it to be not an entirely correct description of the actual situation that prevails in reality. Yes, voters do have a choice but they can vote only for one of the many candidates that the set of competing political parties have chosen for them. It is true that there can be independent candidates but given the reality of the mechanics of the election process, particularly the levels of money spent during elections, it is becoming more and more difficult for independent candidates to contest and get elected. The reality, therefore, is that the *choice of voters is preconstrained by the choices made by a set of political parties.*

The second proof of the stranglehold of political parties on the political process is the complete control that parties have on the voting choices of MPs and MLAs in the Parliament and State Assemblies, respectively. The antidefection law, laid down in the Tenth Schedule of the Constitution with effect from March 1, 1985, under the Fifty-second amendment of the Constitution, says that if an MP or MLA votes against the whip of the party, his/her membership of Parliament or State Assembly can be terminated. This gives political parties *complete* control on the voting choices of the so-called elected representatives.

As greater insight into the exact and detailed mechanics of the election process was acquired, it was discovered that one of the major fundamental reason for the ills of the electoral processes was the opacity of the financial affairs of political parties.

How It All Began?

With the above background and the RTI Act having come into effect in 2005, an application under the RTI was filed on behalf of ADR with the Central Board of Direct Taxation (CBDT) seeking copies of income tax returns (ITRs) of 20 political parties on February 28, 2007. The CBDT transferred the application to the Public Information Officers (PIOs) of the 20 Chief Commissioners of Income Tax (CCITs) under whose jurisdictions the political parties were registered. All the 20 PIOs rejected the applications. ADR then filed the first appeals under RTI Act to the appellate authorities of the 20 CCITs. All the 20 first appeals were also rejected. Second appeals were then filed to the Central Information Commission (CIC). After several hearings in which all the political parties were also heard, the CIC allowed the appeal in its decision[14] of April 29, 2008, and directed the CCITs and the CBDT to provide the "Income Tax Returns of the political parties filed with the public authorities and the Assessment Orders for the period mentioned by the appellant in her RTI-application dated 28.02.2007…within a period of six weeks of this order."

---

[14] accessed on December 28, 2015.

The Next Step

Once copies of ITRs of political parties became available, their scrutiny showed that while *political parties declared large amounts as annual income, they did not pay any tax at all.* Further scrutiny revealed that the Income Tax Department exempted all political parties from income tax, as specified in Section 13A[15] of the Act which is reproduced as follows:

> 13A. Any income of a political party which is chargeable under the head "Income from house property" or "Income from other sources" or "Capital gains" or any income by way of voluntary contributions received by a political party from any person shall not be included in the total income of the previous year of such political party:
>
> Provided that—
>
> (a) such political party keeps and maintains such books of account and other documents as would enable the Assessing Officer to properly deduce its income therefrom;
>
> (b) in respect of each such voluntary contribution in excess of twenty thousand rupees, such political party keeps and maintains a record of such contribution and the name and address of the person who has made such contribution; and
>
> (c) the accounts of such political party are audited by an accountant as defined in the Explanation below sub-section (2) of section 288:
>
> Provided further that if the treasurer of such political party or any other person authorised by that political party in this behalf fails to submit a report under subsection (3) of section 29C of the Representation of the People Act, 1951 (43 of 1951) for a financial year, no exemption under this section shall be available for that political party for such financial year.

This provision was made by the Taxation Laws (Amendment) Act, 1978, which came into effect on April 1, 1979.

---

[15] accessed on December 28, 2015.

Since the earlier provision referred to subsection (3) of Section 29C of the RP Act, 1951,[16] a reference to that became necessary. This is what that reads:

29C. Declaration of donation received by the political parties:

(1) The treasurer of a political party or any other person authorised by the political party in this behalf shall, in each financial year, prepare a report in respect of the following, namely:—

   (a) the contribution in excess of twenty thousand rupees received by such political party from any person in that financial year;
   (b) the contribution in excess of twenty thousand rupees received by such political party from companies other than Government companies in that financial year.

(2) The report under sub-section (1) shall be in such form as may be prescribed.

(3) The report for a financial year under sub-section (1) shall be submitted by the treasurer of a political party or any other person authorised by the political party in this behalf before the due date for furnishing a return of its income of that financial year under section 139 of the Income-tax Act, 1961 (43 of 1961), to the Election Commission.

(4) Where the treasurer of any political party or any other person authorised by the political party in this behalf fails to submit a report under sub-section (3) then, notwithstanding anything contained in the Income-tax Act, 1961 (43 of 1961), such political party shall not be entitled to any tax relief under that Act.

In order to see whether the political parties were complying with the provisions of Section 29C(3) of the RP Act, an RTI application was filed with the ECI asking for copies of the statement of donations filed by various political parties. The total donations over ₹20,000 each, declared by political parties, were compared with the annual income declared by the same parties in their ITRs for the same year. These comparisons revealed the startling information that the

---

[16] accessed on December 28, 2015.

donations declared by political parties accounted, on average, for only 120–25 percent of the total income declared by them. This meant that, on average, *the source of up to 75 to 80 percent of the total income of political parties was not known.*

The Follow-Up

This led ADR to file RTI applications to various political parties requesting them to disclose the sources of their funding, including the 75–80 percent that was not explained by the statements of donations submitted them to the ECI. All political parties responded by saying that they did not need to respond to the RTI application since they were not "public authorities" under the RTI Act. This is when ADR filed a complaint to the CIC for noncompliance of the RTI by political parties and requesting that they be declared "public authorities" under the RTI Act. The CIC asked for data to prove that political parties satisfied the definition of "public authority" given in Section 2(h)[17] of the RTI Act which reads as follows:

(h) "public authority" means any authority or body or institution of self-Government established or constituted,

- (a) by or under the Constitution;
- (b) by any other law made by Parliament;
- (c) by any other law made by State Legislature;
- (d) by notification issued or made by the appropriate Government, and includes any—

  - (i) body owned, controlled or substantially financed;
  - (ii) non-Government Organisation substantially financed, directly or indirectly by funds provided by the appropriate Government;

Since collecting information for all 20 political parties would have been very time-consuming, ADR set about collecting data only for the six national political parties. It took two years to collect supporting data which was collected from authorized government agencies,

---

[17] accessed on December 28, 2015.

again through filing RTI applications. Once again, all political parties opposed declaring them to be "public authorities."

After several hearing, a full bench of the CIC headed by the Chief Information Commissioner, decided on March 3, 2013 "that AICC/INC, BJP, CPI(M), CPI, NCP and BSP are public authorities under section 2(h) of the RTI Act." The CIC further said:

> The Presidents, General/Secretaries of these Political Parties are hereby directed to designate CPIOs and the Appellate Authorities at their headquarters in 06 weeks time.

> The CPIOs so appointed will respond to the RTI applications extracted in this order in 04 weeks time. Besides, the Presidents/General Secretaries of the above mentioned Political Parties are also directed to comply with the provisions of section 4(1) (b) of the RTI Act by way of making voluntary disclosures on the subjects mentioned in the said clause.

The order of the CIC gave detailed reasons for categorizing the political parties as "public authorities." All the reasons can be put into four major groups:

- Direct and indirect benefits by the government, such as subsidized land for party offices, income tax exemptions, free airtime on Doordarshan and All India Radio, supplying electoral roll copies free of cost during elections, etc.
- Political parties are formed only after they are registered such as under Section 29A of the RP Act, giving them statutory status.
- Political parties exercise constitutional authority under the antidefection law as enunciated in the Tenth Schedule to the Constitution of India.
- Political parties perform a public function.

Aftermath of the Chief Information Commission Decision

In a development that many observers found surprising, all the six national political parties decided not to implement the decision of the

CIC and did not appoint PIOs. The government decided to amend the RTI Act to specifically exclude political parties from its purview thereby nullifying the CIC's decision. It introduced a Bill to this effect in the Lok Sabha toward the end of 2013. The proposed amendment of the RTI was supposed to be retrospective in effect. There was a public outcry and the Lok Sabha decided to refer the Bill to a department-related Standing Committee for detailed consideration and recommendation. Though the Standing Committee was reported to have recommended passing the Bill, the report of the Standing Committee could not be discussed in the Lok Sabha before the term of the Lok Sabha was completed. The Bill therefore lapsed.

As the political establishment was trying to amend the law, the original petitioners, ADR and Subhash Chandra Agrawal, filed a complaint to the CIC of noncompliance of its order by the political parties. The CIC conducted two hearings on the matter in November 2014 and January 2015. The political parties completely ignored the CIC, not even acknowledging its notices, including "show cause" notices and decided not to send any representative to these hearings. After the hearings, another full bench of the CIC said the following in a fresh order on March 3, 2015:

- The commission's order of June 3, 2013 is "binding and final. It has not been affected by any judicial or legislative intervention."
- "As per the commission's order, which is final and binding, the respondent national political parties are public authorities under the RTI Act."
- "It is clear that the respondents have not implemented, as public authorities, the directions contained in the commission's order."
- The commission "is bereft of the tools to get its orders complied with."
- "The complainants are at liberty, in view of the facts and circumstances of this case, to approach the higher courts for appropriate relief and redressal."

It was unfortunate that the CIC felt it did not have the powers to get its own lawful order implemented because it is *not* "bereft of the tools to get its orders complied with." Section 20.1[18] of the RTI Act empowers the CIC to "impose a penalty of two hundred and fifty rupees each day till application is received or information is furnished, so however, the total amount of such penalty shall not exceed twenty-five thousand rupees" if the PIO refuses "to receive an application for information or has not furnished information within the time specified." In addition, Section 19(8)(b) says that the CIC "has the power to—(b) require the public authority to compensate the complainant for any loss or other detriment suffered." It was unfortunate because both these provisions of the RTI Act were specifically brought to the notice of the full bench of the CIC by way of written submissions as well as during oral arguments.

After the CIC that formally expressed its inability to ensure proper implementation of the RTI Act, the very purpose for which the CIC has been formed, both the complainants filed a PIL in the SC.[19] In the petition, all the six national political parties have been made parties to

---

[18]

20. **Penalties**.—(1) Where the Central Information Commission or the State Information Commission, as the case may be, at the time of deciding any complaint or appeal is of the opinion that the Central Public Information Officer or the State Public Information Officer, as the case may be, has, without any reasonable cause, refused to receive an application for information or has not furnished information within the time specified under sub-section (/) of section 7 or malafidely denied the request for information or knowingly given incorrect, incomplete or misleading information or destroyed information which was the subject of the request or, obstructed in any manner in furnishing the information, it shall impose a penalty of two hundred and fifty rupees each day till application is received or information is furnished, so however, the total amount of such penalty shall not exceed twenty-five thousand rupees:

Provided that the Central Public Information Officer or the State Public Information Officer, as the case may be, shall be given a reasonable opportunity of being heard before any penalty is imposed on him:

Provided further that the burden of proving that he acted reasonably and diligently shall be on the Central Public Information Officer or the State Public Information Officer, as the case may be.

[19] accessed on December 30, 2015.

the petition, as have been the Union of India and the ECI. Curiously, at the time of writing, only the Union of India had filed its response[20] to the petition, and it has taken a position that political parties should *not* be brought under the ambit of the RTI Act. That the stand of the Government of India is clearly against the principle of transparency should be clear.[21] What is disturbing is the blurring of the distinction between the political party and the government.[22]

Since the matter is still in the SC, the final outcome is unknown at the time of writing.

FOREIGN CONTRIBUTION (REGULATION) ACT AND POLITICAL PARTIES

The last issue to be discussed in this chapter is of the applicability of the Foreign Contribution (Regulation) Act (FCRA) to political parties. Section 4(1) of the FCRA, 1976,[23] reads as follows:

(1) **No foreign contribution shall be accepted by any—**
  (a) candidate for election,
  (b) correspondent, columnist, cartoonist, editor, owner, printer or publisher of a registered newspaper,
  (c) Judge, government servant or employee of any corporation,
  (d) member of any Legislature,
  (e) political party or office-bearer thereof.

While scrutinizing the Donation Reports submitted by political parties under Section 29C(3) of the RP Act, it was noticed that some of the parties had declared donations received from Electoral Trusts. Electoral Trusts were permitted to be formed by the central government in a scheme[24] notified in January 2013.

Two of the leading political parties, the BJP and the Congress, had both declared receiving donations from a particular trust which was

---

[20] accessed on December 30, 2015.
[21] accessed on December 30, 2015.
[22] accessed on December 30, 2015.
[23] accessed on December 30, 2015.
[24] accessed on December 30, 2015.

found to have been set up by three companies. These three companies were found to be 100 percent, fully owned subsidiaries of another company registered in the United Kingdom. Given these facts, it was felt that the two parties had accepted effectively foreign contributions and were in violation of Section 4(1)(e) of the FCRA. A PIL[25] was filed in the Delhi High Court requesting appropriate action to be taken against the two political parties under the FCRA.

After hearing all sides over several hearings, the Delhi High Court gave its decision[26] on March 28, 2014, saying:

> For the reasons extensively highlighted in the preceding paragraphs, we have no hesitation in arriving at the view that prima-facie the acts of the respondents inter-se, as highlighted in the present petition, clearly fall foul of the ban imposed under the Foreign Contribution (Regulation) Act, 1976 as the donations accepted by the political parties from Sterlite and Sesa accrue from "Foreign Sources" within the meaning of law.

The court went on to give a specific time frame to take action in the following words:

> The second direction would concern the donations made to political parties by not only Sterlite and Sesa but other similarly situated companies/corporations. Respondents No. 1 and 2 would relook and reappraise the receipts of the political parties and would identify foreign contributions received by foreign sources as per law declared by us herein above and would take action as contemplated by law. The two directions shall be complied within a period of six months from date of receipt of certified copy of the present decision.

The Ostensible "Action Taken"

Respondent No. 1 was the Union of India and Respondent No. 2 was the ECI. FCRA is administered by the union Ministry of Home Affairs (MHA) and MHA is therefore the appropriate authority to take

---

[25] accessed on December 30, 2015.
[26] accessed on December 30, 2015.

action in this case. The ECI wrote to the MHA to take action according to the judgment. The MHA apparently wrote to the Ministry of Corporate Affairs (MCA) to ask the names of companies falling under the category of "foreign source," who have donated to political parties, namely, Indian National Congress and Bharatiya Janata Party. When the MCA sent such a list to the MHA, the latter merely forwarded that same list to the ECI. This appears to be the action taken in response to the Delhi High Court's judgment! In the meanwhile, both BJP and Congress appealed to the SC against the Delhi High Court judgment.

THE "ACTION TAKEN"

While the earlier ostensible "action taken" was on, the *Economic Times* reported[27] what might in fact be the real "action taken." It was reported that the Home Ministry had proposed to amend the FCRA "to allow foreign companies that are registered in India to contribute to political parties from their corporate social responsibility fund in sectors where FDI is allowed." An earlier suggestion to bring in a notification describing any company registered in India as an "Indian company," irrespective of its shareholding pattern, was turned down during interministerial discussions. Details of this, as analyzed in the media, reveal a three-pronged strategy to not only bail out the two political parties but to also open fresh avenues of finances for political parties.

- If the proposed amendment succeeds and can be made effective with retrospective effect, it will exonerate the BJP and the Congress of what they have been held guilty of by the Delhi High Court.
- If the proposal "to allow foreign companies that are registered in India…in sectors where FDI is allowed…to contribute to political parties" is made into law, then a totally new source of funding will become available to all political parties.
- The proposal to allow such companies to contribute to political parties "from their corporate social responsibility fund" is another

---

[27] accessed on December 30, 2015.

familiar stratagem. Section 135 of the Companies Act specified in August 2013 that

> Every company having net worth of ₹500 crore or more, or turnover of ₹1000 crore or more or a net profit of ₹5 crore or more during any financial year...shall ensure that the company spends, in every financial year, at least two per cent of the average net profits of the company made during the three immediately preceding financial years, in pursuance of its Corporate Social Responsibility Policy.

The MCA initiated a discussion on what activities would be qualified to receive such CSR funds. The initial proposals suggested contributions to political parties as one of the purposes on which CSR funds could be spent. This resulted in an extensive debate after which it was decided that contributions to political parties were kept out of the list of approved CSR activities. The inclusion of CSR funds in the proposed amendments to the FCRA would clearly annul the MCA decision to exclude CSR donations to political parties.

Since the matter of the BJP and the Congress having violated the FCRA is still in the SC, therefore, the jury is still out on how this particular effort will end. But the attempt to amend the FCRA seems to fit into a familiar pattern.

CONCLUSION

Descriptions of several cases given earlier should make it clear that reforming politics and elections through legal changes is certainly possible but is definitely not easy or simple. As is seen in several of the experiences narrated earlier, all political parties seem to sink their differences when it comes to resisting political and electoral reforms. The entire political establishment shows a strong tendency to be unanimous in such cases, a phenomenon which appears to be extremely rare for most other forms of legislation.

For such efforts to succeed, those seeking to follow this course of action have to be persistent and have the perseverance needed to run marathons, for these are not sprints. At the same time, one has to bear the glorious uncertainties of judicial response. While the judiciary on the whole has been generally supportive, its response is always unpredictable.

The best that can be said is that the road to reforming politics and elections through legal changes is long and tortuous.

Chapter 8

Voters and Good Governance

Trilochan Sastry

Democracy is when the indigent, and not the men of property, are the rulers.

—Aristotle

BACKGROUND AND INTRODUCTION

Once in a while, it is pertinent to revisit some basic questions, particularly when times are changing as fast they are now. Many of our unconsciously held assumptions and even beliefs may no longer hold. Some basic questions are: What is democracy in the 21st century? If good governance is a desirable outcome for a democratic form of Government, how do voters define it? Democracy and good governance are more often defined by scholars, thinkers, governments and corporates, but here we look at it from the point of view of the so-called ordinary citizen. While this definition will vary widely from person to person, and country to country, we examine this question using data from India. The Election Commission of India data show that in the 2014 general election, there were 833 million registered voters and 548 million actually voted, making it difficult to say what democracy means to the 'average' person. But as we see later, data reveal that there are some issues of governance on which there is surprising agreement among voters.

What has changed that requires us to revisit this question. In this context, it is relevant to note that rural and working class voters in India outnumber any other category of voters. Rural voting percentages were 15 per cent higher than urban on average in 2014. According to the 2011 census, estimates are respectively that 833 million live in rural areas and 377 million in urban areas. The rural population therefore largely determines the outcome of elections. If we compare this group to that in 1947, the level of education, awareness, availability of information and communication facilities, media reach, mobility from rural areas to urban and so on have seen almost cataclysmic changes. Just one indicator is the number of mobile phones in India, which has crossed a billion, whereas in 1947 the Congress sent volunteers into rural India to inform people that we had won Independence. The last 70 years after Independence have seen 16 National elections and several times that number of State elections. The political awareness and understanding of the citizen has also changed dramatically. There is a lot of progress in reducing poverty though it persists in several pockets. All this has definitely led to higher aspirations in the population, as well as higher expectations from the Government. Meanwhile, the structure of democracy and elections from the official and constitutional perspective has remained largely the same. From the people's point of view, their own role has remained the same since 1947—they get to vote once every few years.

At the same time, less than 10 per cent of the workforce is in the organized sector. One definition is 'the unorganized sector consists of all unincorporated private enterprises owned by individuals or households engaged in the sale and production of goods and services operated on a proprietary or partnership basis and with less than ten total workers' (National Commission for Enterprises in the Unorganised Sector 2008). The voting percentage within this majority is much higher than those in the organized workforce. In addition, there are many small farmers and landless casual labourers. It is easy for everyone in these categories to see the high standards of life enjoyed by a significant minority and contrast those with their own situation.

In this context, what is the end goal of democracy as popularly understood or felt? Perhaps one important aspect is the deep yearning that citizens have for good governance. Unlike perhaps in the West, in India the Government is still seen as the principal provider of basic services, containing inflation and even ensuring employment so on.

Of late, there has been a serious attempt by scholars and thinkers to see democracy from the point of view of the citizen. The traditional scholarly and intellectual understandings of issues no longer suffice. The so-called Arab Spring, and before that the changes in Poland, show that large numbers of people are not satisfied with status quo in several countries. In some pockets, political parties have come up that directly connect to people and choose candidates in addition to using voter preference as a basis for their votes in the Parliament. One example is the El Partido de la Red, or the Net Party, in the city of Buenos Aires. In India, this voter dissatisfaction is expressed by frequent changes in the parties voted to power, both at the National and State levels. For instance, in Uttar Pradesh and in Tamil Nadu, no government has been re-elected since 1989. At the National level, India has had 13 Prime Ministers since 1977. Since the full term of the Lok Sabha is 5 years, the reason for this large number lies in the frequent collapses of ruling coalitions. Only since 1999 has there been some semblance of stability at the Centre.

Is democracy an end in itself for the majority of people? Scholars and political leaders have often argued that the best answer for the evils of democracy is more democracy—implying that dictatorship or some other form of Government is not the answer. While there are several benefits that real democracy brings, the so-called ordinary citizen may or may not be concerned about them. For instance, during chaotic or troubled times, citizens have voted for strong authoritarian or even dictatorial leaders. We are seeing a resurgence of this with the growth of radical parties both on the right and the left in several European countries, and even in the US candidates running for presidency. Several years of economic problems as well as fear of terrorism may have contributed to this. So for many, democracy is not an end in itself. It is perhaps a means to a better life—not for the long run, but for here and now. It is also not clear that people at large would choose democracy over good governance.

In summary, the situation has changed, but the forms and structures of democracy have not kept pace. In India, people's expectations from Government have changed and dissatisfaction has been repeatedly expressed by frequent changes in the ruling coalitions voted to power. A sea change in voter profiles in rural India gives a good opportunity to re-examine these issues.

INDIAN CONTEXT IN ELECTIONS

Indian elections are often said to be more identity based than ideology or issue based. This means that people identify themselves with candidates and political parties based on their personal affiliations to caste, language, religion and region. There are several hundred castes and sub-castes, 15 major languages and literally hundreds of dialects, with all major religions in the world represented here including the Hindu, Islamic, Christian, Sikh, Jain, Buddhist, Parsi and even the Jewish religions, and several regions numbering well over 30 with distinct cultures. In this situation, there are over 1,800 registered political parties, of which 477 contested the National elections and 35 won at least one seat. This makes it the most unique and complex country when it comes to democracy and elections.

Another feature that is distinct from other nations is the role of crime in elections. The Election Commission of India's data reveal that over 30 per cent of elected MPs have some sort of criminal charge against them. Since cases take years to come to a conclusion, charge sheeted MPs are able to complete their full term without being forced to vacate their seat. Even the Supreme Court has taken cognizance of this and issued notice to the Government asking what steps it proposes to take to curb this menace.

A third feature is the use of massive amounts of money in elections. While this is common across nations, there are two features that stand out in India. First, there is a lot of unaccounted money called black money used which does not show up in official expense statements filed by candidates and political parties. Second, given the fact that a majority of the population has relatively low incomes, there is direct bribing of voters. Candidates distributing cash, clothes, liquor, food and so on in return for votes is fairly common in some pockets and constituencies. Two Chief Election Commissioners of India have publicly commented on this while in office. Related to this are some fairly bizarre election promises to distribute free food, laptops, bicycles and so on if voted to power.

GOVERNMENT AND PEOPLE'S PRIORITIES

The citizen sees his/her role as ending after casting the vote. The elected Government takes charge and then decides how the State should run, how the economy managed, budgets allocated and so on. Government's decisions are based on expert advice from economists as well as from bureaucrats and politicians. It is assumed that these decisions are what the mass of voters want, or that it will help the nation—the two not being necessarily the same. While there are social and political issues, we look at how in a modern democracy the economics plays out.

A stream of thought that has gained more traction of late asks a straight question: where is the big money and to whom does it belong? A simple analysis shows that the money is with the Government. No other sector of the economy can compete with that. The RBI data show that in 2014–2015, the total tax revenue of central and state governments was ₹2,585,480 crores[1] or about US$414 billion. This is a growing amount annually. The source of this money is clearly from the people of the country. No other sector of the economy, including the corporate sector, has this kind of funds. The total annual corporate profits are about 8 per cent of India's GDP or $160 billion. While the government funds are for public use, the corporate profits are only for the shareholders. The annual tax revenues come to over ₹18,300 per

---

[1] Available at https://dea.gov.in/sites/default/files/IPFS%20English%20 2015–16.pdf and http://dbie.rbi.org.in/DBIE/dbie.rbi?site=publications (accessed on 3 September 2019).

citizen, or over 20 per cent of the per capita income in India. Over a 5-year period, this is about ₹90,000, roughly the same as per capita income today.

By tradition, the Government manages the economy with the help of politicians, bureaucrats and economists. Depending on the political priorities, economic ideologies and various other considerations, the national and state budgets are prepared. Meanwhile, various lobbies work to get some benefit or the other from the Government. In India, the Central budget, released in February end in time for the financial year starting on 1 April, is a matter of tremendous debate in the media. The divisions in society are along predictable lines—one side arguing for cuts in social spending, reining in budget deficits, cutting taxes, removing regulations, lowering interest rates and so on, and the other side arguing for greater social spending and subsidies to help those in need. Of late, the Government has asked for public suggestions on the debate.

From the point of view of a modern democracy, there are two critical questions. One is whether Government budgets can today take people's inputs into consideration more systematically than a mere call for suggestions. With the growth of technology, it is not difficult to get people to send their suggestions on a large scale. There are several issues around this that need to be worked out, but the critical one is whether people's majority views should prevail, and also whether the layperson has the expertise to manage the budget and indirectly the national economy. At present, the answer seems to be that majority views need not always prevail and that people at large do not really know how to manage the economy. At the same time, expert- and political-led management of the economy has led to the piling up of huge deficits. The central government, for instance, spends over 35 per cent of its revenues on interest payments. This is by far the largest single item of expenditure. The situation in state governments is on the whole worse.

At the same time, there is a question behind this: who sets the priorities and policies based on which budgets are allocated? At present, it is the political system which does this, often under pressure from various lobbies. In some cases, there is a conflict of interest between personal benefits accruing to politicians and the priorities and policies they set. While we can debate about strengthening the conflict of interest laws, technology allows us to cut through it. The Government can simply ask what people's priorities on various issues are. Once the priorities are set, the budget allocations and policies can take it into consideration. There is no doubt that some expertise is required for this. We make an important distinction here between setting priorities and then translating them into budgets and policies.

THE SURVEY: MOTIVATION AND METHODOLOGY

A nationwide survey was conducted by the Association for Democratic Reforms (ADR), a nationwide non-partisan, non-political civil society organization active for a decade and a half in India, in 2013–2014. The focus was on two questions: what are people's priorities? How do they rate the Government's performance on these issues? A laundry list of 30 possible issues was presented to voters in the survey. They included basic essential services, infrastructure needs, law and order, defence and so on. Voters rated each issue as 'very important', 'important' or 'not important'. On each issue, the voter also rated the Government's performance as good, average or bad. The basic premise is that priorities ought to be set by the people who are the source of all Government revenues. The Government should give serious consideration to these priorities. At the same time, it should correct itself on those issues where people are dissatisfied. Demographic data was also gathered along with whether a candidate's criminal record, political background and so on influenced their voting.

ADR is often asked whether fully informed voters will lead to good governance. The response is that structural changes are needed to weed out those with serious criminal charges to properly regulate and make transparent all election spending, and reform of political parties ensuring inner party democracy and transparency. Some then ask whether that will ensure good governance. This is a fair question and reflection shows that this was not sufficient. Indeed some would say that there is no sufficient set of actions that will ensure good governance for all times to come. But a proper consideration of people's priorities in governance is a step forward.

Crisis after crisis has shown that governance is too important an issue to be left only to big Government. Local self-government is one response to this. However, there are issues that cut across local interests and we still need a way to manage regional and national priorities. Different political parties and affiliated organizations appeal to voters telling them why they should be voted to power. In marketing jargon, this is like companies selling their products to customers. But really good companies find out what customers want. Has the time come when modern political parties need to really listen to what voters want? Old-style politics may no longer work with a younger, more aware and more demanding electorate. Recent election results around the country and in several States indicate that the voters are ahead of the political parties in many respects.

The remedy available to voters at present is to vote one Government out and bring in another. But this is not a sufficient remedy. There is little that citizens do to hold Government accountable once it is in power. Hence, we see more and more confrontations between the people, civil society, courts, Election Commission of India and the Comptroller and Auditor General of India on the one hand, and the Government and political system on the other.

The motivation for the survey was in two parts. One is the logic presented earlier: in a real democracy, the people's priorities should count and their rating of Government performance should be important. Second, it is hoped that political parties would learn to reflect people's priorities and pull up their performance where required. Clearly, this is a long-term effort and would need to be repeated several times over years and perhaps decades for any change to be visible.

The samples were chosen based on statistically sound randomization. Responses were obtained from over 260,000 voters in about 525 of the 543 parliamentary constituencies. The remaining constituencies were in very sparsely populated remote areas like the mountains where logistics was a problem. The idea was to get some idea of how governance was perceived in every constituency. The survey was conducted between

October 2013 and February 2014, before the 2014 General Elections, and was the first such survey in India. It was the largest ever survey in India and perhaps anywhere in the world. In contrast, previous voter surveys done to predict election outcomes in India had a maximum of 64,000 respondents, with most such surveys in the range of 14,000 to 49,000 respondents. Gallup polls in the USA use a smaller sample size. They do not address the questions we addressed.

SURVEY FINDINGS

The single most important finding of this survey is that people first and foremost want employment. It cuts across regions, castes, languages, religions, gender, income brackets, age and education levels. Governments need to create policies and an environment where real fruitful employment is generated. There is also a gap between the importance score and the performance score. The average importance of all issues across the country was 7.51 on a scale of 10. Any score above 6.7 is very important. The corresponding average performance rating was 5.68. Any score below 6.7 is below average.

The top 10 priorities are shown in Table 8.1. Employment remains the top priority across regions, religions, castes, income categories and gender. The second set of priorities from rank 2 to 7 are very interesting. These include basic essential services—drinking water, health care, food, education—as well as public transport and roads. It is interesting that an India that sent an unmanned mission to Mars and the Moon still says that basic essential services are top priority. This needs further probing, but other reports speak of 37.9 per cent stunted and 36.3 per cent underweight children in India.[2] The availability of water with persistent droughts in rural areas, and high levels of contamination of rivers and urban water bodies is a pressing problem. The vast majority either do not have access to water or are unable to buy clean drinking water on a daily basis. Comparison of budget allocations for education and health with other countries shows that India lags behind. 'India spends

---

[2] Available at https://data.unicef.org/topic/nutrition/malnutrition/ (accessed on 3 September 2019).

Table 8.1 *Top 10 Priority Issues—All India*

Rank	Issue	Importance (%)	Performance (%)
1	Employment	7.96	5.69
2	Drinking water	7.81	5.88
3	Better roads	7.80	5.97
	Public transport	7.76	6.00
4	Electricity	7.71	5.92
5	Health care	7.70	5.77
6	Lower food prices for consumers	7.68	5.99
7	Better schools	7.66	5.93
8	Law and order/policing	7.65	5.85
9	Security and empowerment of women	7.64	5.79
10	Subsidized food distribution	7.61	5.72

Source: ADR. 2019. https://adrindia.org/content/all-india-survey-governance-issues-and-voting-behaviour-2018-1 (accessed 22 September 2019).

about 1 percent of its gross domestic product (GDP) on public health, compared to 3 percent in China and 8.3 percent in the United States'.[3] Similarly, the education budget has been cut, with the biggest cut coming in primary education—down from ₹46,805 crores to ₹42,220 crores. India lags behind other BRICS countries in education budget allocations as well as literacy levels. The high priority for public transport is perhaps due to the massive increase in travel both in cities and rural areas. Only part of it is due to tourism—the bulk of it is for work. The poor condition of roads perhaps explains the priority of better roads.

What is not in the top 10 priority list is also interesting. These include strong defence, environmental issues, garbage clearance, elimination of corruption, terrorism and reservation for jobs and education. Some are either urban priorities such as garbage clearance and traffic

---

[3] Available at http://in.reuters.com/article/india-health-budget-idINK-BN0K10Y020141223 (accessed on 3 September 2019).

congestion, and others are rural such as agriculture subsidies, and water for irrigation.

VARIATIONS ACROSS VOTERS

India being such a diverse country, we find a lot of variation. One is the rural–urban divide. The rural expectations are slightly higher as reflected in higher scores for Importance, with Rural India at 7.55 and Urban at 7.46. The performance rating of Government is lower in rural areas at 5.58 compared to 5.87 in urban areas. We can infer that levels of dissatisfaction are higher in rural India.

There is no difference between men and women, with both scoring 7.51 for importance and 5.68 for performance for women and 5.67 for men. There is, however, a difference between first-time voters in the age group 18–22 and others:

	Males	Females
First-time voters	7.44	5.54
Other voters	7.53	5.67

First-time voters have lower expectations of the Government and also rate Government performance lower. Whether this is due to some kind of permanent change in the younger generation and will sustain over the years or is due to youthful attitudes is difficult to say.

One of the widely debated issues in India is that of caste. People are generally divided into four categories called Scheduled Castes (SC), Scheduled Tribes (ST), Other Backward Castes (OBC) and General meaning all others. Their scores are given as follows.

State	Importance of Issues	Performance Rating
SC	7.57	5.38
ST	7.51	5.53
OBC	7.57	5.64
General	7.48	5.85

The only clear picture that emerges is that the General category in the population have lower expectations from the Government and also rate its performance higher. This category is about 33 per cent of India's population as the 2011 census was not caste-based, but was estimated by the National Sample Survey. SCs and STs together constitute 25 per cent of the population and OBCs about 41 per cent.

Income-based Expectations and Performance Ratings

Some difference is seen between the rural middle class and the rural poor. Though both rate employment as a high priority, the former gives greater importance to greater farm gate prices for their produce, irrigation programmes, and seed and agriculture subsidy reflecting their peasant status, whereas the latter are more concerned about subsidized food distribution through the Public Distribution System (PDS) and the security of women. This latter is revealing since none of the other rural income categories rate security of women as a high priority. Except for these differences, the top priorities are the same and relate to employment and basic essential services.

The urban poor is the only category that rates eradication of corruption as a top 10 priority. Even in rural areas, this is not rated high. Training for employment and subsidized food from the PDS are rated as high priorities. For the urban well off, facilities for pedestrians and cyclists and better law and order figure in the top 10 instead. The other priorities are the same and again relate to employment and basic essential services.

Regional Variations

There are high expectation regions where most issues are rated as very important, and others where they are not. The high expectation states are Manipur, Delhi, Goa and Bihar, all with scores well over 8.4 in contrast to the All-India average of 7.51. These states are all small except Bihar. Dissatisfaction levels are high with low performance ratings in Manipur (4.28) and Bihar (5.07). Goa (6.58) and Delhi (5.86) have a higher performance rating than the national average.

State	Importance of Issues	Performance Rating
Manipur	9.24	4.28
Delhi	8.88	5.86
Goa	8.82	6.58
Bihar	8.41	5.07

Manipur, Delhi and Goa have a very high level of education, whereas Bihar lags behind national averages. Availability of public services are better in the first three states and low in Bihar. Further research is required to understand this, but it is the gap between expectations and good governance that leads to dissatisfaction. A literate population could rate performance low because of higher expectations, and another population could rate performance low because it is indeed so.

At the other end of the spectrum, we have regions which do not consider the issues to be that important as seen further. The education levels are all higher than the National average except for Meghalaya which is at the average level, and the States are relatively well governed as reflected in higher performance rating. The reasons for low expectations in Meghalaya need to be studied further.

State	Importance of Issues	Performance Rating
Daman & Diu	6.54	6.92
Gujarat	6.52	6.64
Chandigarh	6.45	3.47
Dadra & Nagar Haveli	6.36	6.40
Meghalaya	4.43	4.48

Again these are all small States and Union Territories. The important issue is that the two extremes of regions with high and low expectations are of regions with low populations except Bihar.

In summary, the overall picture that emerges is that employment and basic services such as health, drinking water, education, food availability (either through the PDS or through lower food inflation), transport and roads dominate the priorities. There are regional variations, and variations across income levels. The 'general' population has lower expectations/dependence from the Government and rates its performance higher than all other caste groups. It is largely their point of view that is reflected in the media.

On the issue of tainted candidates with criminal cases, only 55 per cent of respondents gave an answer. About 77 per cent said people should not vote for such candidates. However, 65 per cent said they did not know where to get this information. While they are on the Election Commission of India's website, and there is a fair amount of media coverage, and various civil society watchdog websites, voters at large do not see this information and digest it before voting. The fact remains that such candidates continue to win. This is reinforced by the fact that corruption ranks low in the priority list in the survey. In the face of more pressing issues of day-to-day life such as employment, drinking water, food availability, inflation and so on, tackling corruption takes a back seat.

On the issue of election spending, voters are ambivalent. About 68 per cent say they know distribution of gifts is not legal, while less than 50 per cent admit they know that such gifts are distributed. Further research is needed to unravel this issue. It is widely speculated that some voters accept money from one or more candidates but vote for the candidate of their choice.

IMPLICATIONS

The survey clearly shows that people's priorities are not adequately reflected in the way the economy is managed. The top priorities, namely employment, basic essential and other public services are not adequately addressed. Education and health budgets have been cut and even drinking water availability a major problem is not a priority for Governments. Food security is another priority for people but again not for the Government. Employment is an issue for all Governments around the world, and so is it in India. Some efforts are being made by the Government but the number of jobs created falls short of the numbers joining the workforce each year. The backlog is growing.

In a democracy, people have the right to change governments but do not have a say in their actual functioning as the survey shows. The only remedy available—that of changing Governments once every few years—has been tried by voters several times, for instance, in the States of Uttar Pradesh and Tamil Nadu where no Government has been re-elected since 1989. But this remedy is clearly not working well as governance continues to lag behind expectations.

CONCLUSIONS AND THE WAY FORWARD

This brings us back to the basic question: what is democracy? In India, working class and rural voters have a strong faith in casting their vote, and surprisingly in spite of repeated disappointments, voting percentages have gone up in the recent past. As in other countries, urban voting percentages are low, as it is for those who are well off. For other voters in India, the voting percentages are among the highest in the world and actually growing. There is also a clear increase in voting percentages as we move from National to State elections, and then to local elections. Clearly, there is hope of better governance, and being better connected to the context as in local elections makes a difference to voting percentages.

At the same time, this faith in democracy has not been reflected in good governance as perceived by voters. Is this a failure of democracy as we see it today? Some scholars and thinkers point to the failure of democracy in some of India's neighbouring countries and its continuing success in India for 60 years. We have never had armed conflict when one Government is voted out and another comes in. The fact that 548 million (a 66.4% turnout) voted in the 2014 elections is a record, and no other country comes close. The next highest, numerically, is the United States, where less than 130 million (a 61.4% turnout) voted in the last Presidential election. These facts are put forward to show that democracy continues to thrive in India.

But can India do better? Not only from a macro-perspective, but from the point of view of the voters? Elections are fought on issues framed by political parties whose sole aim is to win. Rarely are the issues of concern to people addressed. Appeals to caste, religious, regional and language-based identities, promises of freebies, direct bribing of voters in some pockets and of late massive mega media campaigns continue to define elections. The role of big money in elections has become critical. Voters have little chance of defining how campaigns are funded or run, and only have the power to choose between the candidates offered by the political parties. The winners feel vindicated that their campaign paid off, and so there is perhaps no real need to address people's priorities.

Election campaigns and voting are largely divorced from governance. The great leap of faith in democracy is that the party that wins will deliver the best governance. However, winning an election requires one set of abilities and governing requires another set. When we go back to the roots of democracy, namely the local participatory systems in ancient India and Greece, the connection between the two—the ability to win votes and the ability to govern—was easy to see. In modern times, with hundreds of millions voting in media and money-led campaigns, that connection is not that clear. Besides, in local government, there is a ready remedy for citizens—direct dialogue with those they have elected. That remedy was not available in modern democracy until recently.

However, that remedy is now becoming more and more possible. Governments can easily get an idea of people's priorities on important issues. One recently elected Government—Delhi—tried this a couple of times, but has now stopped doing it. There are two challenges here—one inherited from the recent past, and another more fundamental. The first is that basic trust between people and elected Governments is low. We started off in 1947 with high trust. But there has been a steady erosion over the years. In this situation, every decision is seen with suspicion and some section of voters may attribute all kinds of motives to the elected leaders. This lack of trust and the increasing scrutiny makes leadership and governance a real challenge.

Many are put off by this and do not want to enter public life. Winston Churchill's more famous quote is about democracy being the worst form of Government, except for all the others. But he too reflected the lack of trust in ordinary people when he said, 'The best argument against democracy is a five-minute conversation with the average voter'. So we see lack of trust on both sides—citizens don't trust the Government and vice versa.

The second issue is more fundamental: whether the majority decision is always the right one. In India, we still see celebrities and powerful persons welcomed by large crowds when they are released from jail after serving their sentence. If things had been left to the vocal majority (or is it minority?), such people would never have gone to jail. Even the economy is difficult to manage and every economic decision cannot be put to a vote. Ironically in India, the few institutions that work reasonably well—the Supreme Court, the Election Commission of India and the Reserve Bank of India to name three—have staff who are not elected. The Constitution protects these institutions from political interference.

The corporate sector's performance is seen as better than that of the Government. Though corporate governance remains an important issue with cases of massive fraud, there is a perception that they are run 'better' than Governments. There is not much democracy here, whether in small proprietary firms or large mega corporations. This better performance leads to demands for running government like a business or even wanting businesses to run Governments. But there is the question of alignment of incentives between the governors and the governed. In business, the incentive for business leaders and the shareholders is closely aligned—to make profits. However, in democracy, the incentive for the ruling parties is to enjoy power, while for voters it is to obtain good governance.

In popular perception, the non-democratic organizations seem to work better than democratically elected Governments. In troubled and chaotic times, this leads to a yearning for strong authoritarian and stable leaders. This goes against the very grain of democracy. So are political parties to blame? Do we need to go back to a system of 'meritocracy' when it comes to important positions in Government and not depend on the popular vote? If we keep faith in democracy, we have to go to the root of the problem—the misalignment between the incentives of those contesting elections and those voting. The one wants power, the other wants good governance.

As hinted earlier, the major task is to restore trust between those in power and the people. A first step surely is to make information widely available. A second is to listen to what the people want. Here, we try to give one way of implementing the oft-heard adage that the remedy for the evils of democracy is more democracy. People cannot participate meaningfully in day-to-day governance. But perhaps they can set priorities. In today's information and digital age, it is not difficult to know what voter's priorities are on various issues as the survey shows. It is important to close the feedback loop and Governments need to periodically report back to the people. Such feedback mechanisms do exist like the continuous monitoring of inflation and, to a lesser extent, of unemployment. But they clearly need to be strengthened and information widely disseminated.

Another fundamental change is needed for democracy to progress. People need to understand that the Government's money is their money. Conversely, Governments also need to understand that the money they collect is the people's money. While there is superficial acceptance of this, at a deeper level this is not yet a societal value. If so-called ordinary voters are willing to be more informed and vigilant, and then hold Governments more accountable, we will move towards better governance.

REFERENCE

National Commission for Enterprises in the Unorganised Sector. 2008. *Report on Definitional and Statistical Issues Relating to the Informal Economy*. New Delhi: National Commission for Enterprises in the Unorganised Sector.

PART III

The Practice of Democracy

Chapter 9

Representing Women
Voting Rights and Women Legislators

Wendy Singer

For a chapter on "women" in a volume on Indian democracy, it would seem logical to look at how women, as a constituency, are represented in the political system, particularly through the electoral process. Especially given the active participation and success that so many women in India have had as candidates and politicians, there is a rich and important story to tell about how Indian democracy can be understood—in theory, process, and practice—with women at the center. Therefore, this chapter focuses on a puzzle. Throughout the history and politics of women's representation, there have been two critical threads: one has to do with voting rights and the other has to do with women's representation in governing bodies. These two very different issues are often intertwined, both by politicians and in social science scholarship. The purpose of this chapter is to examine these as two separate issues and see how they have intersected and influenced one another over time.

Particularly, this chapter argues that there is an uneasy relation between the political arguments to guarantee women voting rights and the arguments to include women as legislators. Voting rights usually have to do with the individual rights that women have as citizens.

This emerged initially as the fight for suffrage, guaranteeing women the right to vote, and, later, in campaigns and court cases about increasing turnout among women voters. But is there a correlative political right for women's representation in governing bodies? This is sometime registered as a "right to run" for office or the need to provide some kind of set aside, such as reservations or nominations, to guarantee women seats in councils, legislatures, and the Parliament. The nature of this demand too has changed over time.

Of course, in raising these questions, the recent example that looms large is the proposed 108th Amendment to the Constitution that would require one-third representation for women in the Parliament and state legislatures. This is a subject on and off in the news and that has received some scholarly attention.[1] In addition, recent studies often link the discussion of reservations to women's participation in elections as voters as well; indeed the numbers of women voters have increased steadily over the past elections.[2] And this is all connected in some literature to women's literacy and women's development.[3] But what is the connection? This chapter takes the long view from the early 20th century fight for the women's vote and the first women representatives in Madras to contemporary elections and debates over the Women's Reservation Bill.

---

[1] See, most recently, Wendy Singer, "Rethinking the Women's Bill: Claims for a 'Level Playing Field'" in *Femininities and Masculinities in Indian Politics: Essays on Gender Archetypes, Transformative Materialities and Resilient Activisms*, ed. Manuela Ciotti (New Delhi: Women Unlimited, 2016), 122–166.

Mudit Kapoor, and Shamika Ravi, "Why So Few Women in Politics? Evidence from India" (August 8, 2013). Available at http://dx.doi.org/10.2139/ssrn.2307482

Virginie Dutoya, "A Representative Claim Made in the Name of Women?: Quotas and the Political Representation of Women in India and Pakistan (1917–2010)," *Revue Française De Science Politique* (English Edition) 66, no. 1 (2016): 41–62.

[2] Mudit Kapoor, and Shamika Ravi, "Women Voters in Indian Democracy: A Silent Revolution" *Economic & Political Weekly* 49, no. 12 (2014, 22 March).

[3] See the government report to the UN for the *Fifth Global Forum on Gender Statistics*, available at http://unstats.un.org/unsd/gender/Mexico_Nov2014/Session%206%20India%20ppt.pdf (accessed on September 4, 2019).

There are several angles of entry into this conversation; however, in the interest of space and time, I am focusing here mostly on the perspectives among women politicians and in legal debates at specific moments in time. To do this, the chapter is divided into three parts; it begins in Madras in the 1920s and 1930s with Muthulakshmi Reddy and Hannen Angelo, two of the first women in political office. Second, it turns to the Constituent Assembly (CA), which produced India's Constitution, and follows the election process as it takes place in the 1950s. Finally, in the last section, it examines the debate over reservations for women in the Parliament in the context of the 108th Amendment Bill.

Before I begin, it is important to acknowledge some caveats to this argument. First of all, the actions and views of women in political office and those contesting for political office do not necessarily coincide with the many interests reflected in India's diverse women's movement. Part of the strength of Indian democracy is the participatory politics that take place outside the electoral arena in terms of nongovernment organizations, movements, mobilization, and protests. The electoral arena, described here, is one slice (though sometimes an overlapping one) of the story of women's democratic activism. Second, this chapter accepts that even among women running for office and holding office there have been different interpretations of the role that female elected officials play, particularly in how—or whether—they represent women as a constituency. That perspective extends to many of the active and powerful elected officials engaged in politics today. However, there is no scope here to talk about them individually.[4]

---

[4] I have addressed this elsewhere. Also see Rajeswari Sunder Rajan's analysis of Indira Gandhi in *Real and Imagined Women: Gender, Culture, and Postcolonialism* (London: Routledge, 1993).

Uwe Skoda, "The Politics–Kinship Nexus in India: Sonia Gandhi versus Sushma Swaraj in the 1999 General Elections," *Contemporary South Asia* 13, no. 3 (2004): 273–285.

Ajoy Bose, *Behenji: A Political Biography of Mayawati* (New Delhi: Penguin Books, 2008).

IS THERE A "RIGHT TO RUN" FOR OFFICE?

One key political argument for increased access to political office has been an idea embedded in Indian elections that the barrier of entry should be low. It is true that running for office requires a deposit, and that candidates who do not receive one-sixth of the total votes forfeit that deposit.[5] But generally independent candidates and minor parties believe they can succeed in getting on the ballot. Popular opinion has resisted added barriers to contesting elections, reminiscent of colonial rules, such as taxpayer requirements or literacy requirements—although various new regulations have been posed in different states.

In March 2016, for example, Sonia Gandhi argued that minimum education requirements for candidates to run for local governing bodies (as passed in Haryana and Rajasthan) "denied a large number of women from SC/ST groups to exercise their constitutional rights."[6] In making this claim that the right to participate in democracy includes the right to run for office, Sonia Gandhi was echoing similar statements by women who advocated for universal franchise 80 years earlier or for expanded electoral rolls, and for (and actually also against) reservations for women. Therefore, to understand the idea of the "right to run" for office, it is critical to examine arguments put forth by women who called for greater access to political office.[7] To illustrate this, I will begin with the first women elected to office following the

---

[5] The requires have increased over time. As of 2014, the deposit was ₹25,000 for a parliamentary constituency and ₹10,000 for Legislative Assembly. This is halved for members of Scheduled Castes or Scheduled Tribes. And a candidate requires support from 10 electors from the constituency.

[6] Available at http://www.dnaindia.com/india/report-women-s-reservation-bill-sonia-gandhi-attacks-govt-says-maximum-governance-means-giving-women-their-dues-2186822 (accessed on September 4, 2019).

[7] My interest in the studying the "right to run" for office, which is so commonly articulated by Indian political activists, was especially prompted by a conversation with a scholar of American election law who challenged the idea. "What does it mean to have the right to run for office, surely that is a competitive process?" He asked. Also, he pointed out that unlike India's policy of reservations, the means that the US Congress devised to increase the numbers of African Americans in office was by constructed districts that were majority Black. This difference in approach reflected, I realized, a different notion of electoral participation and representation.

Montague–Chelmsford reforms in 1917. Madras was a center of these conversations with a number of women competing for office at different levels of government.

HANNEN ANGELO AND WOMEN'S REPRESENTATION IN THE 1920s AND 1930s

As early as the fight for the franchise in India, women advocates connected the right to vote to the necessity of women in public office representing women's interests (including voting rights). As a number of scholars have noted, the fight for the right to vote came in stages with a delegation of women meeting the Montagu–Chelmsford Committee on Constitutional Reforms in 1917. As Geraldine Forbes put it:

> [F]rom the beginning, the demand for "votes for women" was based on the notion that women could bring something new and special to the political realm. Demands were not rooted in the concept of "radical equality," that is, that all individuals are born equal and therefore deserve the same rights, but on notions of "social equality" that stressed the differences between men and women, and insisted on the right to participate fully because of this difference.[8]

It is because of this philosophical claim that these two distinct demands, one for women voting and one for women in political bodies, were sometimes interlinked.

Women's lobbying through organizations such as the Women's Indian Association (WIA), but also through women in the Home Rule League, the Provincial Congress Committees, and the Muslim League did not succeed in effectively gaining women the vote in the Government of India Act of 1919. However, the Act did leave open the possibility of legislation in Provincial Councils. Madras was the

---

This chapter comes, in part, out of my search to sharpen the argument, to go deeper into what Indian women politicians, especially, mean by the right to run for office.

[8] Geraldine Forbes, "Votes for Women: The Demand for Women's Franchise in India 1917–1937," in *Symbols of Power: Studies on the Political Status of Women in India*, ed. Vina Mazumdar (Bombay: Allied Publishers, 1979).

first presidency to give women the vote in 1921 and was one of the first states to allow women to run for seats in the Legislative Council. The first women to run for the Legislative Council in Madras (in elections that took place under the very limited franchise) were Hannen Angelo and Kamaladevi Chattopadhyay, who both lost in elections held in 1926. Muthulakshmi Reddy, a doctor and advocate for social reforms, was then appointed to the Council in 1927. Hannen Angelo, though, then ran and won a seat—the first woman to do so—on the Madras Municipal Council. All three women continued to support voting rights for women's through universal suffrage.

Most women's organizations opposed "reservations" or "appointment" of women to political bodies in favor of equality for women in the election process. In a draft Bill in October 1928 before the Madras Legislative Council, an amendment to the District Municipalities Act 1928, proposed that municipalities too would be opened to women running. At this point, Hannen Angelo had already been elected to the Madras Municipal Council, running on the Congress ticket. As the *Times of India* reported, Hannen Angelo proved the example of success, saying that she

> enjoys, up to the present moment, the unique honour of being the only woman in the whole province who stood for election, faced the opposition of a rival of the sterner sex and was successfully returned. Her election affords sufficient proof that women are capable of contesting seats against men and if this is the case in Madras City it would be absurd to deny the privilege in district Municipalities.[9]

In the Municipal Council, Hannen Angelo pursued an agenda that included advocacy for women, for the Anglo-Indian community of which she was a part, health care, and democratic participation. In April 1927, Angelo questioned the process proposed for preparing voting rolls for the upcoming Legislative Council elections, which some other councilors were trying to hasten and carry out with fewer clerks even then allotted in the current budget. This was a particularly salient concern for women, who were increasingly going to be represented

---

[9] *The Times of India*, "Women Councillors" (1928, 13 October).

on those rolls, as tax records were recorded and scrutinized. Angelo, along with some other members of Council, opposed a reduction in clerks or a speeding of the process.

> I must certainly oppose it for this simple reason: last year all the thirty Divisions were supposed to have been revised. I must certainly say that people dead three years ago are still on the roll. If we are going to appoint these men to revise the lists it is certainly expected that we shall have revised lists and not the same lists over and over again printed with no revising at all. I appeal to the House, Mr President, if they are not going to prepare rolls properly there is no use in appointing them.

Angelo's side did not completely prevail, though the final proposal agreed to revisit the number of clerks in three months.[10] Significant too is that the argument Angelo used to express the imperative for accurate lists was not the increasing number of women voters—though that would happen—but rather the fact that voters who were deceased remained on the list.

At other times, she more explicitly did express the interest of women's rights and welfare in the Council. In 1934, when the council debated the Lothian Committee's recommendations for voting rights, Hannen Angelo supported an amendment for universal adult franchise. When that failed, she proposed to redefine the tax requirement so that it would be based on those who had been assessed a tax, rather than limited only to people who had actually paid. And she proposed to include all forms of taxes, not only property tax. She voted to add literacy as an alternative to the tax requirement since this would add more women to the voting rolls. Her most passionate speech, however, came in opposition to the proposal by fellow councilor S. Satyamurti that the wives of taxpayers be included on the voting list.

> If I rise to oppose Mr Satyamurti, it is because we women at public meetings deliberately declared that we really want our rights on equal terms with the men. This [the proposal for wives of taxpayers to vote]

---

[10] Madras Municipal Corporation, *Municipal Council Debates* (Chennai: Municipal Corporation Record Room, Ripon Building, 1927, 1 April).

will certainly give a woman a vote, because she happens to be the wife of a man who has a vote. If my friends had been liberal enough to give us the literacy vote, certainly many women would have come in. But to give me a vote because I happen to be the wife of a man who happens to have a vote is not doing us justice.... We women have always opposed this method at public meetings. When we went before the Simon Commission, all the ladies who went before the commission opposed it. We sent our Memorandum down to the Parliament and there we opposed it and said that the ladies should not get a vote because they happen to be wives. If women are to have more rights let us use our influence, give us the vote of literacy, so that women who are educated will be entitled to vote.[11]

Satyamurti's proposal failed. However, Basheer Ahmed Sayeed remained adamant. He asked rhetorically if her husband were a taxpayer, "I do not think that as a woman when franchise is to be conferred on her, she would say 'No, we do not want it'." And he pointed out that earlier he supported the WIA request for a representative on Council.[12] "[Women] are entitled to the vote, if they have property. If they are literate, let them also vote. If they are wives of the husbands who have property, let them vote." After all proposals failed, S. Satyamurti responded that despite the intention of the meeting to increase the numbers of Indian voters, the situation remained the same. "The wonderful committee has been so democratic that they have killed every extension of the franchise."[13] In terms of women's vote, this was certainly true. But for Hannen Angelo, the goal had been to

---

[11] Hannen Angelo, *Madras Municipal Council Debates* (Chennai: Madras Municipal Council, 1934, September 7).

[12] While the WIA opposed reservations in general, they did advocate having a representative on the Madras Municipal Council. This did not take the place of elections, but rather since the Council was made up of both elected and nominated members, the WIA had said in an earlier meeting that their representative should be among the communities receiving nominations. For example, another woman, Swarnam Appasamy, was already a nominated member of the Madras Municipal Council at the time, perhaps representing Indian Christians.

[13] S. Satyamurti, *Proceedings of Adjourned General Meeting of the Council of the Municipal Corporation of Madras* (Chennai: Municipal Archive, Ripon Building, 1934, September 6; hereafter, Municipal Corporation Council).

articulate a principle: that women should gain voting rights on their own terms.[14]

The same questions emerged in the CA and then in the first elections of 1952, where both the debates and practice of providing representation for women demonstrated the relationship between voting rights and guaranteed seats in office.

THE LANGUAGE OF CITIZENSHIP IN THE CONSTITUTION

The Constitution used the language of equal citizenship to define the right to vote. It assumed equality under the law as clearly articulated in Article 15 that prevents discrimination on the grounds of religion, race, caste, sex, or place of birth. However, Section (3) of that article also says, "Nothing in this article shall prevent the State from making any special provision for women and children." In this way, the Constitution defines women as a separate category of citizen, just as it contains provisions that guarantee certain rights to religious minorities or reservations for Scheduled Castes and Scheduled Tribes. The rules established for elections and also the practice of post-independence elections demonstrate how these special provisions influenced both the nature of representation and the practice of voting.

In the first elections of 1952 and 1957 (even though the separate electorates of 1937 and 1946 had been eliminated), women remained marked as a special category in government documents. For example, election reports paid special attention to women's participation—even labeling female candidates with a W.[15] And both elected officials and administrators were concerned with the problem of increasing the level of women's participation. However, the special category of women was

---

[14] In this, she did share the general position of women's organizations at the time. A number of sources talk about this process including Anupama Roy, "'The Womanly Vote' and Women Citizens: Debate on Women's Franchise in Late Colonial India," *Contributions in Indian Sociology* 36 (2002 October): 469–493.

[15] This was not the case in the report for first General Election, which contained fewer details in a number of statistical areas. By the 1957 election, both the mechanisms of reporting and (as discussed further) some of the election processes became further refined.

always seen in relation to other groups of citizens—including minorities and Scheduled Castes and Scheduled Tribes—so that gender, caste, and religion were intertwining categories.

I will use two examples to illustrate the sometimes complementary and sometimes conflicting relationships between these categories of citizens in the early elections and how that manifested in legal questions related to women voters and women candidates. The first comes from the debates in the CA that dismantled Separate Electorates and retained Reservations. The second case applied to women voters and especially women's right to separate polling booths. This built on precedents in the 1930s as well, particularly in cases related to women in purdah. All of these suggest ways in which Indian law and political practice were testing ideas about citizenship in the 1950s, and then how the meaning of citizenship played out in elections and legislatures as they applied to representing women.

In the shadow of the Partition, the CA debates over representation emphasized the need for a single electorate as a step toward healing the increasingly apparent social divisions and with the loss of separate electorates for Sikhs and Muslims, so too went the electorates for women. As Pandit Thakur Das Bhargava (East Punjab General Constituency) put it in 1949:

> If this Constitution had been framed in 1947 I know that these reservations must have remained for Muslims and Sikhs also, but the experience of the last two years should not be lost upon us. It is absolutely wrong now to continue this and I for one would beg the House to accept the principle, which they accepted with regard to the coming elections, that there shall be no reservation for the Sikhs and the Muslims.[16]

In that atmosphere, no one was willing to support separate electorates for any group, even though in 1946, as in 1937, there had been separate electorates, not only for Muslims and Sikhs, but for women, Christians, and landlords as well. And constituencies defined by separate electorates

---

[16] Constituent Assembly Debates, October 11, 1949. In the same debate, as a symbolically important statement, Faisal Devji argued for the same position.

had been designated both geographically and by community. For example, Vijaya Lakshmi Pandit, then a member of the CA, first ran from North East *Women's* General Constituency in Kanpur. Members of the CA were not elected directly; rather they were elected by Provincial Legislative Assemblies according to a proportional formula. Therefore, many of them had won election originally based on separate electorates.

PREPARING FOR UNIVERSAL FRANCHISE

But the CA was less clear on how this decision applied to the issue of women's representation. Renuka Ray (who was elected to a General Constituency in Bengal, not a women's constituency) argued against women's reservations as unnecessary and also as a small issue compared to the larger ones of equal rights for women.[17] But the issue gained little attention otherwise. Women were not a separate community or regional block; they did not present a danger of further fragmentation of the Indian state. So the question of women's representation did not hold the potential threat of Muslim and Sikh electorates. This meant that the question of women's representation remained open for years after 1947. Women members of the assembly—some of whom had been elected in separate electorates in the first place—from time to time raised the issue of women's representation.[18] For example, on October 11, 1949, amidst discussion of the transition of the CA into a provisional Parliament, Purnima Banerjee, who represented a general constituency in UP, sought to ensure that the number of women represented in the provisional Parliament should not be less than the number represented in the CA based on the 1946 election. As was so often the case, she tied women's rights to continued representation to that of Sikhs and Muslims as was being proposed in a new article, 312F.

---

[17] Renuka Ray, *Constituent Assembly of India Debates (Proceedings)*, Volume IV (1947, 18 July, Friday).

[18] The actual selection to the CA was through indirect election by provincial legislatures. Nevertheless, some of the women in the CA had been initially elected to the Provincial Legislatures through the separate electorate process.

Sir, I am conscious of a spirit of diffidence in moving this amendment and sometimes feel that in doing so I may be opening myself to a certain amount of ridicule. But, even at that cost I feel I should state my case. The proviso which we are now discussing provides that in respect of the casual vacancies which are to be filled hereafter for the provisional Parliament, those belonging to the Sikh or the Muslim community will be represented by persons of that community. My amendment seeks just to stretch that same provision for women.[19]

Banerjee's argument is based on the recent replacements of women representatives, who had resigned for a variety of reasons, with men, reducing the number of women in the Assembly.

Debate on the article continued with most speakers focusing on the possible precedent this might set for reservations or separate electorates for Muslims and Sikhs. By and large, Purnima Banerjee's amendment was ignored. Only H. V. Kamath addressed it in a meandering response that ultimately supported the amendment. Kamath recounted the concern of "many thinking men and thinking women too" that if government were run by women "the affairs of government might go awry, might not fare as well as we might want them to be." However, he disagreed with this assessment and supported the amendment, saying that more women in the Provisional Parliament would be welcomed.[20]

Once amendments failed—each in succession—to replace Muslims, Sikhs, or Scheduled Caste Members with people from those groups, Purnima Banerjee withdrew her amendment as well. And so Article 312F was adopted without provision for women to be replaced with women. It represented a hiatus—for the next 42 years—of special legislation to assure women places in representative bodies. By contrast in the CA, reservations for Scheduled Castes and Scheduled Tribes

---

[19] Indian Parliament, *Constituent Assembly Debates*, Vol. 10 (1949, October 11, Tuesday). Available at http://parliamentofindia.nic.in/debates/debates.htm (accessed on September 4, 2019).

[20] Ibid. Kamath also expressed confusion about Purnima Banerjee's comment that Sarojini Naidu could not be replaced "among men." Banerjee's statement suggested that Naidu was so preeminent that no one could replace her. But Kamath seemed to hear it in gendered terms.

received an easy endorsement. The next issue, however, was the pragmatic challenges of putting these policies into practice.

The monumental task mandated by universal suffrage was registering every eligible voter. As Hannen Angelo's small-scale debate in Madras in 1927 previewed—on a very small scale—the process of creating voter rolls required considerations of cost, limitations on time, and the necessity of hiring clerks and administrators. And, in 1950, one of the logistical challenges intersected directly with the question of women's voting rights. The states had to hire extra workers and deploy canvassers across every village and community, after which state election officials verified the authenticity of the compiled data.

In the end—though not apparent until polling day—a major discrepancy in the recording procedure had resulted in a considerable number of women being removed from the electoral rolls. Because many women (or their families) gave their names in relation to other family members as someone's mother or daughter or wife, rather than with a surname, they were crossed off the list. "On a directive from the Election Commission, the Electoral Registration Officers were asked to remove the names of women voters who were not registered under their own names but enrolled as wives and daughters."[21] In the language of the Election Commission of India, this was the consequence of a conflict between custom and modernity.

According to the *Report on the General Elections, 1957*:

They [women] had refused to give their proper names to the Registration authorities through some old-world custom and prejudice and they had been entered in the draft rolls not by their own names but by the description of the relationship they bore to some male relation or other, e.g., A's mother, B's wife, etc. The Electoral Registration Officers were instructed by the Commission to substitute the proper names of these women voters in the electoral rolls in place of such entries based on relationship.[22]

---

[21] F1 (16)-H52, Government of India, Ministry of States/Hyderabad Branch, *Report on the Administration of Hyderabad State* (1950–1951).

[22] *Report of the Second General Elections in India*, Vol. 1, Narrative (New Delhi: Government Printing Office, 1957), 42.

However, the Registration Officers did not have alternative names and so those women were unable to vote.

If the expression "old-world custom" had the ironic resonance of a British Government report, it was not without reason. In response to the proposal for universal adult suffrage in the 1930s, the imperial government rejected such a demand resoundingly on the grounds that it was "impractical" and "idealistic," and claiming it would be impossible to implement.[23] This was acknowledged by S. Satyamurti, when he proposed universal adult suffrage for women and men in Madras Municipal elections in 1934. He also claimed that Lothian Committee's decision was made on administrative, not philosophical grounds. The Report rejected universal adult suffrage

> not because they thought it was wrong, not because they thought it was not ideal, but because they put forward certain administrative difficulties which do not exist in a whole Province—difficulties in finding polling officers, returning officers and polling stations, for an organized electorate of tens of lakhs.[24]

And especially, they labeled "the schemes to increase the number of women voters cumbersome and difficult to implement."[25]

But even more significantly, the argument expressed in 1957 *Election Report* also suggests that it was women voters' responsibility to conform to the registration process. This is ironic in another way because the registration process was designed to put the onus of producing voter rolls on the registration officers, not the citizens. Differently from other countries, for example, the USA, where voters were required to register themselves, in India, as required by the Representation of the People Act 1951, the government was responsible for recording all eligible adults onto the rolls.

---

[23] Mrinalini Sinha, *Specters of Mother India* (Durham, NC: Duke University Press, 2006), 224.

[24] S. Satyamurti, *Municipal Corporation Council.*

[25] Geraldine Forbes, *Women in Modern India* (Cambridge: Cambridge University Press, 1996), 112.

The government's failure, in this case to enroll 2.8 million women voters, primarily from Bihar, UP, Madhya Bharat, Madhya Pradesh, Rajasthan and Vindhya Pradesh, was a serious omission. Furthermore, it was not simply that they were not enrolled, but rather their names were struck from the rolls later on because they did not conform to required standards. That means on the day of polling, the women themselves and their families assumed their names would appear on the list at the polling booth. The 1957 canvassers paid special attention to registering women voters in order to show that they could correct the 1952 error. It was similarly important that women voters, once properly recorded in the voting rolls, had access to the polling place. The following case for a separate polling booth for women demonstrated the legal intention for equal access and the court's willingness to enforce it.

SEPARATE BOOTHS FOR WOMEN

In West Bengal, the absence of a separate polling booth for women forced a revote in Maheshtala Constituency in the district of 24 Parganas in 1952. Amiya Mandal, the third place candidate in the election, whose own victory in the Legislative Assembly was not advanced by the verdict, submitted the petition.

The petitioner charged that the Presiding Officer at the local polling station in Panchool village school had without notice closed one of two adjacent polling booths, creating excessively long lines. The petition suggested that there may have been a reduction in numbers of voters and this was indeed true for women.

> The electoral roll shows that there were as many as 618 female voters, i.e., about 38.6%.... [However, it] appears that only 60 female voters could cast their votes. Evidence has been adduced that many voters had to go away without voting owning to inadequate polling arrangements.[26]

---

[26] *N. D. Majumdar v. S. C. Bhandari et al.* Election Tribunal, West Bengal (1953, May 8), in *Election Law Reports Containing Cases on Election Law decided by the Supreme court and the High Court of India, Opinions of Election Commission, and*

To demonstrate that voters—women voters—were unfairly denied their right to vote, the court heard "evidence established beyond doubt that the female voters were mostly purdahnashin Muslims." Therefore, the particulars of the case pertained directly to Rule 18(2) of the Representation of the People Act.

> Provided that the Returning Officer may direct—

> (a) that a polling booth with separate entrance and exit shall be provided for the taking of votes of women electors of any specified polling area and a different polling booth in the same polling station shall be provided for the men electors of that area.[27]

The case therefore turned in part on the women's cultural practice of purdah. It was not only their right as women to vote that was in question but also equal access to the polls for minority voters. In this sense recalled the 1933 case of *A. K. Bijli Sahib Bahadur vs M. K. Muhamed Asan Maracair and Others*, in which women had separate booths, but were asked to remove their veils in front of a candidate. In this instance, the case referred to a District Board election in Tinnevelly (now Tirunelveli) in Madras in which there was one Muslim seat and one general seat open. The election commissioner made a number of accommodations for women, including the provision of women polling officers. Also, the Inspector of Local Boards sent out a circular to all candidates directing that in booths set apart for women, the candidates' agents should be female as well. What could not be accounted for was that the law allowed the candidate himself to be able to witness voting in any polling booth. In this case, candidate Bijli insisted on seeing the faces of the voters who came to the booth. As a consequence, in one polling booth that was administered by a woman agent and in which only women were present, 139 women voted (out of 300 who were eligible). At the same time, in the neighboring two combined polling booths, where Bijli himself was present, out of 613 purdah-wearing

---

Important Decisions of the Election Tribunal, Volume VI, 1953, ed. A. N. Aiyar (Delhi: Government of India, 1954), 197.

[27] Representation of the People (Conduct of Elections and Election Petitions) Rules, 1951, Rule 18(2). In *Bihar Election Manual* (1953), 218.

voters only 14 cast their vote. The judge's ruling in this case, however, sided with the candidate, saying that despite the disability this imposed on potential women voters, a candidate had the right to see and challenge any voter who came to the poll. Commenting on the case, the election commissioner in 1932 simply observed that "franchise and purdah do not go very well together."[28] The observation continued to have resonance.

RETURNING TO ACCESS AND THE RIGHT TO RUN

Two 21st-century cases—a dispute over voter ID cards and the Women's Reservation Bill—have again tested and rehashed the earlier arguments about women's access to the polls and their right to run for office. In a 2010 Supreme Court ruling, the bench specifically drew a connection between the two.

In the Voter ID case, a petitioner argued that it offended a woman's religious commitment for her to remove her burqa in order to be photographed for a Voter ID card. The court dismissed the claim, saying that identification of the voter at the polling booth was a necessity of the voting process. Interestingly though, the court evoked the analogy of running for office. The "right to contest an election is an extension of the right to vote," the judgment said. "Can anyone contest an election saying a photograph of her face not be taken? Can she be photographed in a burqa with a veil and yet contest an election?" Furthermore, the Court explained that voting was a statutory right, rather than a "Fundamental Right," guaranteed by the Constitution. And so, the ruling continued, women chose to vote or not, just as they chose how to practice their faith.

Like the issue of women's access to the polling booth, the case for reservations for women in elected office has also built on arguments that emerged in the early 20th century. In some states, reservations (e.g., in District Municipal Councils) never went away. But women's organizations, who opposed reservations before independence and

---

[28] R. *Pushpam and Others vs The State of Madras*, October 6, 1952, AIR 1953 Mad 392, (1953) IMLJ 88.

afterwards, began to change their positions as the practice of reserving seats by caste, class, and gender reemerged significantly in the 1990s. The implementation of the Panchayati Raj Act and the Municipal Councils Act of 1993 changed the precedents by reserving 33 percent seats for women (and set aside seats for other groups as well). The 108th Amendment (Women's Reservation) Bill that proposed to extend women's reservations to the Parliament and State Legislative Assemblies was, in some ways, an extension of this earlier practice. However, because the Women's Bill challenged the makeup of the Parliament in which it was being debated, it raised the stakes of the argument for representation. Looking at the case of the Women's Bill also shows the inconsistent and complex trajectory of the arguments for women's representation. While one can find, in the Bill, historical remnants of the 1930s and the 1950s, they do not manifest in a linear way.

THE WOMEN'S RESERVATION BILL

Seen through the lens of history, the proposed 108th Amendment to the Constitution, which would reserve for women one-third of the seats in the Parliament and state legislatures, embodies a return to earlier proposals to enable women to participate fully in democratic politics, even when existing structures limit that participation. One key difference is that this incarnation—the debate over the Women's Bill—takes place in a lively democratic environment, both in the Parliament and in public through in election campaigns. Nearly all political parties claim to support the Bill (especially at election time), even though it continues to fail or simply be set aside.

For instance, on March 18, 2016, Sulakshana Sawant, President of the Goa Mahila Morcha (the women's wing of the BJP), announced: "We demand that the bill be passed in the Parliament before Goa's Assembly election" (scheduled for 2017). She told reporters that "the party is committed to give more power to women by passing the bill." While that may be the case, the BJP had been in power for nearly two years when she made that statement and the Bill had not appeared. Indeed her party leader, Prime Minister Narendra Modi, had avoided mention of the Bill in his statement on International Women's Day (March 8), although other political leaders celebrated and demanded it.

For International Women's Day in 2016, the Rajya Sabha gave open time to women legislators to speak out and most called again for the passage of the Bill. These included ministers in the BJP government, prominently Najma Heptulla, Minister of Minority Affairs, as well as opposition members, such as Congress President Sonia Gandhi. The President and Vice President of India both also made statements in support of the Bill. Newspapers, however, pointed out that Prime Minister Narendra Modi—who would have been the key voice—did not join the list.

While the Women's Bill has a long history, what is most relevant here in this chapter is the political rhetoric surrounding it. When Purnima Banerjee argued against reservations for women in the CA in 1949, her claim was based on an assumption that women would have equal access to the electoral process. Strikingly, in fact, the women politicians who have been advocates for the 108th Amendment have her logic—even as they disagreed with her conclusion. Their claim is that equality of participation has not been achieved. As Najma Heptulla put it in 2016:

> Earlier, I was not in favour of reservations, but then I saw they [women] have no voice. There has to be a level playing field for women. Rajya Sabha (the upper house of the Parliament) has passed it and now it is the turn of Lok Sabha to pass it too.[29]

However, Heptulla's comments came as she released a report on widespread discrimination against girls and then announced programs to reserve 33 percent of government scholarships for girls. Linking this to the Women's Bill, she reinforced the idea that women in government

---

[29] *The Times of India*, "Clear Women's Bill for Girls Sake" (2014, November 30). Available at http://timesofindia.indiatimes.com/india/Clear-womens-bill-for-girls-sake-Union-minister-Najma-Heptulla-says/articleshow/45211588.cms (accessed on September 4, 2019).

play a particular role in the development of girls in society. Here, she echoed Muthulakshmi Reddy's claims for women's representation in 1927. In advocating a literacy franchise for women rather than giving the wives of taxpayers the right to vote, Muthulakshmi Reddy said she would rather have a few "high quality" women working for the good of all women than a larger less qualified electorate. Hannen Angelo reinforced this view saying she felt obliged to use her voice specifically as a "woman politician."

The mechanism of elections proposed in the Bill—seat rotation for women's constituencies—seemingly undermined future women politicians' attachment to a geographic constituency and instead seemed to favor the idea of women legislators as representing women citizens. Rotation of seats was controversial from the start and prompted sitting MPs (both male and female) to worry about their own constituencies. According to the Bill, the rotation would take place with each general election on a basis "determined by draw of lots," but assuring that each constituency is reserved only once in a "block of three elections."[30] Although this mechanism of determining women's constituencies was borrowed from the Panchayati system, given that panchayats covered smaller geographic areas and populations, it did not easily fit onto a national template. Furthermore, did a rotating system function like term limits? Would legislators have to change constituencies?

In other words, the rotation of seats undermined two accepted political principles in India first, that Members of Parliament should nurture their constituencies over time and be accountable to the same voters and second that political service to the nation was a long-term commitment and perhaps a career goal. The concern, then, was the instability that might result from MPs shifting constituencies or rotating in and out of the Parliament in an ongoing cycle.

But the case for some women in office being able to represent women's interests more general—and necessarily doing so—was an old one. Muthulakshmi Reddy put this forth in 1919, when she said that educated urban women could and should represent the larger

---

[30] 85th Amendment Bill, introduced in the Lok Sabha, December 1999 (the text did not change from the 81st Amendment Bill).

interests of women in general. "Take any of the reform measures such as child marriage, inheritance laws, property rights, marriage laws in which women are generally interested. These evils apply equally to both the town and village women."[31] Therefore, she demands some women (and in her case she was suggesting urban educated women) could represent women in general.

Several proposals parallel to the Women's Bill placed it in the context of larger electoral reforms, included stricter enforcement of penalties on legislators found guilty of criminal activity, an increase of control over the financing of elections, and greater democratization within political parties. This angle emphasized the barriers in the system that prevented would-be women politicians from running for office. In this context, many reformers both within the Election Commission of India and among activists suggested that political parties should be required to reserve one-third of the tickets for parliamentary or Legislative Assembly elections for women members.[32] Shifting the responsibilities from the Parliament to the Parties—a precedent used in other parts of the world—could eliminate the problem of rotation of seats. More importantly, by putting women's access to the political process at the center of law, policy, and practice, this line of reasoning followed from the arguments of women like Reddy and Angelo and later Heptulla and Sonia Gandhi—a diverse set of political voices—that

---

[31] Forbes, "Votes for Women," 20.

[32] Forum for Democratic Reforms comprises Jayaprakash Narayan (Lok Satta, Hyderabad), Dhirubhai Sheth (Lokayan, Delhi), Yogendra Yadav (CSDS, Delhi), and Madhu Kishwar (Manushi, New Delhi). "Enhancing Women's Representation in Legislature: An Alternative to the Government Bill for Women's Reservation," *Manushi*, no. 116 (2000, August–September). Available at http://indiatogether.org/manushi/issue116/alterbill.htm#sthash.5m4QPIyK.dpuf (accessed on September 4, 2019). In a Consulting Paper presented to the National Commission to Review the Working of the Constitution (January 8, 2001), the Advisory Panel on Electoral Reforms included Gill's proposal in their recommendations for reform of political parties. The Panel included Subhash Kashyap, R. K. Trivedi, P. A. Sangma, and Mohan Dharia, among others. The Consulting Paper was based on a similar paper prepared by the Institute of Constitutional and Parliamentary Studies. This continued discussion of the proposal for reservations within parties demonstrates the enduring appeal of the argument, at least in some circles.

removing barriers to women's participation was the most important mechanism to increased women's representation.

In fact, though the Women's Bill has continued to fail as legislation, small steps in reform have taken place. Both the Indian National Congress and the BJP, for example, amended their constitutions to reserve 33 percent of the seats within the party organization—on committees at the state and national levels—for women in 2007 and 2010. This did not result in one-third of the candidates in elections being women, but a few more women did gain tickets to run for office.

CONCLUSION

Over the century, since women in India gained the right to vote, the question of women's ability to exercise that right and to run for political office has been reinvented for different political moments. Advocates for greater participation among women in the electoral process have continued to balance the contradictions between equal access and the need for special provisions or reservations. The balance in the 21st century has shifted toward a demand for women's reservations. In fact, the demand for reservations more generally for Other Backward Classes and new categories within the Scheduled Caste communities suggests a shift in the political tactics.

Attention to women's participation as voters remain a subject of both policy and academic debate. Writers link voter participation to development, education, and women's independence. However, as the Women's Bill keeps the question of women's representation in governing bodies as part of electoral discourse, it is the latest vehicle to move beyond the question of "how do women vote?" to "how can women participate more fully in the political system as candidates, legislators, and political leaders?" Especially at election time—though also on other political occasions—the Women's Bill has become a conduit for rethinking women's political participation in the electoral arena. In doing so, it allows politicians to move back and forth between two different notions of women's representation—the voter's right to be represented and the right to run for political office (or to actively represent).

However, what the history provided here—of women's advocacy for greater access to the political process—demonstrates is that a common set of arguments are being reconstituted for a new historical moment. Contemporary politics borrows significantly from the earlier debates about women's franchise. Who would (or should?) women legislators represent? And how does the form and mechanism through which women's seats might be established influence the larger question of what is a woman politician's constituency? As most women politicians show, in their legislative agendas and political influence, their interests are diverse. How can that diversity balance with the mechanisms proposed to increase women's representation? This chapter ends with questions because the story has not finished. For example, the Women's Bill has not passed in the Lok Sabha; and it is not clear what effects it might ultimately produce. Yet the chapter does suggest that while Muthulakshmi Reddy and Hannen Angelo rejected reservations as the mechanism for women's participation, the historical process they set in motion has returned to a solution that would seem familiar to their own political aspirations: that being a part of the legislative arena is a necessary democratic right.

Chapter 10

Democracy as Emancipatory Politics

R. Azhagarasan

Self-government and democracy become real not when a Constitution based on adult suffrage comes into existence but when the governing class loses its power to capture the power to govern.

—Ambedkar (1990: 448)

Democracy as a form of government is threatened by democracy as a form of social and political life and so the former must repress the latter.... Democracy is neither a form of government nor a form of social life. Democracy is the institution of politics as such, of politics as a paradox.

—Rancière (2005: 50)

The increasing debate on the role of money and muscle power in electoral politics seems to create suspicion about the nature and functioning of democracy in India. This suspicion occupied centre stage among the Western intellectuals such as Jacques Derrida, Jacques Rancière, Tzvetan Todorov, Slavoj Žižek and others. The suspicion of democracy comes from different quarters. In Europe, it was raised during the first decades of the 20th century by the surrealists. The surrealist artist Alfred Kupin came out with a series of paintings titled, 'Birth and Death of Democracy'. It again surfaced during the late 1990s and during the early 2000s. Among those who initiated these debates, Todorov sees two different attitudes: one is internal and the other is external. While the internal critique chooses to adopt the perspective of democracy towards the practice of democracy, the external critique, especially Žižek's, attacks the very idea of democracy itself. Todorov says:

> …. democracy secretes within itself the very forces that threaten it, and the novelty of our time is that these forces are superior to those attacking it from outside. Combating and neutralizing them is all the more difficult because they claim to be imbued with the democratic spirit, and thus have every appearance of legitimacy. (Todorov 2014: 6)

This is very much true in the context of India as well. While the debates on nationalism in the wake of students' unrest in JNU becomes a political and an external critique of BJP's regressive measures, the Dalit critique (which refers to a perspective invoked in the Dalit literature, activities of the Dalit movements and the Dalit studies at large) remains a social and internal critique of the function of democracy. There is a basic paradox here. While the suspicion on of democracy is on the rise among intellectuals worldwide, marginal communities in different cultures fight for a space within the institution of democracy. Aboriginal action groups in Australia have conducted a huge campaign among aborigines to encourage Aboriginal Australians to vote in elections and to participate in parliamentary democracy. The Dalit activists in different parts of India strongly criticized Indian democracy for preserving caste practices during the 50th-year celebration of Indian Independence. A Dalit journal (August 1997) from Pondicherry carried Kupin's painting criticizing democracy in its special issue on the golden jubilee of Indian independence. Many were arrested under the National Security Act 1980. But in 2000, the Dalit movements participated in the 50th year of the Republic Day celebrations, claiming that the day marked the achievements of Dr Ambedkar, who chaired the Drafting Committee of the Constitution of India. They were partly inspired by the speeches of the then President of India K. R. Narayanan. This shows the complex nature of the Dalit critique (its sensitivity to the local social codes and hence its diversity) of democracy in the Indian context.

It is against this backdrop that this chapter attempts an elaborate account of the nature of the Dalit critique of democracy both during colonial and post-colonial India. It tries to demonstrate this idea by invoking the history of the activities of the Depressed Class in colonial Tamil Nadu in the first section and then offers a close reading of the speeches of President K. R. Narayanan in the second section. If the former adopts a seemingly pro-state (pro-colonial) attitude, lauds the state for its emancipatory measures and then criticizes the state for its dubious stand on the issues concerning the depressed class, the latter criticizes the state for its silence on the issues of the deprived from a constitutional position of the President of India. In both cases (the colonial and republican contexts), democracy remains a mode of fighting for the cause of the lowly and justice for the deprived. By juxtaposing these critiques found in two different contexts separated by a century, the paper tries to highlight the participatory nature of the Dalit critique of democracy. From this perspective, the chapter tries to argue, democracy functions as a mode of emancipatory politics. The third and last section hints at the implications of such a critique and offers the possibility of challenging the strict opposition between political democracy and social democracy, and thereby tries to extend the scope of reading Dr Ambedkar's vision of democracy.

SECTION I

The revival of the caste question, enunciated by the uprising of the Dalits in India in the post-Mandal and post-Ambedkar centenary celebrations of the 1990s, gave a renewed context not only for the Dalits but for all to rethink our understanding of democracy as well. Scholars who worked on the operations of rival colonial powers focus mostly on the difference between the British and the French colonial policies. They have pointed out the violent nature of the British administration and the policy of appropriation adopted by the French government. Such a view is shared even among nationalist leaders such as Aurobindo, the poet Bharathi and B. G. Tilak. The recorded history of the British

Indian and the French occupied territories—that include Pondicherry, Mahe, Karaikal, Yanam and Chandannagar (earlier Chandernagore)—may clearly show this difference.

But the rise of the caste question offers a totally different perspective on the colonial powers. Notwithstanding the differences in the handling of the caste question, the rival colonial powers seem to have understood the fact that *caste is part of the national question in India.* This is very clear in the East India Company's system of trade with the natives. The foreign traders were expected to have their dealings only through the *qaspa*, the entrepôt of the trading communities. The Marikayars (Tamil-speaking Muslims), Chettis and Pillais were the major trading communities in South India, whereas Marwari and Multanis in Rajasthan, Banias in Gujarat and Bengal were the major traders in North India. While the British disturbed this 'caste-based trade', the French never tried to interrupt the *qaspa* system (Alalasundaram 1998: 309). In fact, the Governor of French Pondicherry Joseph Dupleix, besides building houses for the Mudaliars, the weaving community, supplied tax-free yarn and cotton for two years when the community threatened to leave the territory (Alalasundaram 1998: 356). So the fact that the participants in the early uprising against the British India were mostly from traditional trading communities is not just a coincidence. This may help us understand that silence about French colonialism in India is not due to the 'policy of assimilation' but due to our failure to understand colonial powers' handling of the caste question.

Contrary to such a history of colonial powers, the underprivileged sections both in British India and in the French-occupied territories give us a totally different vision of colonialism. Those sections of Indian society usually looked at the colonial powers—both in British India and in French India—as a boon. Sources concerning their activities are readily available for those interested in re-examining their own assumptions of nationalism vis-à-vis colonialism. The archival sources regarding the activities of the untouchables in the two territories seem to alter our perceptions of colonialism and democracy. This chapter tries to reflect upon such sources concerning the Depressed Class in colonial Tamil Nadu in order to move beyond our conception of political democracy and get an understanding of social democracy as insisted on by Dr Ambedkar. It also tries to argue that *social democracy* remains only a *critical reading* of the principle of political democracy and does not stand in opposition to political democracy. The history of the Depressed Class in colonial Tamil Nadu and their continuous criticism of the activities of the National Congress provide us such a nuanced understanding of colonialism and democracy.

It is in this context that we must look at the various Depressed Class conferences and Adi Dravida conferences conducted between 1891 and 1926. The conduct of the conferences in the late 19th and the early 20th centuries was a significant shift from the culture of giving petitions to the colonial government—a practice that had existed earlier. This is very clear in the references made in the conference resolutions to the petitions and may help us identify the *culture of petitioneering*. A close reading will show that the petitions do not remain pleas to the government as they hinted at the power of the colonial authority and its responsibility over its subjects. The petition submitted in December 1779 states:

> ... to whom can your petitioners repose and implore for success but to God and to your Honor &c., as absolute and patron of the place, convinced and not doubting in the least that your Honor &c., are far superior in humane dispositions for aiding, relieving the poor and oppressed.... (Government of India 1779)

By way of attributing 'Godly' power to the colonial authority, the petitioners seem to suggest that authority—whether Godly or of Governmental—means 'responsibility'. The same tone could be found in the petition submitted in 1810:

> At the government of Major-General Meadows, Major Mall the Chief Engineer at that time have continued to take your petitioners addressed to Marquis Cornwallis and Major General Meadows their grievances after perusing your petitioners case, those *noble gentlemen* have passed a minute on the government records expressing that during the flag of the Hon'ble Company your petitioners shall not be troubled hereafter—your petitioners can live in quietness without paying any tax. (Kamalanathan 1985: 4)

The colonial responses to these petitions, conference resolutions and their memoranda show the organized movement of the Depressed Class during the 19th century. Besides raising voice for their safeguards, the untouchables played a significant role in making a section of colonial officers to raise ethical issues regarding colonialism. In his 'Note on Pariahs of Chingleput' (1892), the district collector J. H. A. Tremenheere says:

> It is sometimes asked why the State should do anything for the lower castes; why they, should not be left alone to find their own level. The answer is that the policy of the State in the past has do grade them, and the State must retrieve its mistakes. We have permitted ancient privileges to survive until they have become anachronisms, and we have created now privileges. These at least can be confined to their minimum range of harm; and the classes who have been kept back in the race of life can be given a new start. (Tremenheere 1892: 45)

The reference to 'ancient privileges' shows that he is not just criticizing the colonial government but hints at the alliance between colonialism and Brahmanism. This is clear when he says: 'The concessions asked for the Pariahs alone (e.g., in the proposed Settlements) are not very great when it is remembered that until so late as the Settlement of 1875, special advantages in the tenure of land were being conceded to the Brahmans' (Tremenheere 1892: 45).

It is within this century-old organized struggle that we must place the activities of the untouchables in the 20th century and their 'seemingly pro-colonial' standpoints. The Farewell address presented to the Viceroy Lord Willingdon in 1924 notes:

> ....that the British government should on no account sacrifice the interests of the Depressed and Minority Communities, out of deference to the wishes and sentiments of a majority community; that the British character of administration through the agency of the British people must be maintained at any cost. (Quoted in Rajah 1925: 79)

These details, placed in their culture proper, will demand that any discussion of democracy in the Indian context must go beyond a critique of a government (colonial or native government) and take into account the operations of power vis-à-vis caste.

Sources concerning the activities of the Depressed Class suggest that during the turn of the 19th century and in the beginning of the 20th century, the tension between the nationalists and the Depressed Class was so strong that they challenged each other's activities. Knowledge of this tension may help us situate the petitions of the untouchables and Tremenheere's report in a renewed context. Pointing out the colonial government's acceptance of the system of Mirasidars, which does not allow pariahs to own land, and the caste Hindus' prejudice against them, which led to the oppression of untouchables, he suggested major reforms in the fields of land and education. It is apt here to quote at length the reasons that he gave for establishing special schools:

1) That the Mirasidars and other masters of the Pariahs get their face against this education.
2) That the parents of the caste pupils object to their children frequenting schools where Pariahs are admitted.
3) That the schoolmasters share this prejudice, making the Pariah children sit outside school, and teaching them from a distance.
4) That the children have to tend cattle or otherwise work during the day.
5) That they are often too poor to pay fees or buy books.
6) That there are no trained Pariah masters (for no Result Grants are given unless masters have passed the Primary Examination): Even untrained masters can hardly be obtained.
7) That even if masters could be obtained, they could not keep themselves on the Result Grants, though these are 50 per cent higher for Pariahs.

The remedies I propose are:
   a) To increase the number of special Pariah day and night schools so that every large Paracheri have one;
   b) To attract Pariahs by scholarships into the Normal schools;
   c) To abandon the Result Grant System and pay salaries in these special schools;

d) That Provincial administration, which alone can stand the financial strain, and which can maintain a sympathetic policy in favour of the low-castes much more consistently than the Local Boards, should assume the control of the special Pariah schools. The measures which I recommend in connection with the land question would ensure an ample supply of funds. (Tremenheere 1892: 32)

Contrary to this report that shows concern for the untouchables, missionaries like Annie Besant shared the views of caste Hindus and insisted that untouchables should not be mixed with 'high caste' children in schools:

The children of the depressed classes need, first of all, to be taught cleanliness, outside decency of behaviour, and the earliest rudiments of education, religion and morality. Their bodies, at present, are ill-odorous and foul, with the liquor and strong-smelling foods out of which for generations they have been built up; it will need some generations of purer food and living to make their bodies fit to sit in the close neighbourhood of a school-room with children who have received bodies from an ancestry trained in habits of exquisite personal cleanliness, and fed on pure food-stuffs. (Besant [1909]1913: 46–47)

It is ironic that while the colonial official could ignore the prejudices of caste, the missionary, who is expected to have concerns for the natives, shares the caste prejudice. Annie Besant was one of those missionaries who were manipulated by the nationalists and the Brahmins. The 19th-century Buddhist Pundit Iyothee Thass said that the so-called Brahmins manipulated a section of missionaries, 'gave them certain palm-leaf manuscripts, encouraged them to translate the materials into English and constructed a "hindu philosophy"' (Thass 1999: 70).

In addition, the Brahmins and the caste Hindus also campaigned against those colonial administrators who (like Tremenheere) tried to ameliorate the condition of the Depressed Classes. This is very clear in the report published in the nationalist paper *Swadesamitran* on

17 July 1897[1] against the appointment of Tremenheere as the district collector in Madras Presidency and urged the government to send him to northern states. Challenging this report, *Parayan* on 24 July 1897[2] cited the welfare measures taken up by Tremenheere and made the colonial government appoint him as the collector of Chengleput.

Since there are differences even among the colonial officials and among the missionaries, the binary native vs colonial (constructed in the nationalist debate and in the post-colonial discourse) seems too limiting for an understanding of colonialism and democracy in the Indian context. This becomes apparent in the demand for simultaneous examinations for civil services in India and London, campaigned under the headship of Dadabhai Naoroji and in the reports on the famous Dandi March led by Gandhi. When Gandhi conducted the famous Dandi March demanding abolition of salt tax, the untouchables headed by Rettaimalai Srinivasan (who was the close associate of Dr Ambedkar and accompanied him in the Round Table conference) demanded for the imposition of salt tax. They suggested that the tax may be used for the welfare measures for the untouchables.

The fourth resolution passed at the First Congress Maha Jana Sabha (1885) demanded that the civil service examination may be conducted both in London and in India to enable Indian natives to appear for the examination and join administrative services under colonial rule (Bharathi 1985: 11). Continuous campaign for this demand was taken up by Dadabhai Naoroji. In the magazine *Parayan*, Rettaimalai Srinivasan launched a counter campaign demanding that the examination should not be conducted in India. Exposed to these activities of the Depressed Class, a wide range of scholars including missionaries, magistrates, even some of the nationalists, and non-Brahmin ideologues, continuously wrote in the *Indian Review* between 1900 and 1909, suggesting that the caste question is a national question in India.

This renewed understanding of caste within the colonial context may help us view the colonial government as just 'another authority'

---

[1] From native newspaper reports submitted to British, Tamil Nadu state archives, Chennai.

[2] Ibid.

that assumes 'responsibility' over its subjects. It was this 'responsibility' that was suggested in the petitions of the untouchables during the 18th and 19th centuries. This authority/responsibility nexus sometimes became a source of power in the colonial/missionary gestures of compassion and emancipation. The post-colonial discourse (following the nationalists) chose to focus only the authoritarian power assumed within colonialism and ignored this aspect of 'responsibility'. It was with this understanding that Dr Ambedkar criticized the nationalist claims of *swaraj* and questioned the activities of the Indian National congress:

> Philosophically it may be possible to consider a nation as a unit but sociologically it cannot be regarded as consisting of many classes and...it is foolish to take solace in the fact that because the Congress is fighting for the freedom of India, it is, therefore, fighting for the freedom of the people of India and of the lowest of the low. (Ambedkar 1990: 202)

This argument of Ambedkar and the activities of the Depressed Class may force anyone to regard the untouchables as having a pro-colonial attitude. That was how it was described by the nationalists during their struggle for political freedom of India in the early decades of the 20th century. Such a pro-colonial nature of the archival sources poses serious problems for those of us who want to talk of colonialism as well as issues concerning the Dalits. Dr Ambedkar takes into account these intricacies involved in the perception of colonial government and refutes the nationalists' charge in his chapter, 'Are Untouchables Tools of the British?' He criticized Congress' view that 'freedom of India from British Imperialism to be the be-all and end-all of Indian nationalism', and clarified the matter thus:

> The British government admits India's right to freedom, even to independence, if Indians so desire.... There can be no greater proof of this new angle of vision than the Cripps proposals. The condition precedent laid down by the British Government for India's freedom is that Indians must produce a Constitution which has the concurrence of the important elements in the national life of the country. Such is the stage we have reached. The Untouchables cannot therefore understand why the Congress, instead of trying to achieve agreement among

Indians, should keep on talking in terms of a 'Fight for Freedom' and maligning the Untouchables in not joining in it. (Ambedkar 1990: 177)

So the real issue, according to Dr Ambedkar, is not colonialism but 'what one regards as proximate and what as ultimate. Others regard the question of constitutional safeguards as ultimate. I regard as proximate' (181). Refusing to believe that the constitutional safeguards as ultimate, Dr Ambedkar seems to hint at the limited scope of the political democracy envisaged by the Congress.

SECTION II

In order to maintain constitutional decorum, the presidential addresses of the former President K. R. Narayanan, the first Dalit president of India, tried to create a space for dialogue between the mainstream and the marginalized, the grand and little traditions of Indian history. Failing to notice this complexity, his addresses to the nation were read either as a desperate cry of a veteran Congressman or as a direct critique of the state by a radical Dalit intellectual. Both views fail to see how he went beyond such crude and rigid ideological positions and how he released the 'word' from its boundaries from the position of a statesman and a President of a nation within the constitutional powers assigned to him.[3]

What we desperately miss in such ideological readings is the situatedness of the speaking subject. While we are inclined to read him ideologically for his being the first Dalit President at the time when the country witnesses the rise of the Dalit movement following the centenary celebrations of Dr Ambedkar, we fail to see the singular position that he occupies in the history of independent India. As a President, he was in a situation where:

1. He was bound by the constitution and his speech must not be regarded anti-national and anti-constitutional.

---

[3] The comments on K. R. Narayanan appeared in the journal *The Dalit* (March–April 2003).

2. He needed to be careful in not carrying the voice of a Congressman at the time when the country was being ruled by a Right-wing government.

3. He had to resist being reduced to being a spokesperson for the Dalit cause by the mere fact of being a Dalit.

4. While voicing concern for the underprivileged, he could not devalue the mainstream of which he himself was part, holding the highest position in the state.

5. He must be aware of the context of his address and its possible reception by the media and the state machinery. In addition, he had also to be aware of his reception in the neighbouring countries and the world at large, where India occupies a status in the South Asian region and represents a position in international affairs.

6. At the individual level, he had to also recognize the achievements of various social and cultural movements. He was therefore forced to take recourse to the strategy of a 'quoted speech' with a view to create a dialogue among the divergent forces of culture.

Hence, he had to carefully choose quotes from nationalists and traditionalists such as Gandhi, Vivekananda, Nehru, Rajendra Prasad, Raja Ram Mohan Roy and even the then Prime Minister of the Right-wing government, Atal Bihari Vajpayee, and resituate their words in a different context so that the caste Hindus and the 'weaker majority', as he would like to put it, could engage in a fruitful dialogue. In other words, he had to place the 'word' with a side word glance offering a new meaning and diverse possibilities. It is an awareness of the situation and one's own position in that situation where the speaker cannot speak, but can only quote other's words and speak through the established voices of authority. Here, the word is placed in a context where it could create a dialogue between opposing forces within the realms of the dominant political culture.

While making the masses realize their power, their capacity to subvert the state power, he as the head of the state had to instruct the government of this possibility of subversion and uphold the spirit of democracy. He thereby tried to create a dialogue not just between the dominant culture and the unrecognized cultures but also between the state and civil society, which otherwise would continue to remain binaries of the colonial form of democracy. As the Constitution provides only limited powers to the President, he could not directly refer to the communal violence sparked by the Right-wing government. Therefore, he coached it thus: 'especially today when the poison of communalism has caused so much violence and hatred in some parts of our country'. Again, indirectly referring to the then BJP government's attempt to review the Constitution, he reacted through the words of India's first President of independent India.

> Today, when there is so much talk about revising the constitution or even writing a new constitution, we have to consider whether it is the constitution that has failed us or whether it is we who failed the constitution. Dr Rajendra Prasad, as President of the Constituent Assembly, had pointed out, 'If the people who are elected are capable men of character and integrity, they should be able to make the best of a defective constitution'. I believe these words are wise words which we should pay heed to. (Narayanan 2011: 160)

The quotes and Narayanan's comments on the quotes gave a different twist to the whole exercise of power. It offered a vantage point from which the listener was expected to read the quotation. As he could not overtly disagree with Gandhi's parallel between parliamentary system and the traditional system of village panchayats, Narayanan referred to how Dr Ambedkar saw this parliamentary system as originating from the Buddhist sanghs and allows us to think of ancient India as Buddhist. Unable to talk directly about the role played by Dr Ambedkar as it would be reduced in the context of the Dalit uprising, especially during the late 1990s, he avoided mentioning Ambedkar's name and referred to him as one of the 'founding fathers'.

While talking about the policy of reservations, Narayanan seemed quite conscious of the negative connotations of the word 'reservation' in the Indian context. Hence, he used terms closely related to it such as 'social policies' and the 'provisions we have already given' or the popular American expression 'affirmative action' and so on. In order to be heard by all sections of society and to keep his distance from anti-Brahmin rhetoric, he carefully avoided the word 'Brahminism' but referred to it as 'self regarding purity ignoring others have been the bane of our culture' (Narayanan 2011: 147).

By way of regarding 'water', 'education' and other basic amenities not only as needs but as 'fundamental rights' of the people, he tried to empower the disempowered masses, who otherwise remain voiceless within the discourses of democracy. When he says, 'the economic reforms through liberalization and globalization should not ignore this weaker majority', his use of the phrase 'weaker majority' refers to the power and not the powerlessness of the masses. At the same time, he felt the necessity to warn the state of the consequences of the uprising of this 'weaker majority'. So he said, using the old adage, 'beware of the fury of the patient and long suffering people' (Narayanan 2011: 146).

Again, when he talked of the youth, he accommodated the spiritual dimension of Indian vision of democracy, by referring to Swami Vivekananda's call for reviving the potential of our youth: 'If only we could release and set in motion the bottled up potential and energy of our youth we can change India, if not change the world' (Narayanan 2011). He also felt the need to empower the suffering masses without simply expressing sympathy for their condition. Cautious of the reception of his words in the media, Narayanan says, 'Violence in society has bared a hundred fangs as advertisements–driven consumerism is unleashing frustrations and tensions in our society' (Narayanan 2011: 146).

He is conscious that his direct words would only feed the demands of the dominant attitude and the already commodified consumer culture of the media. The situation in which Narayanan was placed as Head of the state and was condemned to defend the spirit of Indian democracy at the time of the rule of the Right-wing government was similar to Dr Ambedkar's position in the Constituent Assembly when he defended the Hindu Code Bill. Regarding India 'as a country of one billion people (the most vibrant democracy of the world) that has achieved self-sufficiency in food for the first time in modern history', Narayanan said, 'In our state, supreme power is exercised not by some remote monarch but by the people' (Ambedkar 2011: 145).

The powerless masses are at the same time seen as powerful agents of democracy having the capacity to overcome the social divisions. Recalling his personal experience of his acquaintance with people, he said in his Farewell speech:

> At Ottapallam I experienced the essential goodness of people, their capacity to forget all communal, religious and social divisions of our society, when an occasion was presented to them. It is up to our social and political leaders to present the people with such occasions, especially today when the poison of communalism has caused so much violence and hatred in some parts of our country. (Narayanan 2002)

Combining the moral and pragmatic aspects of this tolerance (that Gandhi and Vivekananda praised so much), he says:

> Prime Minister Jawaharlal Nehru wrote to the Chief Ministers of India during the dark days of 1947 and I wish to quote excerpts from that letter: 'We have a Muslim minority who are so large in numbers that they cannot, even if they want to, go anywhere else. They have got to live in India. That is a basic fact about which there can be no argument'. His words are true and relevant even today and we can ignore these words of wisdom at our risk. (Narayanan 2002)

Such comments appended to the quotation make the quote a double-voiced speech, which leaves space for the other, the opponents to participate in the discourse. It is this participatory nature of our democracy that gets a verbal expression in K. R. Narayanan. Because the words expressed by K. R. Narayanan our own, expressing our anguish. Despite being the head of the state, he functions merely as an agent within the constitutional powers of the president and chooses to give form to our anxieties over the dangers of democracy.

These views of Narayanan were read as a direct attack on the then BJP government during the early 2000s. While traces of criticism on the government could be identified in his speeches, we cannot reduce it to an oppositional act. Such a view may benefit the radical politics. But it will not help us understand the emancipatory politics of his critique from the perspective of the constitutional authority of a head of the state. It will also ignore his continuous engagement with such a kind of critique. He echoed a similar view even earlier. Speaking at

the Commonwealth Club of California on 23 March 1983, Narayanan
had said:

> Pessimism about India continues to persist. Some of the problems are
> still with us, but in minor and manageable forms. What is remarkable
> is that India, with all its differences, has consolidated itself as a stable
> and united political entity, and is today a rapidly changing, developing
> economy. It has weathered successfully many a fissiparous threat to
> its unity, and demonstrated its age-old genius of accommodating and
> reconciling differences, and living together in peace and co-existence,
> notwithstanding occupational eruptions of social, economic or political
> trouble in one part or another of this vast country...India has man-
> aged some very critical transitions in political power, through peaceful
> democratic means making democracy in India no longer an experiment,
> but an established fact. (Narayanan [1984]1998: 15)

This poignant statement of Narayanan clarifies two significant points:
(a) his indirect and participatory critique of the government expressed
in his presidential addresses cannot be reduced to a direct attack on the
BJP government, (b) his views cannot be construed as part of the Dalit
ideological critique invoked at the national and local level. In fact, it
radically alters any oppositional critique and invokes an emancipatory
and participatory politics. It is this kind of participatory and responsible critique that we could find in the history of the Depressed Class
in colonial Tamil Nadu. The paradoxical position of President K. R.
Narayanan shares something in common with the ironical relationship maintained by the Depressed Class with the colonial government
(which was reduced to a pro-colonial standpoint by the nationalists).
The commonality goes much deeper and it helps us transcend the
opposition between the idea of social democracy and political democracy suggested by Dr Ambedkar.

SECTION III

Here, one faces another question: How did Dr Ambedkar manage
to arrive at this vision of social democracy? While arguing that
Dr Ambedkar's social identity (as a member of untouchable community

and the difficulties he faced in his personal life) leads to this alternative vision of democracy, we should also remember that there were untouchable leaders even within the Congress who never questioned Gandhi and his praise of the Varna system. This may prove that our focus on the personal/social identity of Dr Ambedkar would fail to recognize his philosophical–political vision.

Let us not forget that Dr Ambedkar was exposed to a wide range of European intellectuals, political philosophers like John Stuart Mill and classical thinkers like Theocritus. He was also very clear about the importance of reading these intellectuals without subscribing to the colonial vision and to an anti-colonial sentiment. Meera Nanda has pointed out the influence of John Dewey on Dr Ambedkar and suggested the possibility of tracing the impact of various Victorian intellectuals on him (Nanda 2004: 181–203). Only then we will be able to understand that Dr Ambedkar's vision of social democracy remains part of the political democracy that he was vehemently criticizing. While those who follow the vision of political democracy could easily criticize J. S. Mill's Orientalist views on Eastern culture and regard him as racist, Dr Ambedkar helps us reread Mill's views on Representative Government, according to which both the governing class and the governed are responsible for establishing democracy.

Challenging the strict binary of autocratic and democratic forms of government, Mill said that order and progress are two fundamental principles of any form of government. Besides pointing at their interdependency, he said that the government alone could not be held responsible for maintaining these principles (of order and progress) and made civil society accountable:

> The first element of good government, therefore, being the virtue and intelligence of the human beings composing the community, the most important point of excellence which any form of government can possess is to promote the virtue and intelligence of the people themselves. The first question in respect to any political institutions is how far they tend to foster in the members of the community the various desirable qualities, moral and intellectual, or rather (following 's more complete classification) moral, intellectual, and active. The government which

does this best has every likelihood of being the best in all other respects, since it is on these qualities, so far as they exist in the people, that all possibility of goodness in the practical operations of the government depends. (Mill [1861]1977: 9)

Dr Ambedkar is interested not just in Mill's views on government but in the social vision inherent in his discussion of representative government and of political democracy. While Mill's views of representative government may seem to justify the values of a colonial, despotic government, Dr Ambedkar's reading of Mill extends the idea of democracy through an internal critique. In his last speech at the Constituent Assembly on 25 November 1949, Ambedkar expressed it as warnings against the narrow understanding of democracy and nationalist politics. He said:

> If we wish to maintain democracy not merely in form, but also in fact, what must we do? In my judgement we must do is to. It means we must abandon the bloody methods of revolution....we must do is to observe the caution which John Stuart Mill has given to all who are interested in the maintenance of democracy, namely,...Bhakti in religion may be a road to the salvation of the soul. But we must do is not to be content with mere political democracy. We must make our political democracy a social democracy as well. Political democracy cannot last unless there lies at the base of it social democracy. (Ambedkar 2011: 217)

This may help us understand that Dr Ambedkar's vision of social democracy does not stand in opposition to political democracy but suggests the need to rethink the political concepts like 'Nationalism' and 'Democracy' through a critical reading of existing forms of political democracy. Such a reading of the archival material concerning the Dalits, moving beyond the confines of the Dalit history, may help us broaden our understanding of colonialism and democracy. It may also demand us to recognize such moments in our colonial and national history that sought to break the opposition between the social and the political for achieving an emancipatory politics. It will also demand that we challenge the comfortable binaries within which we invoke discourses of nationalism in the present context.

REFERENCES

Alalasundaram, R. 1998. *The Colonial World of Ananda Ranga Pillai 1736–1761: A Classified*. Pondicherry: The author. *Compendium of His Diary*. Pondicherry.

Ambedkar, B. R. 1990. *What Gandhi and Congress Have Done to the Untouchables. B. R. Ambedkar: Writings and Speeches*, Vol. 9. Mumbai: Education Department, Govt. of Maharashtra.

———. 2011. *Thus Spoke Ambedkar: A Stake in the Nation*, Vol. 1. Edited by Bhagwan Das. New Delhi: Navayana.

Besant, Annie. (1909, February) 1913. 'On Untouchables'. *The Indian Review*. Reprinted in *The Depressed Class*, Government Archives. Chennai Egmore.

Bharathi, Subramania. 1985. *Bhartha Jana Sabha (Congress Jana Sabha's Caritiram)*, 2nd edition. Sivaganga: Bharathi Mandalam.

Government of India. 1779, 31 December. *Public Consultation*, Vol. 122. Government Archives, Chennai Egmore.

Kamalanathan, T. P., comp. 1985. *Scheduled Caste's Struggle for Emancipation in South India*. Tirupattur: The South India Sakkiya Buddhist Association.

Mill, J. S. [1861]1977. *Principles of Representative Government*. Toronto: The University of Toronto Press.

Nanda, Meera. 2004. *Prophets Facing Backward: Postmodernism, Science, and Nationalism*. Delhi: Permanent Black.

Narayanan, K. R. [1984]1998. *India and America: Essays in Understanding*, 2nd ed. New Delhi: Asia Books.

———. 2002, 22 July. 'The Freedom to Err and Correct is the Essence of Democracy'. Farewell Address delivered in the Central Hall of the Lok Sabha. Available at http://m.rediff.com/%0D%0Anews/2002/jul/25guest.htm (accessed on 19 February 2019).

———. 2011. *In the Name of the People: Reflections on Democracy, Freedom and Development*. New Delhi: Viking.

Rajah, M. C. 1925. *The Oppressed Hindus*. Madras: Huxley Press.

Rancière, Jacques. 2005. *Dissensus: On Politics and Aesthetics*. Translated by Steven Corcoran. London: Bloomsbury.

Thass, Iyothee. 1999. 'Vesha Brahmana Vivaram'. (Details on Fake Brahmin). *Iyothee Thasar Cinthanaikal*. Palayankottai: Folklore Research Centre.

Todorov, Tzvetan. 2014. *The Inner Enemies of Democracy*, Translated by Andrew Brown. Cambridge: Polity Press.

Tremenheere, J. H. A. 1892. 'Note on Pariahs of Chingleput', submitted to the British.

Chapter 11

Gender Equity in Education among Muslims in India

Josephine Anthony and Sudarsan Padmanabhan

INTRODUCTION

In the new millennium, there is a clearly discernible emphasis on inclusive development in India's educational sector. The Sarva Shiksha Abhiyan (SSA), launched in 2001, is the first-ever major policy measure to ensure free and compulsory elementary education in India. The Right to Education Act (RTE Act), 2009, is a momentous effort in India that mandates legal obligation on the central and state governments to provide elementary education to all children between 6 and 14 years. The implementation of Rashtriya Madhyamik Shiksha Abhiyan (RMSA) in 2009 and Rashtriya Uchchatar Shiksha Abhiyan (RUSA) in 2013 are important policies which make access to secondary and tertiary education a right, especially to the marginalised groups, who have been traditionally left out of the education system. In the recent past, accessibility to primary schools has substantially improved. A historic record of about 95 per cent of children in rural India are attending primary schools (ASER Centre 2011). However, poor quality of education and large number of dropouts continue to pose a great challenge at the elementary as well as secondary level. These problems are exacerbated by increased enrolment due to the policy of universalisation of education. It should be noted that out-of-school children are predominantly from the marginalised groups such as Dalit, tribal, rural, urban slum and Muslim minority communities, migrants, child labourers, street children, children with disabilities, children in conflict zones, nomadic groups and girl children. The SSA identifies these children as 'Special Focus Groups' and implements specific programmes for them. However, retention of these children in schools is a major challenge. This chapter examines multidimensional factors affecting Muslim girl children in India, which create obstacles to uninterrupted access to school education.

Achieving universal enrolment, retention and quality education, concurrently, implies equity in education. Ensuring equal opportunities without discrimination and creating a level playing field entails inclusion, equity and social justice. Equity is ensuring fairness in access and quality. It indicates distributive justice, implying unequal distribution of resources and opportunities to a vast section of people, hitherto. Thus, inequity and inequality may not differ, when the outcomes are assessed. Unlike inequity, inequality is measurable and hence, differences in equal distribution can be considered as inequity (UNDP 2014). Thus, this chapter discusses inequity among Muslim women in education in terms of gender disparity in enrolment rate and other statistics that highlight the backwardness of Muslim community, particularly Muslim women in education.

Gender inequity in education is a major concern, which requires deeper analysis of causes inhibiting their opportunities to have access to quality education. The World Economic Forum (2010) highlights the fact that 70 per cent of 130 million out-of-school adolescents in the world are girls. The education of girls has often been neglected, while their right to education is denied due to gender discrimination prevailing in the social structure, practices, norms, culture, institutions and systems. In India, gender disparity in primary education is vastly narrowed down by creating universal access to primary schools and conducting vigorous enrolment drives. Data show impressive increase in enrolments after the implementation of RTE Act, with significant percentage being Muslim and SC/ST children. This indicates that the largest chunk of out-of-school children are from these communities. However, vulnerable groups, like Muslim minority girl children, continue to experience educational deprivation despite the efforts of the government.

The Government of India has been implementing various schemes aimed at the Muslim community, which is considered to be one of the most vulnerable groups in India. There is a heightened understanding of backwardness of the Muslim community in comparison to other socio-religious groups in India, as per the report of Prime Minister's High Level Committee, Cabinet Secretariat, Government of India (2006), which brought out the backwardness of Muslim community in comparison to other socio-religious groups in India. This chapter locates 'group-based analysis' of inequalities within Frances Stewart's Horizontal Inequalities (HIs) framework. This helps us to further our analysis of gender inequity in education among Muslims in India. This chapter argues that achieving the goal of gender equity in education for Muslim girl children requires multidimensional intervention in social, economic and political domains in dialogue with the Muslim community broadly, along with specific need-based programmes for Muslim girl children in schools. The first section of the chapter describes Frances Stewart's approach on HI, while the second section deals with the historical context of Muslim women's education in India, followed by an analysis of the current status of the education among Muslim women. In conclusion, this chapter discusses policy implications of HIs for addressing gender inequities among the Muslims as a socio-religious group.

HORIZONTAL INEQUALITY AND GENDER INEQUITY IN EDUCATION

This section discusses Frances Stewart's (2001) approach on HI as an analytical framework to expound gender inequities in education among Muslims in India. HI is the existence of inequalities between groups, while 'Vertical Inequality' implies inequalities between individuals. HIs are multidimensional. Social, economic, environmental and political elements affect an individual's well-being and social stability seriously, in a way that is different from that of vertical inequality. Stewart (2001) describes how HIs affect the individual well-being differently as follows:

> [T]he unequal access to political, economic or social resources by different cultural groups can reduce individual welfare of the members in the losing groups over and above what their individual position would merit, because their self-esteem is bound up with the progress of the group.

Along with this psychological determinant, Stewart also describes two more aspects of HI that affect individuals' well-being. First, individuals' inability to overcome problems independently due to the influence or limitations of group practices on them, for example, gender discrimination; and second, the need to address group inequalities to protect social stability, as providing 'direct welfare' to individuals, may trigger conflicts within groups (Stewart 2001). Since some of the factors mentioned above affect individuals in a group and do not address the problems that affect the group as a whole, Stewart's emphasis on understanding HI assumes significance if public policy interventions have to be effective in reaching out to them as collectives.

Another salient feature of HI is 'persistence'. The characteristics of persistence and multidimensionality of HIs are coeval, one deepening the other. The multidimensionality of HIs through a range of elements of economic, social, political and cultural boundaries that interact within them determines persistent deprivation. To illustrate, social inequality, which deprives access to education, affects income, creating economic inequality, which in turn blocks access to social agency and political empowerment. Persistent deprivation is multidimensional and complex, and individuals feel trapped being part of a social group. Stewart explains the complex dynamics and interaction between financial capital, human capital and social capital in persisting deprivation or inequalities (Stewart 2008, 56–62). The dynamic complexities in HIs are utilised to delineate gender inequities that affect access to education among Muslims in India. Stewart differentiates groups as 'fragmented' and 'polarised' according to the nature of groups and their size (Stewart 2001, 12). Fragmented groups are of numerous types, but generally small, as in the case of caste-based groups in India, while large size divisions of men–women, Hindus–Muslims or urban–rural connote polarised typification. This chapter considers socio-religious communities, groups which show inequalities, namely Hindus, Muslims, other religious sects and SC/ST categories in India, as a polarised group. These classifications could themselves be problematic as fragmentation and polarisation could criss-cross various groupings and could be dynamic and asymmetrical.

Gender Inequity in Education

In the new millennium, gender inequality in education has gained global attention. The Millennium Development Goals (MDGs) 2 and 3 focus on universal primary education and gender equality, respectively. The MDGs combine the goals of gender equality to influence the rapid realisation of other goals and adopt a strategic approach to reduce gender disparity in school education. The Sustainable Development Goals (SDGs) 4 and 5 on quality education and gender equality, respectively, follow similar strategy to reduce gender inequity in education which would enhance achievement of other goals. With the increasing enrolment of girls in schools, the gender gap in primary schooling narrowed down from 57 per cent in 1999 to 53 per cent in 2008 globally (United Nations 2010). In India, the share of girls in the total enrolment has increased substantially with more than 95 per cent of girls and boys attending schools in rural India (ASER Centre 2011). However, reducing gender disparity does not achieve gender equity or inclusive education. Inclusive education that aims at equalisation of opportunities without discrimination is a process of empowerment for female children who experience systematic deprivation and multi-layered discrimination in society. The social attitude towards girl children as an economic liability, cultural bias, discriminatory norms, restrictive practices and socialisation process that ordain girl children as the protector of customs and rituals often target the self-esteem of girl children. Gender discrimination and poverty systematically deny women's participation in every sphere, from family to society, even affecting their capacity to make decisions for their own self. Such kind of incapacitation suffered by women could only be redressed by gender-equitable, gender-responsive and gender-sensitive education. Gender equity in education implies providing 'Quality of education experience and its ability to maximise the potential of every child, build self-esteem and develop capacities to function fully as citizens' (Sayed et al. 2007, 4). Women in Muslim community experience multi-layered inequities. Such inequities are further widened by cultural and religious practices that are gender-biased, which, in turn, hamper social agency and obstruct the process of empowerment.

Relevance of Horizontal Inequality to Analyse Gender Equity in Education

Frances Stewart's approach on HIs contrasts vertical inequality, which is individual-centric. The HI approach provides a framework that does not consider a group as a mere collection of individuals, but rather an organic unit, with its own characteristics. Individuals undergo a transformation when they come together as a group, in which they are influenced or affected differently. The characteristics of individuals affiliated to a group could echo the group's nature rather than their own and individuals tend to imbibe the characteristics of the group osmotically. The HI-based perspective provides a broader understanding of individuals as a collective in a group and the nature of inequalities within groups. Thus, HI provides a sound framework to bring out the nuances of gender discrimination and inequities that plague women's development as a group. The HI approach would be able to address the issue of marginalisation of Muslim women as a group and effectively engage with the multi-layered and multidimensional inequalities and inequities they face. The following section provides a historical context for Muslim women's education in India, commensurate with changes in social status or lack thereof.

HISTORICAL CONTEXT OF MUSLIM WOMEN'S EDUCATION IN INDIA

Muslims are the largest minority group in India, with the population of about 150 million according to 2011 Census. It is the second biggest

Muslim population in the world next only to Indonesia. This section deals with the historical understanding of the Muslim society in India, which is essential to locate the position of women within the Muslim community and in the broader Indian society. Medieval Indian history sources indicate that Muslims had a prominent political role for about eight centuries; the number of converts to Islam increased steadily and, at the same time, social distinctions due to caste, class divisions created inequalities, affecting the lower class Muslims, particularly women.

The contributions of the Muslim community to politics, economy, administration, culture, religion, science, art, architecture, commerce and language, during the medieval period, influenced modern India significantly (Sen 2005, 59). The Arab Muslims were the first to enter India in the 8th century, followed by the Turkish-Afghan invaders who founded the first Muslim dynasty in 1206, known as the Sultanate of Delhi. Five dynasties with 35 sultans ruled Delhi until 1526, which marked a period of strong Hindu–Muslim social, political, cultural, economic and religious interaction. The Turks introduced Arab and Persian languages and a unique Indo-Saracenic architectural form by combining Islamic–Indian architectural styles. The Muslim rule in India changed from the Sultanates to the Sayyids and then to the Lodis, followed by the Mughals. While the Mughal rule officially ended in 1857, however, the Mughal Empire was powerful only until 1707. The Mughal period is considered by some scholars as non-constructive since they attribute India's lack of encounter with modernity to the continuation of medieval practices (Kazi 1999; Singhal 1983, 155–180).

The hierarchical social structures and social relations created by the Muslim nobility essentially comprised of the upper caste elite and systematically excluded ordinary Muslims. 'Muhammed Shah, the Mughal noble laid stress on social distinctions and judged anyone's work in proportion to his place in the social hierarchy…he was extremely disdainful towards those below him in the social scale', remarks M. S. Jain (2000, 4). The social class distinction laid immense burden on people, particularly on the lower class. The elite Muslims were very wealthy, indicating a sharp socio-economic divide. However, they sustained wealth by collecting taxes from the ordinary, poor and downtrodden of the society. The condition of people, particularly the lower class, was such that they revolted against the nobility and ruling dynasties, who collected at least one-third of their hard-earned money regularly. Wilfred Smith remarks that there was at least someone found in discord with Akbar at any particular time, regarding payment of *taxes* or *revenue*. Smith further highlights, 'Aurangzeb and his court were thoroughly alarmed. For one thing, we are told that the grain supply at Dilhi was becoming scanty, which reminds us how dependent was the empire on its control and exploitation of the villages' (Smith 1998, 226, 236).

Besides social class division, the caste system divided Indian Muslims, regardless of Islamic egalitarian principles. Indian Muslims systematically adopted a version of the caste system around the 12th century, revealing their assimilation with Indian culture and life. The caste system sowed divisions among the Indian Muslims and also estranged them from the Hindus. D. P. Singhal remarks, 'Islam failed to demolish caste in India. Muslims, in fact, became another caste for the Hindus, and despite identity in culture, remained a distinct social group' (Singhal 1983, 164). The two major divisions among the Indo-Muslim society was the Ashraf, the upper class, the undoubted descendants of foreign Muslims, converts from the upper castes Hindus and the Ajlaf, the ones involved in menial jobs. The social division among Muslims was very distinct. The Ashrafs were more stringent than the upper caste Brahmins as they excluded communities by virtue of birth as well as economic status, while Brahmins excluded communities only by virtue of birth (Jain 2000, 5). The class differences pervaded the caste system, creating powerful space for the noble and the elite to impose control over the poor and ordinary people. 'Not religious belief but social snobbery preserved social distinctions', emphasises Singhal (1983, 165). These kinds of social distinction further created more caste-based groups or caste-analogous groups, according to Imtiaz Ahmad. There were several small caste-analogous groups of varying social status, apart from the two broad dichotomous groups of Ashraf–Ajlaf (Ahmad 1967, 890). Some of these groups were: Sayyid, Shaik, Mughal, Pathan, Malik, Momin, Mansoor, Rayeen, Qasale, Raki, Hajjam, Dhobi, Teli and Bhat (Singhal 1983, 165). Arzal, who rank the lowest on the ladder of social stratification, considered equivalent to the untouchables by leaders like Ambedkar (Ambedkar 1946; Dyrhagen and Islam 2006). The untouchables among Muslims, called the Arzal or Bhangi, were treated like their Hindu counterparts. Singhal (1983, 165) remarks:

> ...although the Islamic ideal of human equality was a major reason for the conversion of many caste-ridden and oppressed Hindus to Islam, in practice the inequality was the same. Muslims of higher status would not generally accept food from them; sometimes they were not allowed in the village mosque to pray.

At the same time, this kind of exclusion practice was also a consequence of massive conversion. Singhal (1983, 166) states, 'Large communities converted to Islam from among Hindus carried with them Hindu customs and usages, and often passed them on to other Muslims'. This ultimately created social instability and tension, even though some Muslim rulers were known for tolerance and peace. According to Zahiruddin Malik, 'The political and economic inequalities further deepened the social tensions between various endogamous units...and prevented a unified and harmonious growth of society' (Jain 2000, 6). Thus, the Muslims adopting the discriminatory practices of the caste system created more havoc in the Indian society, adding to the already entrenched divisions among the Hindus.

The contemporary scenario discussed by the Sachar Committee reveals that about 32 per cent of Muslims in India belonged to OBC in the year 1999–2000, which increased to 41 per cent in 2004–2005. The report explains that more Muslims belong to OBC because of the Presidential Order 1950, which restricted the status of Scheduled Caste (SC) to the Hindus of unclean occupations while their non-Hindu equivalents were considered OBCs. This led to the formation of two major OBC groups among Muslims, namely the 'Arzals' the 'untouchable converts' and the Ajlafs, the converts from 'clean' occupational castes. Correspondingly, as estimated by the NSSO 2005, about 41 per cent of Muslims in India belong to OBCs, which forms 15.7 per cent of the total OBC population in the country (Prime Minister's High Level Committee, Cabinet Secretariat, Government of India 2006, 192–193, 213). The OBC Muslim group includes a small percentage of

SC/ST community. Khalidi (1995) estimates that there are about 350 ethnolinguistic Muslim groups in India. Thus, we find a heterogeneous group of Muslims living in India.

Muslim Women in India

In Islam, the status of women is regarded as low, even though women held a better position at the time of its inception in Arabia. Some of the accepted norms in Islam include male offspring having access to a larger share of property than females; stringent practices in granting a divorce to females even if they were treated badly; men being allowed to take four wives and his female slaves as concubines and considering the object of marriage as progeny (Singhal 1983, 154). The practice of polygamy, early marriage and religious conservatism and system of 'purdah' placed control over women's sexuality and opportunities for development. During the Mughal period, women were kept away from public life for which 'purdah' was symbolically used.

> The ideology of purdah (female seclusion) derived from the idea of women as Fitna (potential disorder). The 'disorderly' effects of women upon men's lives could be relegated to the private, walled-off regions of the household. Purdah later transformed into a marker of female 'respectability' among upper-class women. The practice of purdah combined with social ideas of women as primarily wives and mothers, prevented female education. (Kazi 1999)

The purdah system proved unfavourable to women's development in Indian society. Singhal remarks that some Hindu community, who gave their daughters to Muslims in marriage, also adopted this practice. 'The institution of purdah, led to the seclusion of women, child-marriage and further deterioration in the position of women in Indian society', remarks Singhal (1983, 164). Even today, veiling is used as a practice to keep women away from their public participation. In Hyderabad, Andhra Pradesh, women tend to use purdah these days more and some colleges have made it compulsory recently. This practice is due to the influence of many men from this area working in the gulf countries (Hasan and Menon 2005, 112). The use of purdah physically secludes women from society and tends to hinder them from accessing opportunities.

The caste-analogous social divisions worsened the plight of the Muslim women. The Islamic education system catered only to the upper class Ashraf, and Persian was used as the medium of instruction. While the Hindu elementary schools used Indian languages, the Muslim schools did not use Urdu or any other Indian language, inhibiting access to education to ordinary Muslim communities. Moreover, the elitist and exclusive practices among the Ashraf led to the problem of unmarried youth, both male and female, and particularly a large number of widows during 18th and 19th centuries. The problems of child widows, unmarried girls below the age of 10–15 years and widows of 15–40 years were large, which hindered the progress of Muslim women (Jain 2000, 7–8). Even though inter-caste marriage among Muslims was accepted, it rarely took place, particularly among the Ashraf. Singhal (1983, 164) remarks, 'Intermarriage and inter-dining between Hindus and Muslims did not become a part of their mutual social contact and behaviour. Some Muslim rulers, however, married into Hindu houses for political reasons....' To name a few, Akbar, Jahangir and Alauddin married Hindu women. This again did not bring any significant change in the status of Indian Muslim women, as it was largely politically motivated. In fact, the Hindu nobles gained significant reputation for their gallantry if they refused to give their daughters in marriage to the Muslims.

In India, Muslim children, both boys and girls attended *Maktabs* (Muslim elementary schools) for primary school and Madrasas for upper primary education, in which girls were not enrolled. This led to the lack of access to education for girls and they were restricted to memorising Quran. However, the elite arranged for private tuitions at home for the girls. For instance, the Mughal emperors educated their daughters at home. Babar's daughter, Gulbadan Begum, authored *Humayun Nama*, and wrote about the social realities of Mughal women, while Zeb-un-Nissa, Emperor Aurangzeb's eldest daughter, was a scholar in theology and poetry (Kazi 1999). Access and scope for education further receded for Muslim children, at the introduction of English as the medium of instruction in schools, in 1835. The inaccessibility to

Urdu medium schools was vastly responsible for the backwardness of the Muslim children in education (Hasan and Menon 2005, 78; Prime Minister's High Level Committee, Cabinet Secretariat, Government of India 2006, 18). However, currently, Muslim parents show greater interest in educating their children in English medium schools than Urdu to create a level playing field (Hasan and Menon 2005, 98).

The spread of modernism in India during the 18th century triggered critical debates on various social issues pertinent to Muslim women, including gender bias, purdah system, education, marriage and women's freedom in decision-making. However, modernists and philosophers such as Mohammed Iqbal, Maulana Abul A'la Maududi and Syed Ahmed Khan encouraged 'Quranic education' instead of modern education for Muslim women. This was emphasised by 'Ulema', the Muslim theologians, who strongly believed in women being ruled and controlled by men in order to lead a proper religious life. The modernists viewed access to education and women's freedom in the West, irrelevant for the Muslim women (Kazi 1999). At the same time, the social reformers among the Hindus targeted sati, widow seclusion, child marriage and female illiteracy which were abominable practices foisted on the Hindu women. However, the Muslim women, who shared all the problems of their Hindu counterparts except sati, did not have direct support or representation. Further, the Muslim women, unlike the Hindu women, had the legal rights for divorce, remarriage and property inheritance, so they were never in the forefront of social reforms. Post-independence, the Hindu community demanded their lawful rights, which resulted in the Hindu Code Bill 1956, thus ensuring Hindu women's access to legislative equality. Such representations never happened in the case of the Muslim women (Lateef 1990, 10–11). With regard to education, Islamists of the pre-independence period considered their women as 'incapable of learning or of producing knowledge' (Kazi 1999). However, the British authorities proposed egalitarian educational measures through English and vernacular medium of instruction and prioritising the needs of females, particularly Muslim girls. The British made more funds available for primary education and for educating women. Despite the efforts, the enrolment of girls in public schools was as low as 444,470, in 1901–1902, which was nine times less than the enrolment of boys. The 1901 Census revealed that one-tenth of male and seven in a thousand female population were literate. Also, an extensive work on documenting the spread of education revealed that only 1 in every 40 girls in schooling age attended schools (Ghosh 2000, 123). The analysis of the Fourth Quinquennial Report (1897–1902) (Nathan 1904) and the Memorandum on Progress of Education in British India (1928) reported that in the Muslim community, which was about 24 per cent of the total population in British India, only 24 per cent received an education. However, there was a gradual progress with Muslim girls attending school, surpassing all other communities at the national level, and the Tenth Quinquennial Report in 1932–1937 revealed that the enrolment of Muslims increased in secondary schools and in colleges (Lateef 1990, 49–52).

The Hunter Commission (1883) identified Muslims and women as educationally backward classes and recommended promoting indigenous Muslim schools at high, middle and primary school levels as well as instituting scholarships and studentships from primary to college level. Moreover, to promote Muslim girls' education, the Hunter Commission suggested providing more grants to girls' schools, instituting a simple curriculum at primary level, creating funds to support *zenana* teachers and a separate inspectorate for girls' education (Ghosh 2000, 98). In addition, the Muslim Educational Conference in 1896 emphasised the issue of educating their women. Similarly, the Calcutta University Commission (1917) recommended 'purdah schools' for Hindu and Muslim girls, a special board for women's education to look after courses suited for women and cooperative arrangements for teaching in women's colleges (Ghosh 2000, 146). Some of the enlightened Muslims and Hindus supported government's initiatives and started schools to cater to their own community children. Sheikh Abdullah and his wife Wahid Jahan founded Aligarh University for women in 1906 in Calcutta that currently serves more than 3,000 students. Similarly, the British established the 'New Zenana School' in Hyderabad in 1907 by hiring Florence Wyld from England, along with three more teachers in 1909, a remarkable effort from the British with the help of Nizam of Hyderabad (Hasan and Menon 2005, 114–116, 183). In West Bengal, the British missionaries and reformist established many schools for girls in the beginning of the 20th century attracting Muslim girls. Also, West Bengal is known for its more than 500 Madrasas that are classified into junior, higher secondary and senior levels. These Madrasas follow state board syllabus with the compulsory addition of Arabic language. The 'Calcutta Madrassah College', established in 1780, is first of its kind in the country to provide modern education (Hasan and Menon 2005, 40). Even though education was accessible to Muslim girls in the beginning of the last century, they were highly restricted in their freedom of thought. 'At the Mohammedan co-educational college at Madras, girls were required to wear their burqas (veils) and at Aligarh, male teachers sat behind a curtain' (Lateef 1990, 80). The enactment of the Shariat Act or 'Muslim Personal law' in 1937 followed by 'Dissolution of Muslim Marriages' in 1939 set a positive precedent. However, the Hindu Code Bill in 1956 highlighted the drawbacks of the Shariat Act, as the law was not protecting women against polygamy and unilateral divorce, implying legal sanction to continue such practices. To avoid such loopholes, while formulating the Muslim Women's Protection Bill 1986, the legislative changes were left to the Muslim community themselves. But the government did not ensure an unbiased approach towards women's issues, which led to the continued approval of the practice of polygamy and unilateral divorce, although they are banned in many Muslim countries (Lateef 1990, 163). The Muslims in India had sharper community divisions and practice of segregation among their community members based on caste and class, and they were backward (Jain 2005, 6–7). The Muslim women in India continue to experience multidimensional exclusion and deprivation of rights due to inadequate state measures and legal provisions. However, in the past decade, the Government proposed initiatives to reduce inequalities according to vulnerabilities of groups are noteworthy.

State Measures to Reduce Inequalities: Focus on Vulnerable Groups

In a globalised society, increasing inequalities and inequities are a major concern. The extent of inclusiveness in the society in the view of the so-called development is debatable. Emerging issues, which are offshoots of globalisation, digitalisation and other transformatory processes, as well as unequal distribution of its benefits in the society, create, deepen and perpetuate the chasm between the privileged and the less privileged. It also cuts across the resilient and entrenched inequalities of caste, class and gender, and increases the vulnerability of marginalised groups. Muslim women in India, particularly those who belong to low caste and poor families, face vulnerability to a greater extent.

For a more nuanced understanding of a vulnerable segment of population, it has to be examined within the context of groups with which it is affiliated, as proposed by Stewart. Lately, analysis of group inequalities has wider reach, especially in developing countries. The UNDP (2014) underscores that as per Minorities at Risk Project, about 300 minority groups in more than 90 countries experience a range of political and economic exclusion and increased HI in terms of discrimination in access to jobs, justice and services (UNDP 2014, 22). The report focuses on challenges in addressing vulnerabilities of groups while sustaining human progress. The UNDP (2014) indicates the need to examine 'structurally vulnerable groups' along caste, class, gender and indigeneity, as the complexity of vulnerability deepens with inter-sectoral layers. 'For example, those who are poor and also from a minority group, or are female and have disabilities, face multiple barriers which can negatively reinforce each other' (UNDP 2014, iv). Moreover, the report by the UNDP discusses link between the intensity of vulnerability and inadequate investment in different life stages of life to build capabilities, as in the case of children or adolescents who are deprived of school education. The report says, '…conditions experienced before age 18 including structural vulnerabilities such as poverty and group inequality contribute to about half the inequality in lifetime earnings' (UNDP 2014, 60). It recommends that policies addressing vulnerabilities should focus on preventing risks of childhood development by providing education, promoting gender and group equality and building social competencies (UNDP 2014, 26). While current programmes of the state for the Muslims have a focus on promoting children's education, it is important to evaluate the trajectory of state welfare measures and approaches to strengthen the capability of Muslim minority.

Post-independence, the Constitution of India mandated the Government of India with the protection of the rights of minority and socially excluded groups. The term 'minority groups' generally represent Muslims, Christians, Sikhs and Buddhist among whom Muslims are the largest, while the SC and Scheduled Tribe (ST) represent socially excluded groups. Despite the constitutional mandate, no specific policies were formulated for minority welfare and Muslims did not get much focus even as equivalent to the SC/ST. This is evident from the Five-Year Plans that had devised specific economic assistance for the SC/ST under the provision for marginalised communities. Ritu Dewan and Sandhya Mhatre (2015), who analysed minority budgeting, highlight negligence of minorities in the Five-Year Plans for almost half a century. The first five Five-Year Plans (1951–1978), which focused on reducing inequalities and promoting equality and social justice, generally concentrated on SC/ST welfare, as compared to Muslim minorities. The Sixth Plan and Seventh Plan had a special focus on SC/ST welfare and the Seventh Plan came up with Special Component Plan (SCP) for SC and Tribal Sub-Plan (TSP) for ST which hugely invested in improving basic facilities in SC/ST areas. The Ninth Plan (1997–2002) spelt out programmes for the welfare of minorities but no schemes were implemented during this period. The Tenth Plan (2002–2007) and the Eleventh Plan (2007–2012) had a sharp focus on inclusive development of marginalised groups including Muslim minority population, women and children. During this period, the Sachar Committee came up with the first-ever high-level commissioned Report in 2006. The Sachar Committee Report provides a thorough analysis of the socio-economic, educational and political status of Muslims in India. As per the Sachar Committee Report, the Muslims are the worst performing socio-religious group in India in comparison to other religious groups and SC/ST groups; they are more backward in education—elementary to higher education, employment status particularly with regard to service sector and political representation; there is considerable increase in the number of Muslims categorised under OBC and SC communities.

In 1992, the National Commission for Minorities was established which was expanded to the Ministry of Minority Affairs in 2006. The Ministry coordinates schemes and policies of different departments for the benefit of Minority with a focused approach. Two important programmes are implemented by the Ministry of Minority Affairs are Prime Minister's New 15 Point Programme and the Multi-Sectoral Development Programme (MSDP), as Post-Sachar response. The Prime Minister's New 15 Point Programme focuses on the well-being, protection and development of minorities. Seven Ministries are involved in the implementation of this scheme. These ministries stipulate about 15 per cent of physical targets and financial outlays under schemes proposed by the ministry to be earmarked for minorities, review the progress on a monthly basis and send quarterly reports to the Ministry. The MSDP is a centrally funded comprehensive scheme for the minorities which invests in improving infrastructure facilities, health, sanitation, housing, drinking water, education, skill development and income generation activities.

Also, the Ministry focuses on coordination with different Ministries to optimally benefit Minorities with schemes, particularly in the Minority Concentration Districts (MCD). The idea of MCD to reach out to the minorities came up in 1987 and about 41 districts with 20 per cent and more minority population was listed out. However, in 2009, 90 districts were categorised into MCDs and the Ministry reached out to the people with various schemes to improve infrastructure facility, provide basic amenities and ensure livelihood opportunities through a coordinated effort.

While there is a focus on minority concentrated areas, Kundu's Report for Diversity Index (2008) brings out issues around concentration of minorities. In fact, among 90 MCDs, Uttar Pradesh alone has 50 MCDs of Muslims, all of which indicate poor standard of living. Kundu's Report essentially focuses on this aspect and the need to have diverse groups living together. Kundu's Report recommended providing incentives to housing builders, who promote 'composite living spaces for socio-religious communities' (2008). Madrasa modernisation and promotion of Urdu language are important initiatives in improving education of Muslim children. The earlier initiatives of the Government of India to reduce vulnerability of minorities, particularly the Muslim population, is located within the understanding of group inequality as proposed by Stewart.

MUSLIM GIRLS' ACHIEVEMENT GAP: GENDER EQUITY ANALYSIS

The above section analysed the Muslim girls' educational status as a group-based issue, and highlighted the disparities in Muslim women's education in comparison to other socio-religious communities in India. As Stewart advocates, group comparisons are significant to understand the location of excluded communities. As the chapter focuses on gender equity in education for Muslim girls, it examines various factors that contribute to their achievement gap, moving beyond physical access to schooling. Stewart's HI provides the lens to consolidate these factors within the domain group characteristics, interactions and dynamics. As Stewart argues, identifying the characteristics of groups such as persistence and multidimensionality enables critical understanding of inequalities prevailing in groups. Also, defining group boundaries in relation to long-term cultural markers would enable us to identify the existence of inequalities in a group at a particular time and to understand the relevance of such cultural indicators at the time of inquiry (Stewart 2008, 54–55). Stewart mentions that persistent HIs exist only if cultural markers defining group boundaries remain and they are continuously reinforced. The multidimensionality of HIs describes economic, political, social and cultural dimensions with a whole range of elements associated with each of the dimensions. The interactions between these dimensions are extremely vital in understanding persistent deprivation.

Recognising the multidimensional problems of Muslim women in India is important to understand inequities that hamper quality education. Figure 11.1 shows the multidimensional issues that affect Muslim women from experiencing quality education. The layers are shown in circles, one entangled with the other. Some of these layers of inequalities are typical of women's suppression in India, such as caste and class divisions. Also, spatial inequality, which describes exclusion based on the place of residence, is another feature of inequality, as rural and remote areas are a neglected lot. As seen in the analysis of Socio-Religious Communities (SRCs), rural Muslim women showed the least progress in education, as rural areas lacked adequate or competing resources for development while also being plagued by social problems such as mass illiteracy, unemployment, gender discrimination

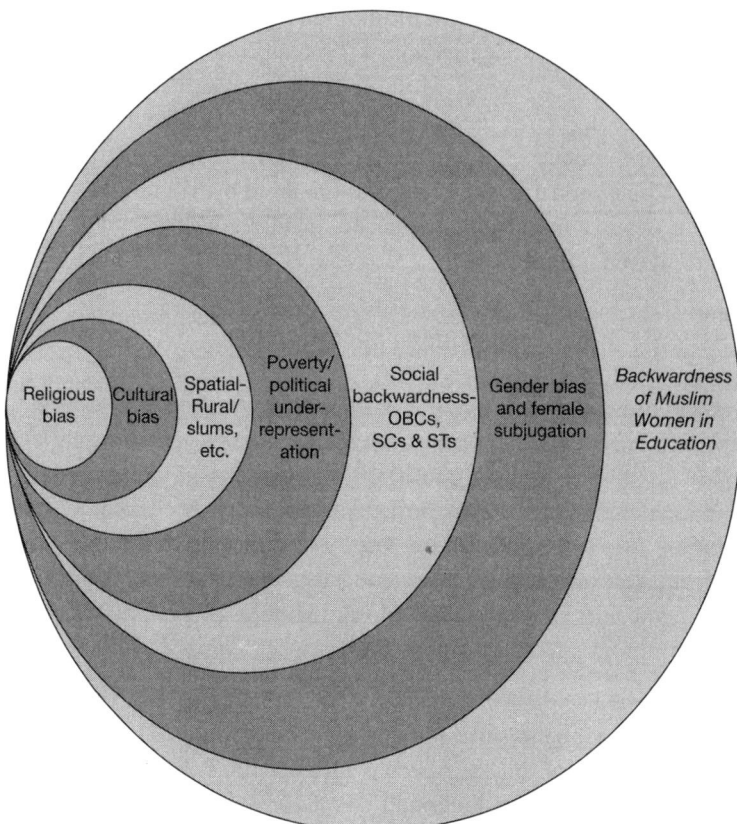

Figure 11.1 *Multidimensionality of Inequalities Experienced by Muslim Women in India*

and poverty. Although caste, class and spatial gender-specific issues are common to women all across India, the variation in the intensity of the occurrence of inequalities manifest differently for different groups.

As shown in Figure 11.1, in the case of Muslim women, the fundamental layers of inequalities such as gender discrimination, caste, class and spatial exclusion are entangled with each other as well as with other inequalities distinctively. The cultural norms, practices of the Muslim community and religious conventionality significantly affect Muslim women's backwardness in education in combination with other inequalities. The cultural markers that indicate discriminatory practices compounded by norms against Muslim women over a period of centuries establish persistent deprivation. The inequalities that have persisted over a long period among Muslim women show the intensity and extent of the deepened divide, affecting their development differently than other women's groups in India. A comprehensive understanding of multidimensional nature of inequalities faced by Muslim women in India is essential in pursuing the goal of gender-equitable and gender-responsive education.

CONCLUDING OBSERVATIONS

Frances Stewart's HI provides a critical framework to address group inequalities within the broader context of a socially, economically and culturally diverse Indian population. It necessitates multidimensional understanding of factors that perpetuate inequality. A nuanced understanding of the HI informs activists, academicians, researchers and policymakers with a multi-layered understanding of group inequalities. The inequalities experienced by Muslim women are multidimensional and HI provides a critical lens to understand it comprehensively.

Addressing vertical inequalities even in a liberal and egalitarian society may not be feasible. However, in a multicultural, multilingual and multi-religious society, which is also hierarchically stratified, there is a need for a concerted effort to tailor any redress according to the specific characteristics of traditionally neglected groups. Different socio-religious groups have different issues. Muslim women are a unique socio-religious group, long suffering due to neglect and deprived of access to quality education. Their condition typifies HI. So, any measures to ameliorate the HI should be need-based and relevant to specific groups to address the challenges that are specific to their social, political, economic and cultural dimensions.

The educational backwardness of the Muslim society should also be addressed within the framework of HI. Need for Urdu schools, appointment of Urdu teachers in the vacant positions must be done immediately. This is a serious issue in different parts of the country. There is an explicit connection between poverty, illiteracy and gender inequality among the Muslim community. Rural Muslim women are ranked the lowest in educational attainment. Hence, the central and state governments have to come up with policies that would tackle the entire gamut of problems instead of looking at the solutions in isolation. Reservations for women in education, employment and political participation based on SRCs could be one of the solutions to handle these combinations of problems effectively. Economic programmes for rural Muslim women are very important along with education and awareness campaigns to reduce the dropout rate of female children; reservation in the public sector jobs, which is politically fraught, could be one of the measures explored for empowering educated Muslim women and men in India. The political participation of Muslim community needs to be enhanced considerably at the local and national level.

Policies on addressing inequalities should aim at enhancing inclusion and participation, building social cohesion, respect for diversity and a capability harnessing inclusive space. This requires a comprehensive understanding of existing inequalities and social exclusion. Gender inequity is HI (Anthony and Padmanabhan 2010). Gender equity in education is an ideal goal that requires social inclusion and participation of women at all levels and fields.

REFERENCES

Ahmad, Imtiaz. 1967, 13 May. 'The Ashraf and Ajlaf Categories in Indo-Muslim Society'. *Economic & Political Weekly*: 887–891. Available at www.epw. in/system/files/pdf/1967_2/19/The_Ashraf_and_Ajlaf_Categories_in_ IndoMuslimSociety.pdf (accessed on 7 April 2019).

Ambedkar, B. R. 1946. *Pakistan or the Partition of India*. New Delhi: Thackers Publishers.

Annual Status of Education Report (ASER). 2012. *Annual Status of Education Report (Rural), 2011, Provisional*. Mumbai: Pratham.

Anthony, Josephine, and Sudarsan Padmanabhan. 2010. 'Digital Divide And Equity In Education: A Rawlsian Analysis'. *Journal of Information Technology Case and Application Research* 12(4): 37–62. DOI: 10.1080/15228053.2010.10856195.

Dewan, Ritu, and Sandhya Mhatre. 2015. *Minority Marginalisation and Sustainable Livelihoods: Implementation of Development Schemes in Minority Concentrated Districts of Uttar Pradesh*. Mumbai: Centre for Study of Society & Secularism.

Dyrhagen, Gitte, and Mazharul Islam. 2006. *Consultative Meeting on the Situation of Dalits in Bangladesh*. Dhaka: Bangladesh Dalits' Human Rights and International Dalit Solidarity Network. Available at http://idsn.org/wp-content/uploads/

user_folder/pdf/New_files/Publications_from_network/Bangladesh_full_report_FINAL_VERSION.pdf (accessed on 7 April 2019).

Ghosh, S. C. 2000. *The History of Education in Modern India*. New Delhi: Orient Longman.

Hasan, Zoya, and Ritu Menon. 2005. *Educating Muslim Girls: A Comparison of Five Indian Cities*. New Delhi: Women Unlimited.

Indian Education Commission Report (Hunter Commission Report), 1882–83. 1883. Calcutta: Government Printing.

Jain, M. S. 2000. *Muslim Ethos: As Reflected in Urdu Literature*. Jaipur and New Delhi: Rawat Publications.

———. 2005. *Muslims Political Identity*. Jaipur and New Delhi: Rawat Publications.

Kazi, Seema. 1999, February. *Muslim Women in India: A Minority Rights Group International Report*. London: Minority Rights Group.

Khalidi, O. 1995. *Indian Muslims Since Independence*. New Delhi: Vikas Publishing House Pvt. Ltd.

Lateef, Shahida. 1990. *Muslim Women in India: Political & Private Realities 1890s–1980s*. New Delhi: Kali for Women.

Memorandum on Progress of Education in British India between 1916 and 1926. 1928. India: Department of Education, Health and Lands.

Nathan, R. 1904. *Progress of Education in India 1897–98 – 1901–02*. Calcutta: The Superintendent of Government Printing, India. Available at https://archive.org/details/in.ernet.dli.2015.35185/page/n2 (accessed in September 2019).

Prime Minister's High Level Committee, Cabinet Secretariat, Government of India. 2006. *Social, Economic and Educational Status of the Muslim Community of India, A Report*. Sachar Committee Report. Available at http://minorityaffairs.gov.in/newsite/sachar/sachar_comm.pdf (accessed on 7 April 2019).

Progress of Education in India 1927–32: Tenth Quinquennial Review (vol. 2), 1934. Delhi: Manager of Publications.

Progress of Education in India 1932–37: Eleventh Quinquennial Review (vol. 1). 1940a. Delhi: Manager of Publications.

Progress of Education in India 1932–37: Eleventh Quinquennial Review (vol. 2). 1940b. Delhi: Manager of Publications.

Sayed, Yusuf, Ramya Subrahmanian, Crain Soudien, Nazir Carrim with Sarada Balgopalan, Fhulu Nekhwevha, and Michael Samuel. 2007. 'Education Exclusion and Inclusion: Policy and Implementation in South Africa and India'. *Researching the Issues* 72. London: DFID.

Sen, Amartya. 2005. *The Argumentative Indian: Writings on Indian Culture, History and Identity*. London and New York: Penguin Books.

Singhal, D. P. 1983. *A History of the Indian People*. London: Methuen London Ltd.

Smith, W. C. (1998), 'Lower-class Uprisings in the Mughal Empire'. In *The Mughal State 1526–1750* (pp. 323–346), edited by Muzaffar Alam and Sanjay Subrahmanyam. New Delhi: Oxford University Press (first published in *Islamic Culture*, vol. 20, no. 1, 1946).

Stewart, Frances. 2001. Horizontal Inequality: A Neglected Dimension of Inequality. Helsinki: *UNU World Institute for Development Economics Research*.

———, ed. 2008. *Horizontal Inequalities and Conflict: Understanding Group Violence in Multiethnic Societies*. New York, NY: Palgrave Macmillan.

UNDP. 2014. *Sustaining Human Progress: Reducing Vulnerabilities and Building Resilience*. Human Development Report. New York, NY: UNDP.

United Nations. 2010. *The Millennium Development Goals Report*. New York, NY: United Nations.

World Economic Forum. 2010. *Global Gender Gap Report*. Available at http://www3.weforum.org/docs/WEF_GenderGap_Report_2010.pdf (accessed on 7 April 2019).

Chapter 12

Organic Agriculture and India's Food Security

A. V. Balasubramanian

PROLOGUE

Although matters of agriculture, including agricultural science and the range of agricultural practices, are apparently matters of science, custom and practice, the political nature of agriculture has been highly significant in many regions of the world for several decades now. The Second World War was crucial in the adoption of food security as a major element in state policy whether in industrial democracies or state socialist systems like the Soviet Union, or even in fascist societies such as Spain under Francisco Franco (Pinilla, 2013). This inevitably involved, as it still does, education and research policy, national priorities and public cooperation and participation. Especially in democracies, public knowledge and public education campaigns are central to these processes and are linked with the accountability of public institutions and elected representatives. This issue has strong resonances with, for example, voter education as analysed in Chapter 2.

Since the early 1980s, sustained efforts to disseminate knowledge of agricultural production processes and of the dangers of, for example, excessive pesticide or fertiliser use, as well as problems of overproduction or wasteful consumption, have been, so to speak, put on the global political agenda by environmentalist campaigning groups and even by some private businesses involved in the mass production of food (Hamilton, 2005; Pinilla, 2013). This chapter, among other things, shows the importance of a well-informed public to the sustainable production and consumption of food. The term 'food democracy' has even gained wide currency (Norwood, 2015).

It has been said for several years now that agriculture in India is in a state of crisis. This is tantamount to saying that India is in a crisis since about 70 per cent of our population is still in rural areas with agriculture as their main livelihood source. This crisis manifests itself as increasing impoverishment of the farmers and lack of options for rural non-farming employment. There is an alarming degradation of the resource base of agriculture, especially of soil, increased pressure and demand on land from non-agricultural activities, erosion of biodiversity in terms of both species and varieties of cultivated crops and decline in cattle population. This has led distress migration to the cities and caused scarcity of labour in rural areas for agricultural activities. Along with this there is also a recognition that while the food production has been increasing, we are far from the goal of achieving food security. It is possible to achieve food security and what could be the sustainable pathway to do this?

The perception of the policymakers towards 'sustainable agriculture' remains ambivalent today. On the one hand, there is an increasing realisation about the environmental costs and the unsustainable nature of the chemical path to food production and an increasing awareness among the consumers about the health hazards of chemical produce. On the other hand, there are a set of concerns—real as well as exaggerated and even imaginary—about the capacity of 'sustainable agriculture' to provide yields of grain keeping pace with the increasing demands of the rising population. How does one make a comparative assessment of the potential of sustainable/organic farming as against chemical farming?

THE EFFICACY OF ORGANIC FARMING

In the following section, we looked at three different dimensions that are relevant in where we compare chemical and organic farming.

1. Field performance data
2. External costs of chemical agriculture
3. Subsidies and support available for chemical agriculture and required for sustainable agriculture

The above three factors are discussed in the following sections.

However, before we look into these aspects, we would like to spell out the vision and approach of the Centre for Indian Knowledge Systems (CIKS) which has been building on indigenous knowledge, practices and wisdom in the area of sustainable agriculture.

CENTRE FOR INDIAN KNOWLEDGE SYSTEMS' VISION AND APPROACH

The CIKS has been in existence since 1995. It works with the vision of—'Indigenous Knowledge and Resources for Sustainable Growth in Organic Agriculture with Food and Nutritional Security for Farmers'. We would state at the outset that when we refer to 'sustainable agriculture', it may be considered as organic farming but in a sense it is more than organic farming. It is more than organic farming in the sense that we do not see this as an end in itself. It is a form of sustainable agriculture making the best use of resources, knowledge and wisdom available with our people.

The CIKS provides support for organic farming in at least three different ways:

1. Providing knowledge (training and publications)
2. Providing materials—seeds (certified, indigenous), Vermicompost, neem cake, organic liquid nutrients, biopesticides and biofertilisers
3. Services (soil testing, soil health card, credit and revolving fund)

This support is provided based on the understanding that currently while a lot of support and subsidies are provided for chemical farming, such support is not available for organic farming.

The work of our centre has been built around the potential and possibilities of traditional knowledge of agriculture. In the following section, we draw extensively from a recent article by Balasubramanian (2015) on this topic.

India has one of the largest networks of organisations and infrastructure for agriculture anywhere in the world. Nevertheless, traditional Indian agriculture has hardly any space in the research or extension and dissemination services of the Central or State Governments. The achievements of the modern chemical model of agriculture have been so dazzling that little attention has been paid to the relevance of indigenous agricultural knowledge and practices. India is richly endowed with plentiful natural resources and tremendous density and diversity of bioresources. Its cultivable area of 160 million hectares is about 60 per cent of the total land area, as against the world average of 10 per cent. The average rainfall throughout India is 105 cm per year, higher than the amount that other large areas of the world receive. Almost all parts of India have rich traditional knowledge of agriculture and sustainable utilisation of natural resources with a history of continuous land cultivation over long periods with little decline in soil fertility. This knowledge tradition is both oral and textual.

Today's scepticism about traditional knowledge is based on the view that such knowledge cannot be trusted since it has not been subject to testing and validation as per modern scientific norms. In this connection, it is very interesting to see that a vast body of traditional knowledge of agriculture was indeed very recently put to scientific examination.

The Indian Council of Agricultural Research (ICAR) launched a nationwide mission mode project on collection, documentation and validation of indigenous technical knowledge (ITK) under the National Agricultural Technology Project (NATP) in 2000. Information on ITK was collected from primary sources through voluntary disclosure and collection and compilation of ITK volume was made from available literature, books, journals and theses. The compilation has five documents in seven volumes, which were published between 2002 and 2004. The first two documents, consisting of four volumes, listed 4,879 indigenous practices. The third and fourth documents describe efforts at validating and cross-validating these practices. Of the 4,879 practices documented, a set of 111 practices were selected and subjected to experimental testing and validation in efforts that were conducted by ICAR institutes and state agricultural departments and universities. These pertain to various topics such as pest control, crop protection, farm implements, weather forecasting, etc. The results of these validation experiments were published as separate volumes. These volumes do not contain an overall analysis of the results; hence, our centre has compiled the results in Tables 12.1 and 12.2.

This shows that slightly more than 80 per cent of these practices were valid and about 6 per cent of the practices were partly valid. About 9 per cent were classified as being not valid. There were a few cases where scientists felt that experiments need repetition. In some cases, the results were not declared. *In sum, there was an overwhelming evidence in favour of the validity of these practices.* However, it is strange that this entire exercise seems to have left no impression whatever on our body of scientists. None of these tested and validated practices have found their way towards larger dissemination through our extension services.

FIELD PERFORMANCE DATA

The CIKS has been working since 1995 to initiate, support and strengthen efforts relating to sustainable agriculture building on traditional knowledge, wisdom and practices. Our field activities have taken place in Tamil Nadu in the districts of Kancheepuram, Tiruvannamalai, Dindigul, Ramanathapuram and Nagapattinam. In the following section, we share some key results from case study.

To begin with, we can share the results of what may be considered as a case study of organic farming. In this case study, we look at some specific aspects such as costs, yield and income. After that we take note

Table 12.1 *Tabulation of Results of Document III (Validation Volume) in Terms of Efficacy Grouped Thematically*

S. No.	Theme	Total Number of Experiments	Analysis of Results of Experiments					
			Proved Valid	Partially Valid	To Be Repeated	Not Valid	Results Not Declared
1	Rainwater management	3	3				
2	Soil and water conservation	2	1	1			
3	Tillage practices	1	1				
4	Crops and cropping systems	5	4	1			
5	Pest and disease management	13	9		1	2	1
6	Farm implements	4	3	1			
7	Grain/Seed storage	8	8				
8	Horticultural drops	18	16	1		1	
9	Veterinary science and animal husbandry	34	23	3	1	7	
10	Fisheries	3	2				1
11	Food product development	5	5				
12	Natural yarns and dyes	2	2				
13	Ethnic food	7	7				
14	Thermal efficiency	1	1				
15	Weather forecasting	4	3		1		
16	Low-cost housing materials	1	1				
	Total	111	89	7	3	10	2

Source: Das et al. (2004).

Table 12.2 *Practices Tested by Indian Council of Agricultural Research: Overview of Success Rate*

Total	Number	Percentage
	111	100
Proved valid	89	80
Partly valid	7	6
To be repeated	3	3
Not valid	10	9
Results not declared	1	1
	111	100.0

Source: Das et al. (2004).

of certain other observations emerging from the field which indicate that there are several other factors which need to be taken into account.

This particular case study is based on an intervention that was focused in three villages in Kancheepuram district of Tamil Nadu state. The total area studied is about 80 acres. The two crops on which the study was carried out were groundnut and rice. The factors examined were costs, yields and the overall income for the farmers in respect of both types of crop.

Difference in Price

Organic production brings greater financial returns, as the examples below demonstrate.

- In the case of groundnuts, around 75 per cent of the sample organic growers have fetched a higher price for their produce. The incremental price ranges from ₹2.50 per kg to ₹5.50 per kg—the average incremental price being ₹3.95 per kg.
- In the case of paddy, around 90 per cent of the sample organic paddy growers have realised a higher price for their produce. The incremental price varies from 0.20 per kg to ₹4.70 per kg. The average incremental price is ₹1.16 per kg.

Thus, it is seen that a vast majority of the farmers have been able to realise a higher price for organic produce.

Net Incremental Income

Seventy-five per cent of the organic cultivators had incremental net income. The incremental net income per acre varied from ₹400 to ₹10,000. The average incremental net income was ₹4,980 per acre. Remaining 25 per cent of the farmers have not realised incremental income through organic cultivation of groundnut. Similar effects were also seen in the case of paddy.

ORGANIC FARMING: RETURN ON INVESTMENT

Are all the benefits captured by factors such as costs, yield and income? Discussions with farmers and our observations show that while some of the benefits can be reduced readily to financial terms, several other factors may not be reducible to financial terms at all. For example, several of the following factors were cited frequently by farmers:

- Improved health for the farmers, farm labourers and cattle
- Improved health for those who consume organic food
- Improvement in taste and keeping quality
- Decreased cooking time
- Long-term increase in soil fertility
- Lower water consumption

The fact that these could not be readily converted to financial terms does not mean that these are only subjective or qualitative observations. Very often, these were reported by a large number of farmers and the experiences shared were based on rich and detailed descriptions. For example, with respect to a factor such as 'increase in soil fertility', the following were among the observations shared:

- The water holding capacity of the soil has increased—fields that had to be irrigated on alternate days now have to be irrigated only once or twice a week.

- The soil is soft and rich, and it has lost its hard/dry quality which was commonly observed when it was under chemical farming when we walk across the field with our bare feet, the foot marks are seen imprinted very clearly.
- A large number of natural predators such as spiders, honeybees may have a reappearance and they are seen in great abundance.

EXTERNAL COST OF CHEMICAL AGRICULTURE

It is generally recognised that chemical agriculture imposes a heavy burden on the society at large as a consequence of chemical use. However, for several decades, it has been held that it is not easy or possible to assign specific figures to this damage. While studies from India are not as yet available, currently there are studies available from the United States and the United Kingdom—these are summarised further.

Estimation of Costs—The United States

This study was carried out by a team at the Economics Department of the Iowa University. The views and findings of this team may be summarised as follows in their own words:

> Agricultural production effects environmental and human health. Many consequences are borne involuntarily rather than chosen because no formal market trading takes place for ecosystem functions or health attributes. These impacts, or externalities, may be quantified indirectly by assigning dollar values through a process called valuation, which informs agricultural production and policy decisions. This study estimates external costs of agricultural production in the United States in the areas of natural resources, wildlife and ecosystem biodiversity and human health. Valuation studies are reviewed and revised to compile aggregate figures. External costs are estimated at $5.7 to $16.9 billion (£3.3 to £9.7 billion) annually. Impacts due to crop production are figured to be $4,969 to $16,151 million per year. Livestock production contributes $714 to $739 million to external costs. Using 168.8 million hectares of cropland in the United States, external cost per cropland hectare is calculated at $29.44 to $95.68 (£16.87 to £54.82). (Tegtmeier & Duffy, 2004, p. 1)

The authors recognise and list various categories of resources that are damaged as follows:

- Water resources
- Soil resources
- Air resources
- Wildlife and ecosystem biodiversity
- Human health pathogens
- Human health—pesticides

Based on the above study, the authors conclude:

> Many in the United States pride themselves on our 'cheap' food. But, this study demonstrates that consumers pay for food well beyond the grocery store check out. We pay for food in our utility bills and taxes and in our declining environmental and personal health. Furthermore, the estimates presented in this paper are conservative. Political intention is required to reassess and reform agricultural policy. Programmes that highlight sustainable methods rather than destructive, risky practices would be a start in internalizing the true costs of the present system. (Tegtmeier & Duffy, 2004, p. 14, 16)

AN ASSESSMENT OF TOTAL EXTERNAL COSTS OF UK AGRICULTURE

This chapter is the result of a collaboration between a team of academics in the UK and the Netherlands. In the words of this research team:

> This trans-disciplinary study assesses total external environmental and health costs of modern agriculture in the UK. A wide range of datasets have been analysed to assess cost distribution across sectors. We calculate the annual total external costs of UK agriculture in 1996 to be £2343 m (range for 1990–1996: £1149–3907 m), equivalent to £208/ha of arable and permanent pasture. Significant costs arise from contamination of drinking water with pesticides (£120 m/year), nitrate (£16 m), *Cryptosporidium* (£23 m) and phosphate and soil (£55 m), from damage to wildlife, habitats, hedgerows and drystone walls (£125 m), from emissions of gases (£1113 m), from soil erosion and

organic carbon losses (£106 m), from food poisoning (£169 m), and from bovine spongiform encephalopathy (BSE) (£607 m). This study has only estimated those externalities that give rise to financial costs, and so is likely to underestimate the total negative impacts of modern agriculture. (Pretty et al., 2000, p. 113)

According to the authors, the following are the significant environmental costs:

- Contamination of drinking water with pesticides and nitrate
- Damage to wildlife habitats and hedgerows
- Emission of gases
- Soil erosion and organic crop losses
- Food poisoning
- Bovine Spongiform Encephalopathy (BSE)

The authors conclude that 'The study has only estimated those externalities that give rise to financial costs. This is likely to under estimate the total negative impacts of modern agriculture' (Pretty et al., 2000, p. 113).

SUBSIDIES TO CHEMICAL FARMING AND THE LACK OF SUPPORT TO SUSTAINABLE AGRICULTURE

It has been extensively documented and noted that there is a large amount of subsidies that are provided to chemical farming. For example, it has been noted in a study published by Greenpeace that (Rupela & Gopikrishna, 2011) with respect to soil fertility the maximum investments by the government are put into subsidies for chemical agents for soil fertility.

However, more recently a report from the Parliament of India relating to the National Project on Organic Farming, presented to the Lok Sabha on 13 August 2015, provides extensive information (National Project on Organic Farming, Committee on Estimates, 2015–2016). In the following section, we quote extensively from the report of this Committee, which provides information about the origins of intensive investments into chemical agriculture and the problems caused thereby.

As per this report, while the Green Revolution was initially successful in increasing productivity, the long-time impacts were disastrous in terms of the negative ecological effect and gradually decreasing yields. There was also a cascading effect of degradation of soil health, low yields and new pests and diseases. The committee stated that while in the 1960s we could get 50 kg of grains for every 1 kg of nitrogen, phosphorus and potassium, currently this is reduced to 10 kg. It recognises that the chemical fertilisers received by subsidy in the range of ₹70,000–100,000 crores each year and it recommended a financial assistance of ₹20,000 per acre for a three-year period to support organic farming (National Project on Organic Farming, Committee on Estimates, 2015–2016, pp. vii, 58).

Committee further note that the representative of the Ministry of Agriculture also admitted that the extant fertilizer subsidy regime has done the maximum damage to the Indian agriculture. An eminent expert deposed before the Committee that during the sixties before the Green Revolution, we got 50 kg of grains from 1 kg of Nitrogen, Phosphorus and Potassium as of now we get only 10 kg grain from the same nutrients. The expert also testified that ideal Nitrogen, Phosphorus and potassium ratio should be 4:2:1 but it has come to 7:3:1 all over the country and shockingly to 39:9:1 in the Punjab. The expert therefore stressed the importance of organic farming which while building the ecology increases production and quality of the items produced. Having examined the adverse impact of chemical fertilizers and subsidy thereon to their manufactures, the Committee come to the inescapable conclusion that the present incentive of fertilizer subsidy needs to be revisited on urgent basis. (National Project on Organic Farming, Committee on Estimates, 2015–2016, p. 61)

Later, the Committee goes on to make a recommendation about the kind of financial assistance that needs to be extended to organic farming in order to make it sustainable.

Having regard to the testimony of the representative of the Ministry of Agriculture that the allocations for organic farming were quite insufficient vis-a-vis conventional farming which receives subsidy on chemical fertilizers usually in the range of ₹70,000–100,000 crores each year, the Committee find that the current level of allocation for organic farming does not provide a level playing field for promotion of organic farming. Further, the financial assistance of ₹20,000 per acre upto 3 years needs to be extended as soil treatment and refurbishing takes 3 to 5 years and only after that the produce becomes profitable. The Committee therefore recommend that the allocations for promotion of organic farming be scaled up substantially to meet the intended objective of sustainable agriculture which has the potential to increase 30 per cent more employment by way of resource recycling, certification process, product marketing and packaging. (National Project on Organic Farming, Committee on Estimates, 2015–2016, pp. 60–61)

The Committee, therefore, recommend that Government need to take urgent steps to incentivise production of green manure of approved standards by the farmers and the entrepreneurs. They also urge the Government to go for management and production of organic manure from millions of tonnes of organic solid waste being produced every day in urban and rural households and elsewhere in the country. (National Project on Organic Farming, Committee on Estimates, 2015–2016, p. 62).

IMPLICATIONS

Let us now sum up the implications of various of these reports and data:

- Calculations that compare the relative costs and benefits of organic and chemical farming are flawed unless they recognise that chemical farming is subsidised in the above manner at a policy level.
- Today when farmers seek to undertake organic farming, they are unable to utilise subsidies of this kind since there is no equivalent subsidy or support for organic farming.
- The micro-picture that emerges from the case study shared is that while some costs can be readily calculated, there are other costs that are more involved and it needs quite a bit of an effort to calculate them.

THE WAY FORWARD

We sum up our observations about the way forward.

- In terms of comparing the costs of benefits of organic farming, a detailed analysis is required and such an analysis should take into consideration factors that are not easy to quantify or assign a monetary value.

- The external costs of chemical agriculture are seen to be significant both in monetary terms as well as their impact—work needs to be initiated on this topic under our conditions.
- Significant steps need to be initiated in an imaginative manner for providing support of various kinds to sustainable agriculture.

It is clear that sustainable agriculture can play a significant role in the progress towards food security provided there is a 'level playing field'.

REFERENCES

Balasubramanian, A. V. (2015, 19 May). A hand to the plough. *Financial Chronicle*: 114–115.

Das, P., Arya, P. S., Das, S. K., Geetha Rani, M., Mishra, A., Verma, L. R., … Subha Reddy G. (2004). *Cross sectoral validation of indigenous technical knowledge in agriculture*, p. 259 (Document 4). New Delhi: Publication and Information Directorate, Indian Council of Agricultural Research.

Hamilton, N. D. (2005). 'Food democracy II: Revolution or restoration?' *Journal of Food Law & Policy*, *1*(13): 13–42.

National Project on Organic Farming, Committee on Estimates. (2015–2016). *Ninth Report*. New Delhi: Sixteenth Lok Sabha, Lok Sabha, Secretariat. Presented to the Lok Sabha on 13 August 2015.

Norwood, F. B. (2015). 'Understanding the Food Democracy Movement'. *Choices*, *30*(4): 1–5.

Pinilla, V. (2013). 'War, agriculture, and food: Rural Europe from the 1930s to the 1950s'. *Reviews in History*, *1445*. Retrieved from https://history.ac.uk/review/1445.

Pretty, J. N., Brett, C., Gee, D., Hine, R. E., Mason, C. F., Morison, J. I. L., …, G. Van der Bijl. (2000). 'An Assessment of the Total External Costs of UK Agriculture'. *Agricultural Systems*, *65*: 113–136.

Rupela, O. P., & Gopikrishna, S. R. (2011, February). *Of soils subsidies and survival: A report on living soils*. Mumbai: Greenpeace India Society.

Tegtmeier, E. M., & and Duffy, M. D. (2004). External costs of agricultural production in the United States. *International Journal of Agricultural Sustainability*, *2*(1): 1–20.

Chapter 13

India's New Intellectual Property Policy
Passive Sovereignty

Chamundeeswari Kuppuswamy

INTRODUCTION

Intellectual property rights (IPRs) constitute a justified concern globally, and the approaches taken to them by researchers and governments,
not to mention multilateral organisations, vary. Broadly characterised,
one approach has it that IPRs can serve to enhance democracy, as the
protection they provide constitutes an incentive to innovation and also
provides an element of economic stability in civil society (McKenna
2006: 2). This is countered by arguments that IPRs amount to the
'globalized construction of knowledge scarcity' (Tyfield 2010: 63).

Other significant IPR issues are generated by tensions between
states, one notable example being those between China and the United
States; these kinds of tensions arise partly because there are no clear
international standards for cyber relations (Liao 2019).

Given that context, India's Intellectual Property (IP) Law and innovation sector is of significance nationally as well as globally. India's IP
Policy reflects the exercise of both democracy and sovereignty, as these

are two sides of a coin. They are interlinked and develop by feeding off each other. This chapter explores the fascinating coming together of strong forces from within and without and melding to produce the effect of passive sovereignty. This may be expressed thus:

External Pressure + Strong Judiciary = Passive Sovereignty

These elements of the equation are meant to act as symbols rather than as actual scoped-out terms. External pressure signifies unilateral nudging or political commands from states such as the United States, and also refers to institutional pressures such as harmonisation drive of World Intellectual Property Organization (WIPO). Strong judiciary signifies both the actual judiciary in action in India as well as the grass-roots movements which judge the system by embracing it or puncturing it with their interventions. This chapter argues that the National IPR Policy is an exercise in passive sovereignty, with potential to harm the development of the country.

The context within which the policy is being drawn is discussed in the first section. The pressures and concerns about changes in laws prevailed throughout the drafting period. The process of appointment of the Drafting Committee (the IPR Think Tank), the consultation and the final draft have raised issues of transparency, conflict of interest, ideological controversies and insipid content. The second part of the chapter compares the Baseline Draft with the Think Tank draft, followed by the last section on assessing the final version of the National IPR Policy. This is done under four themes, namely Frugal Innovation, Traditional Knowledge (TK), Pharmaceutical Patents and TRIPS-Plus Policy.

It is argued that even if some of the concerns have been assuaged in the final draft, the scene has been set in the long term that could bring these concerns back.

PRESSURES AND CONCERNS ABOUT INTELLECTUAL PROPERTY LAWS IN INDIA

IP Law in India has a long history, having been promulgated during the time of the British Raj. The controversial area of IP law has been patent law. Soon after Independence, these rules were reviewed and a new system put in place in 1970. Further changes came since the liberalisation of the Indian economy in the 1990s, culminating with India's accession to the World Trade Organization in 1995 and the controversial treaty on trade-related IPRs which was implemented into Indian law in 2005. Yet again, the threats to IP law, in particular patent law, come from the pharmaceutical sector which seeks to protect its investment in R&D fiercely. Drug patents have come under constant scrutiny because of their impact on health, and hence a matter of public interest. While legislators have exercised caution in incorporating international standards into Indian IP law, many concerns come from the health care sector which worries that there will be a lowering of standards for the efficacy threshold for the grant of a patent under Article 3(d) of the Patent Act, 1970, which will consequently bring more drugs into patent, and thereby make them more expensive for procurement.

Evidence of the brittle nature of patent policy in India is available in the oscillating statements from the commerce ministry. India's chief economic adviser, prior to appointment, testified to the US Trade Commission that Article 3(d) was problematic because defining efficacy can be arbitrary and other policy tools may be available to achieve better control over thresholds of patentability.

So why is the threat to Article 3(d) so worrying? It is because of a practice that has been commonly referred to as evergreening (Dwivedi, Hallihosur and Rangan 2010). Article 3(d) of the Indian Patent Act, 1970, is strictly interpreted by the courts and does not allow incremental changes or modifications to be considered inventive enough to cross the patenting qualification threshold. In the context of active substances in drugs, which can be patented, Article 3 (d) has made it a significant barrier for 'new uses' of these compounds to be patented separately. If it were allowed, then the compound which is already protected for addressing one problem would be patented over again, thus paving the way for keeping the patent protection alive for longer, and perhaps indefinitely, hence the tag of evergreen. Patents have been applied for, and rejected under Section 3(d), for example, for tablets that have been converted to syrups, for heat stable version of drugs, for new use of known substance, and these have all been rejected (Brougher 2013: 54–55). Only under rare circumstances would a patent be granted for showing improvements in efficacy. This Indian policy was pronounced to be compliant with the TRIPS Agreement, and in the Glivec case, the court declared that 'Section 3(d) sets an obviousness standard which member states are free to define in a manner consistent with their national policy' (Brougher 2013: 57).

Harmonisation of IP law to a certain minimum standard of protection was stipulated under the WTO Agreement on Trade-Related Aspects of IPRs, TRIPS and signed up to by India. The fear is that the WIPO is pushing to harmonise IPR beyond the WTO minimum standards (Biadgleng 2007), as the pressure comes from the WIPO Quad group (Canada, the USA, Japan and the European Union). It has been time and again discussed that premature harmonisation of IP law is detrimental to the developmental needs of developing countries (Ncube 2016). In fact, it has been argued that IP is not necessary for innovation and would hinder growth and prosperity (Boldrin and Levine 2007).

NATIONAL IPR POLICY

The National IPR Policy is a report published in 2015. It is the first of its kind in India and has been produced in response to the need for an 'all encompassing' IP Policy. It is not very clear where the need comes from, for the report also states that there are already robust IP laws and a strong IP jurisprudence (Sridevan et al. 2015: i–ii) in India. *India has implemented the provisions of the TRIPS Agreement* (World Trade Organization 1994) *when it signed up to becoming a member of the World Trade Organization.* The laws are considered to be balanced and fit for purpose and 'are notable for their far-sightedness and have also anticipated international developments' (Sridevan et al. 2015: 2).

Politically, IP laws in India have been controversial. In a speech in 2015, the Prime Minister Narendra Modi labelled IP laws as underdeveloped. He talked of 'bringing our intellectual property rights at par with global parameters' (Mishra 2015). *In response, the United States*

Trade Representative (USTR) 'encouraged India to expeditiously undertake this initiative'. Such slurs on robust laws have been criticised as pandering to the monopolist models of IP.

Perhaps the clearest indication of the policy purpose is revealed in its aim to create an IP culture. The report commodifies creativity and casts intellectual creations as IP, right from the start. In one fell swoop, the policy creates intellectual 'property' out of intellectual 'creations' by stating 'India's range of intellectual creations is as diverse as its people, from patents to plant varieties, trademarks to traditional knowledge, copyright to designs and geographical indications'.

It is difficult to reconcile an IP culture with developments in India surrounding frugal innovation (Bound and Thornton 2012) and informal economy. Frugal innovation recognises the environment within which inventions and works are created, and is designed to offset novelty and inventive concept with social impact. A lesser amount of novelty or inventiveness is offset by the presence or greater amount of social impact in an invention or a work that is then granted patent or copyright protection. The IP culture that allows this to thrive may not sit well with an IP culture proposed by the new policy. The proposed spread of IP culture could also act counter to existing culture around stewardship or common proprietorship of innovation. One widely prevailing value system in India does support this IP culture. The Bhagvad Geeta is purported to state 'that one should not claim proprietary rights over anything or attach the pronoun "mine" to anything, since the true owner of all things is no one but God, from whom everything originated' (Ganapathi and Pullaǐ 2015: 16). While faith-based property theories are under researched, there is also not enough research into the benefits of property models for intellectual creations, and therefore to disregard knowledge in the public domain by stating that 'it is merely laudable and altruistic' (Sridevan et al. 2015: 5) is to blindly put faith in proprietary models for intellectual creations.

This report is soon to be published as the new National IPR Policy for India in 2016. It consists of two major parts. The first sets out the objectives in seven sections, namely IP Outreach: awareness and promotion, Generation of IPRs, Legal and legislative framework,

Administration and Management, Commercialisation of IPR, Enforcement and Adjudication, and Human Capital Development. The second part deals with particular themes, known as special focus areas and there are nine such areas, namely Agriculture and Food, Creative industries, Geographical indications, Information and communion technology and electronics, New and renewable energy, Public health, Science and Technology, Textiles and Traditional Knowledge.

THE IPR THINK TANK

The National IPR Policy was brought to fruition by a six-member think tank appointed by the Department of Industrial Policy and Promotion (DIPP) at the Ministry of State for Commerce and Industry (CI). This new Think Tank committee was chaired by a former Chairperson of the Intellectual Property Appellate Board (IPAB), Justice Prabha Sridevan. She gave such momentous decisions as *Yahoo v. Controller and Rediff*, *Tata v. Unilever* and *Financial Times v. Times Publishing House* and named one of the top 50 to influence IP law in the world. The members include corporate lawyers, a judge, an academic from a business school and the chair of an IPR committee at the business and commerce council. Some members are said to feature on the panel because of connections to the Ruling party rather than because of their IP expertise. There are issues of transparency and incompetence surrounding IP adjudication in India. The issues of transparency around the Think Tank only add to these concerns.

The handling of the process by the Ministry is in itself telling of the differences that surround IP Policy in India. A committee was first appointed, made up solely of IP academics, which then seems to have been replaced by a fresh committee devoid of IP academics. This turnaround perhaps reflects two strands of thinking within the commerce ministry that is responsible for commissioning the IPR Policy report. Critics see that the output from such a committee 'marks a shift from the earlier emphasis on policymaking in favour of multinational corporations and a neoliberal vision of "development"'. Poor communication and poor planning by the Department of Commerce seems to have led to the side-lining of this earlier committee. Having a good mix of academic and other sectors is ideal for the purpose of policy-making, especially because Indian IP academia is making waves in the world and is known for its rigour and quality. The lack of transparency around the process 'smacks of arbitrariness and ad hocism in policymaking both in the choice of experts and in the manner in which it was constituted', this being the sharp and rightly warranted response to a shoddily managed policymaking, with possible serious consequences for the economy and India's leadership in the IP policymaking world. Where is the representation on the committee from the 20 odd chairs of IP created by the Indian government, asks Rema Rangarajan in her article, that is now only available through other sites, after seemingly been supressed by the publishers.

THE PROCESS

The Think Tank was constituted to draft an IPR Policy in 2014. The IPR committee went through a very busy consultation period from Christmas 2014 to March end 2015. In total, the committee received 290 written submissions from across a wide spectrum, governments departments, including from representatives of foreign governments to business and industry associations, law firms, academics and research organisations and the general public. In addition, the committee benefitted from oral hearings, or 'in-person meetings' as it is referred to, 132 delegates from 60 organisations and according to the chairperson, 'Stakeholders' comments were diverse and in some cases diametrically opposite'. Since its submission to the Commerce ministry, it has been on its rounds to other ministries, with a release date in March 2016.

DIFFERENT POLICY VERSIONS

This section will discuss differences in the policy drafts in December 2014 draft and April 2015 final version. It will then consider the IPR policy draft submitted by the IP academic group, prior to the December 2014 version of the Think Tank.

The most noticeable difference between the draft and final versions of the National IPR Policy submitted by the Think Tank is the presence of 'Special focus areas' in the final version of April 2015. These areas of the economy have been selected based on the relevance IP holds for them. The effect of the consultations seems to have been for the better as there is a bit more clarity and categorical reiteration of the objectives in the Policy.

There are small but significant additions if one were to observe the trend in the type of additions made to the final version. It seems to appease those who are suspicious of the need for such a policy. Additions such as the 'promotion of public interest', international but also 'South–South cooperation', implementation and enforcement of IP rights as 'not adversely affecting India's developmental objectives', the recognition that 'IP will sub-serve the current and future national priorities', patents for 'improvements and modifications' strike the right balance between protection of innovation and the larger goal of betterment of society.

The final version of the draft IP Policy proposes introduction of 'multidisciplinary' IP courses/modules in all major training institutes such as Judicial Academies, National Academy of Administration, Police and Customs Academies, Indian Institute for Foreign Trade (IIFT), Institute for Foreign Service Training and Forest Training Institutes. The recognition of multidisciplinarity can be beneficial for India's development needs; however, given the lagging behind support for social sciences and humanities in India, this multidisciplinarity might not be far reaching enough to reach what might be its intended purpose.

In the Legal and Legislative section, the sentence 'as well as promote further research and development in products and services based on traditional knowledge' has been replaced with 'as well as promote their future development'. This shows the subtle shift in how TK needs to be viewed, not as a provider of products and services, but worth protecting for its own ends. This may or may not bring innovation benefits, but innovation is only one side of TK, identity, culture and the commons are the other characteristics of TK that are worth protecting. It would be interesting to see if the shift is a paper tiger or a real one, when the discussions for the proposed sui generis system for protection of TK and traditional cultural expressions (TCEs) gets under way. A stipulation under the revolutionary new Schedule 7 (Corporate Social Responsibility) of the Companies Act 2013 (Sarkar and Sarkar 2015; Singh and Verma 2014) to include TK preservation is a welcome addition in the final version, that is, if it doesn't get drowned out by all the other additions to strengthening IPR rights.

Making IP teaching compulsory, developing teaching through collaboration with WIPO, WTO and foreign universities, formulation of institutional policies and strategies for IP in government departments, higher education, research and technical institutions, etc.

The establishment of a new ministry or a department of IP is being proposed. The new ministry 'will be the nodal authority in the Government responsible for bringing cohesion and coordination among various Ministries/Departments on IP matters under their charge' and 'be responsible for laying down priorities for IP development in accordance with the National IPR Policy'.

Now, looking back further at the very first policy document commissioned by the DIPP and wondering if the reason the whole project was restarted from scratch, with no acknowledgment whatsoever of the work done before, although ideas were borrowed from that publication, was because of the values it embedded. The principled and clear approach adopted by the authors stands out in contrast to the Think Tank April 2015 document (Basheer and Pai 2014).

The Baseline Draft	Think Tank Draft
The aim of the IP policy is to identify a set of core common principles underlying these various IP categories.	The Policy aims to foster predictability, clarity and transparency in order to augment research, trade, technology transfer and investment. It will protect concerns such as public health, food security and environment, and encourage generation and diffusion of knowledge by laying a roadmap for holistic, effective and balanced development of the Indian IP system.

The Baseline Draft	Think Tank Draft
will unearth fundamental philosophies that reflect what is unique about Indian IP	....this does not fit with the global regime of strongly protected IP.
India is committed to ensuring TRIPS compliance and will avoid any TRIPS plus measures, purely at the behest of a trading partner. Unfortunately, TRIPS-plus norms have become the order of the day, proliferating rapidly through bilateral/plurilateral and regional free trade and investment agreements. Where possible, India will be guided by the 'Principles for Intellectual Property Provisions in Bilateral and Regional Agreements' issued by the Max Planck Institute for Intellectual Property and Competition (MPI).	In future negotiations in international forums and with other countries, India shall continue to give precedence to its national development priorities whilst adhering to its international commitments and avoiding TRIPS plus provisions.
Intellectual property will not be considered in isolation but in relation to other elements of an innovation ecosystem, namely financing, venture capital, education, infrastructure etc. In short, a holistic approach will be adopted so as to situate intellectual property in its proper context, and not as an end in itself.	It (IP Policy) shall weave in the strengths of the Government, research and development organizations, educational institutions, corporate entities including MSMEs and other stakeholders in the creation of an innovation-conducive environment.
Given that intellectual property is merely one of the tools to help incentivize innovation,	Increased IP generation will play a significant role in establishing a vibrant innovation ecosystem in India.

(Contd...)

(Contd...)

The Baseline Draft	Think Tank Draft
IP linkages through authorities that have next to no expertise in IP will be discouraged. Similarly enforcement by authorities that do not have clear statutory mandate to oversee IPR infringement will be discouraged.	Engaging with all levels of industry, including e-business, in order to create respect for IP rights and devise collaborative strategies and tools.
The rapid proliferation of ex parte injunctions in patent cases is a case in point. The Government will review such trends (after appropriate data collection in this regard) and explore the idea of legislation that would help balance IP enforcement against civil liberties, particularly criminal enforcement.	In recent times, India has witnessed an increase in IP disputes. Patents have a limited term and patent disputes need to be adjudicated expeditiously.

Technology transfer is firmly embedded in both documents. Recommendations for trade secrets law are common to both policies. Harnessing IP from publicly funded research features in both the Baseline and Think Tank drafts. Education and going a step further by romanticising IP are espoused enthusiastically by both policies!

ASSESSING THE IPR POLICY 2016

Frugal Innovation

In assessing its value and intent, it needs to be understood that this is an IP policy for the long term. While it may not have disturbed the current arrangements around compulsory licensing (in the National Manufacturing Policy and Section 84 of India's Patents Act) and Section 3(d) of India's Patents Act (preventing evergreening of drug patents), it will bring ever-increasing pressure to change these provisions, as the ethos of the policy is one of global harmonisation of IP and stronger protection of IP rights, based on weak evidential foundations for such an approach in a developing and populous economy. The foundations it has laid in the conception of the IP system as a fundamental system for economic growth is in itself an important statement. Under the prevailing circumstances in the global arena, this is inevitable and necessary. While the Commons values are what prevailed in pre-WTO India, exclusive property ownership is firmly embedded in the formal economy and will continue to provide the foundations of policies.

The support for the utility patent among government departments is evident from the Think Tank report and also being picked up by media before the anticipated endorsement of National IPR policy. While utility patents are inconvenient for the IPR system, it is a need felt in informal economies. The world body for the promotion and harmonisation of IP laws, WIPO, has been discussing IP in informal economies at the behest of low- and middle-income countries. India is among the top countries where the informal economy contributes to the Gross National Product (GNP), around 50 per cent. Along with economic growth, there is a rise in informal economy, not a fall. This is an indication that it needs to be recognised and studied. Base of the pyramid (BoP) innovation and the jugaad phenomenon have led to groups such as Honey Bee Network cataloguing over 140,000 grassroots innovation in India. The National IPR policy should pull its weight on this subject, which it currently does not do. In fact, informal innovation promotion should be the centrepiece of the policy. The policy has a role to play in strengthening the growing movement on responsible IPR in the world. The policy needs to lay out and promote development-friendly IPR initiatives as is already done in respect of utility patents. The IPR Policy should join forces with the National Commission on Labour Policy, which recognises informal workers and looks at incorporation of innovation clauses into the policy.

It seems the dangerous status quo in IP law and enforcement has been accepted by the Think Tank draft. But accepting status quo is dangerous as IP policy needs to change and needs to change globally. It does not sit well with informal economies and with frugal innovation. The knock-on effect that innovation in the field and innovation in Indian IPR law and policy has in the world is also something that needs to be considered in India's IP policy. As the British High Commissioner for India in 2012 wrote in his introduction to a good breaking report commissioned by NESTA, 'India's potential as a laboratory for frugal innovations and the knock-on effect this could have not just on Indian or UK societies but on the global community' (Bound and Thornton 2012).

What about the two-way development of global IP law? 'India should market its distinctive expertise in frugal innovation to the world', says the NESTA report (Bound and Thornton 2012: 9). The Think Tank draft should have given precedence to formulating policy that envisions Indian IP policy taking the lead on reforming global innovation policy through this new policy. It is a lost opportunity in creating soft power, at the very least.

How is the grass-roots sector represented, promoted and envisioned for the future in IP policy? There are a number of obstacles that need to be removed, what does the IP policy do or say about that? In the Baseline draft, one of the first special focus areas was 'inclusive intellectual property'. Basheer and Pai put 'informal innovation' centre stage as it forms 90 per cent of the Indian economy and state that current IPR laws do not cater to this sector. They are of the view, and rightly so, that 'Data driven studies need to be undertaken to explore innovation and creativity within these informal sectors to locate the role of incentives, build on them and help create local, national and international markets for the creative segments within India's informal economy' (Basheer and Pai 2014).

Given that such products are not always using frontier technology, there are IP policy issues that arise in this field relating to both speeding up technology transfer and ensuring that efficient markets operate for the use of existing IP via licences where the 'frugal innovation makes use of old technology' (Greenhalgh 2013: 9). Otherwise dubbed as Asian innovation (*The Economist* 2012), the technology transfer provisions don't take cognisance of these developments demonstrating that the ethos of IP policy is different from the grass-roots concerns and needs of the Indian populace.

TRADITIONAL KNOWLEDGE

There is little mention of making the IP system responsive to TK in the proposed National IPR Policy. A harmonised IP policy in India should demand that the sequence be the other way round, for TK to adjust to IP. This was exactly the World Bank recommendation in its report on sustainable development and inclusive growth in 2007. It recommended that for TK

> a policy-oriented intellectual property rights think tank be set up, which will establish India's leadership on this issue, and reinforce its image as a country taking bold, novel approaches to developing its innovation system, and its burgeoning role as a leading player in the global knowledge economy.

The policy needs to provide leadership in fields that we are leaders of, such as in TK and farmers' rights. The setting up of an appellate body for People's Biodivesity Register (PBR) rights is a welcome move. The emphasis on development of TK and TCE is welcome, but the devil is in the detail. The changes in the final version which seem to signify that TK and TCE would be promoted for their own ends is promising. However, we come up against an IP culture, which is also promoted by the National IPR policy, which may not be conducive to the growth and development of TK and TCE for their own ends. How are we envisioning our leadership in these aspects as the future unfolds?

There is nothing on equity in the TK section in the policy (Sridevan et al. 2015: 33–34). The Indian policy, as it is being discussed as a special theme TK in the report, is a follower, rather than a leader on TK policy. It comes from rehearsed options on TK policy, without addressing it from scratch. The proposal for a new sui generis law on IP is a way forward, but how is it going to deal with the sticky issues that we know will arise, from observing the difficulties that WIPO is having putting together a global convention on TK, TCE and genetic resources. There are no indications as to innovation. We need, as the NESTA report suggested, 'a research programme on the 'science of science and innovation policy' and for it to 'be tailored to distinctive

Indian strengths: its focus should be on developing new metrics that capture the breadth of India's innovation (including in design, training, organizational or process innovation etc.) and provide new tools for charting India's progress' (Bound and Thornton 2012: 74–75).

Three options were discussed in the World Bank report. The first option seems to be favoured by the IPR policy. This is also the most fraught in terms of difficulties and, given the need for movement, might a more graduated process of protection be suited? The second option of the report was to institute a blanket license for TK IPR. This would reduce complexity of administration but will leave enough incentives for its protection and use. But issues around international coordination, enforcement and distribution will remain. However, this helps separate the urgent from the less urgent, which is a step better than the first option which is effectively a committee issue, rather than a grass-roots issue, and the positive step forward in the IPR policy would reach the frugal innovators yet.

An important change would be to make patents contingent on obtaining a TK non-objection certificate. This proposal on prior informed consent and benefit-sharing is languishing in the WTO–TRIPS committee and will be a major step change in recognising TK. There is no mention of this at all in the policy. A revival of this discussion will bring it closer to determining a more globally centralised and harmonised solution to TK appropriation, and more importantly put the onus of decisions on TK in the mainstream patent forums, which have effectively cut off some dead weight discussion by sectioning the innovation sectors into inventions and TK. Although this makes historical sense, this is causing major issues in the arena of IP policymaking and causing IP debates where countries like India have a lot at stake.

There is no mention of TCE in the special themes section titled 'Creative Industries' (Sridevan et al. 2015: 24–25). The model being aspired to is not sui generis but one of harmonisation with existing IP systems, hence the policy that is oblivious to the contribution of traditional culture to the modern world of entertainment and creative industries. There should be a recognition that traditional arts contribute hugely to the creative industries in India and they need to be fostered using a welfarist model of IP.

PHARMACEUTICAL INTELLECTUAL PROPERTY RIGHTS

India has come to be known as the pharmacy of the developing world. India's generic drug industry supplies medicines to large parts of the developing world and contributes significantly to the health of all. The patent laws in India are compliant with international law in this area while also seeking to utilise the flexibilities provided by international law in order to suit the development pace of the country. Tensions have been created with this approach as there is dissimilar global harmonisation of patent law, and it has resulted in a more welfarist (Pugatch 2011: 73)[1] model of IPRs, as opposed to a capitalist model of IPRs.

The new National IPR Policy can be seen as the latest effort by supporters of a capitalist model of IPRs to capture policy space. Thus far, it is the judiciary in India that has been at the forefront of determining IP policy by interpreting the scope of IP law. It will soon have to share the space with its parallel pillar of democracy, the executive, to determine and shape IP policy. The methods adopted by these two pillars of democracy are very different and the consequences are yet to be seen. Issues of transparency plague the executive initiative. The influence of pharmaceutical IP sector on the development of IP law is significant. To the outsider, it might seem like the tail wagging the dog, and that is just the case. This sector of innovation holds sway over IP frameworks not just in India but in other countries too.

The role of the Indian judiciary has been praised and recommended in other jurisdictions that are implementing the TRIPS Agreement 2005. The issue of access to medicines is an important debate in the implementation of patent law in India. India's patent laws have radically changed twice within the last hundred years. Following the Ayyangar report which criticised the then patent law for leading to very high

---

[1] See a discussion of three approaches to IP Social Welfare, Industrial and Global.

drug prices, the then government set about dismantling the patent system that existed from before the Indian Independence. It succeeded. But since the ratification of the TRIPS Agreement by India fears have surfaced that this is the beginning of the reversal of the Ayyangaresque policy on IP, especially in relation to patent law. The judiciary have, within the powers they exercise, taken an independent and unique approach in interpreting provisions of the TRIPS Agreement. A change, of course, seems to be looming on the horizon if the New IPR policy manages to create a different culture for interpretation of IP norms. Will the policy steer a course towards a pre-independence IP rights protection regime, which was shunned post-independence. Have we not been there and done that already?

In times of soaring prices and unaffordable health care, does the government not have an obligation to investigate, like the Nehru government did via the establishment of the Ayyangar commission? Instead all hands are on the deck for an IP policy that seeks to strengthen patent rights.

A passive compliance-oriented policy is not useful in addressing innovation challenges in India. The policy aims to foster predictability in the system. This should raise concerns. TRIPS is being continually interpreted in various jurisdictions and the flexibilities are necessary in order to respond to growing and evolving scenarios. Developed and developing countries perceive TRIPS as complete and unfinished products, respectively. In fact, there are more objections to TRIPS after its signature than there were before it came into existence. IP Policy needs to be shaped over time, more discursively, become tried and tested.

TRIPS-PLUS PROVISIONS: MISSION CREEP THROUGH PASSIVE POLICY?

India risks passivity in international negotiations with the new National IPR Policy. The reform of global IP, particularly in the context of flexibilities and in the WIPO, has only come from actively questioning existing IP regimes and their impact on growth, innovation and development. Whither India's voice when it would be following an

IP policy that is compliance-oriented rather than being world leading and development-oriented? After the failure of the WTO Doha Development Round, it is going to be harder to find policy space for discussing development issues in IP and trade and this is detrimental for IP policy. But then again, WTO cannot to do very much if states do not actually initiate what they want (Lester 2016), hence having robust policies at the State level becomes even more important. With WTO being a victim of its own success, various regional and bilateral forces are at play in the trade, innovation and liberalisation arena. This is a further need to develop robust indigenous policy.

The section containing Objective 3: Legal and Legislative Framework (Sridevan et al. 2015: 9) of the IPR Think Tank report reads like a student textbook discussing IP rationale rather than providing a policy stand. It merely states 'To have strong and effective laws with regard to IP rights that are consistent with national priorities and international obligations and which balance the interests of rights owners with public interest' (Sridevan et al. 2015: 9). The specifics are missing, prioritisation and urgency are missing from the policy statement. Granted that the policy is a long-term vision, it should build on current situation, and suggest solutions and directions. While it is specific about the past (being TRIPS compliant and using flexibilities) when it comes to the future, even the near future, it loses specificity. There is just mention of more research needed (Sridevan et al. 2015: 10). Compare this with what could have been achieved had had the original IP Think Tank continued. The original IP Think Tank was going to offer 'guiding principles while negotiating with international partners for free trade agreements' (Dutta 2014). In Section 3.3 of the new Think Tank's IPR Policy, the objective is to 'engage constructively in the negotiation of international treaties and agreements in consultation with stakeholders' (Sridevan et al. 2015: 10). The former approach provides a basis rooted in the rule of law and would act as a bulwark against political exigencies that arise as part of negotiations. In the same vein, a commitment to 'ensuring TRIPS compliance and avoiding any TRIPS-plus measures, purely at the behest of a trading partner' (Dutta 2014) would be a welcome policy objective.

The National IPR Policy is parrot-like in its insistence on no TRIPS-plus provision, but might that come about in another guise? Nothing about the policy is reassuring that it would not do so.

CONCLUSION

India's IP Policy is a passive compliance-oriented policy, uninspiring and populated by 'to-do' lists, rather than taking a principled policy stand on protecting national interests. The glimpses one gets of policy are nothing new. In the main, it seems like India is starting from a clean slate through this policy, or is the intention to wipe the slate clean? The measures taken to harmonise the Indian IPRs system with that of external international rights systems is adopted unquestioningly, leaving little room for the recognition of stark incompatibilities and incongruence between sui generis systems and mainstream IP. If eventually it is the judiciary that is then going to decide on incompatibilities and incongruences, and are left to perform the balancing act, then what direction can the policy give in this regard? It is a lost opportunity, at least as matters stand at the time of writing.

While any attempt to indicate improvements in the current Indian national policy must necessarily be tentative if not speculative, it is clear that the public debate—in a country noted for its expertise in and widespread use of information technology—must be widened and strengthened without delay. Elected governments can play a significant role here, at least in initiating a better-informed public discourse, as has been shown in Chapter 3. The involvement of the Indian public—in their role as the voters who make Indian democracy work in its most elemental ways—by turning out to vote at every level of the Indian state deserves nothing less.

REFERENCES

Basheer, S., and Y. Pai. 2014, 3 December. *Indian Intellectual Property Policy, a Baseline Draft.* Available via Swaraj Paul Barooah. *The Draft IP Policy That's MIA, & More on the Think Tank.* Available at http://spicyip.com/2014/12/the-draft-ip-policy-thats-mia-more-on-the-think-tank.html (accessed on 12 January 2016).

Biadgleng, E. T. 2007. *Analysis of the Role of South–South Cooperation to Promote Governance on Intellectual Property, Rights and Development*. Geneva: South Centre.

Boldrin, M., and D. K. Levine. 2007. *Against Intellectual Monopoly*. Available at http://levine.sscnet.ucla.edu/general/intellectual/againstnew.htm (accessed on 14 July 2014).

Bound, K., and I. Thornton. 2012. Our Frugal Future: Lessons from India's Innovation System. London: National Endowment for Science, Technology and the Arts (NESTA).

Brougher, J. T. 2013. 'Evergreening Patents: The Indian Supreme Court Rejects Patenting of Incremental Improvements'. *Journal of Commercial Biotechnology* 19 (3): 54–58.

Dutta, S. 2014, 12 December. 'Breach of Promise on IPR Policy?' *The Frontline*.

Dwivedi, G., S. Hallihosur, and L. Rangan. 2010. 'Evergreening: A Deceptive Device in Patent Rights'. *Technology in Society* 32 (4): 324–330.

Ganapathi, J., and V. Pullaī. 2015. 'Intellectual Property Rights and the Ancient Indian Perspective'. *Space and Culture* 3 (2): 15–24.

Greenhalgh, C. 2013. 'Science, Technology, Innovation and IP in India—New Directions and Prospects'. Discussion Paper Series, Department of Economics, University of Oxford.

Lester, S. 2016. 'Is the Doha Round Over? The WTO's Negotiating Agenda for 2016 and Beyond'. *Free Trade Bulletin* 64 (11): 3.

Liao, Rebecca. 2019. 'IP Rights: The Pressing Need for Standards'. *Democracy* (Spring). Available at https://democracyjournal.org/magazine/52/ip-rights-the-pressing-need-for-standards (accessed on 14 June 2019).

McKenna, Mark P. 2006. 'Intellectual Property, Privatization and Democracy: A Response to Professor Rose'. *St Louis University Law Journal* 50: 829–842. Available at https://scholarship.law.nd.edu/law.faculty_scholarship/266 (accessed on 14 June 2019).

Mishra, A. R. 2015, 24 April. 'Need to Bring Our Patent Laws on Par with Global Standards: Narendra Modi'. *LiveMint*. Available at http://www.livemint.com/Politics/vW6RzcArtqHi6tUNFyoMqO/Need-to-bring-our-patent-laws-on-par-with-global-standards.html (accessed on 24 February 2016).

Ncube, Caroline B. 2016. *Intellectual Property Policy, Law and Administration in Africa: Exploring Continental and Sub-Regional Co-Operation*. Abingdon: Routledge.

Pugatch, M. P. 2011. 'Intellectual Property Policy Making in the 21st Century'. *The WIPO Journal: Analysis of Intellectual Property Issues* 3 (1): 71–81.

Sarkar, J., and S. Sarkar. 2015. *Corporate Social Responsibility in India—An Effort to Bridge the Welfare Gap*. Mumbai: Indira Gandhi Institute of Development Research.

Singh, A., and P. Verma. 2014. 'CSR@ 2%: A New Model of Corporate Social Responsibility in India'. *International Journal of Academic Research in Business and Social Sciences* 4 (10): 6990.

Sridevan, P., P. Singh, N. K. Sabharwal, P. Bhargava, R. Srinivasan, and U. P. Pandit. 2015. *National IPR Policy* (Final Draft). New Delhi: Department for Promotion of Industry and International Trade.

The Economist. 2012, 24 March. 'Asian Innovation'. Schumpeter Column. Westminster: The Economist.

Tyfield, David. 2010. 'Neoliberalism, Intellectual Property and the Global Knowledge Economy'. In *The Rise and Fall of Neoliberalism: The Collapse of an Economic Order?* Edited by Kean Birch and Vlad Mykhnenko, 60–76. London: Zed Books.

World Trade Organization. 1994, 15 April. Agreement on Trade-Related Aspects of Intellectual Property Rights Marrakesh Agreement Establishing the World Trade Organization. Annex 1C. *The Legal Texts: The Results of the Uruguay Round of Multilateral Trade Negotiations 320 (1999)*, 1869 U.N.T.S. 299, 33 I.L.M. 1197. Geneva: World Trade Organization.

Dutfield, G., and Sutharsanen, U. 2005. 'Harmonisation or Differentiation in Intellectual Property Protection? The Lessons of History'. *Prometheus* 23 (2): 131–147.

Reichman, J.H., and Dreyfuss, R.C. 'Harmonization without Consensus: Critical Reflections on Drafting a Substantive Patent Law Treaty'. *Duke Law Journal* 57 (1): 85–130.

Subramanian, S. 2015. 'The Changing Dynamics of the Global Intellectual Property Legal Order: Emergence of a "Network Agenda"?' *International and Comparative Law Quarterly* 108 (4).

Stewart, H. *After Doha: Why the Negotiations Are Doomed and What We Should Do about It.* http://www.theguardian.com/business/2015/dec/20/doha-is-dead-hopes-for-fairer-global-trade-shouldnt-die-too (accessed 22 September 2019).

'Institutional Developments in the WTO: Recent Trends and the Challenge Going Forward'. *European Yearbook of International Economic Law* 6: 375–389.

Chapter 14

The Practice of Democracy
Chennai Floods, 2015

Arappor Iyakkam

No one can forget images from the Chennai Floods, 2015: neck-high water, boats on the roads, the airport flooded—powerful visual imagery which moved the nation. Lakhs of residents were affected, hundreds of lives lost and thousands of crores worth of property was destroyed. While there was unprecedented rain, heavily concentrated into a few days, the Chennai flood was not a natural disaster, but a man-made one resulting from years of neglect of the natural drainage and waterbody systems of Chennai, Kanchipuram and Tiruvallur district of Tamil Nadu, in all consisting of more than 3,600 waterbodies and four rivers.

The Chennai flood of 2015 was an inflection point in invoking the civic consciousness of Chennai's citizens. The immediate aftermath of the flood brought about an upswelling of humanitarian efforts, but the effect did not stop there. It was a wake-up call to the citizens to realise the extent to which mechanisms of urban governance and water management had broken down, about the catastrophic impact of citizen apathy and the need for common people to stay aware and continuously engaged in the practice of democracy. In the days and months after the flood, civil society groups came together as never before and began making concerted efforts to understand water management in Chennai and take proactive steps to reclaim the waterbodies of the city through various democratic tools and processes such as Right to Information, Social Audits, Awareness and Outreach, Public Hearings, Continuous Engagement with elected representatives and the bureaucracy and non-violent, peaceful protests.

This chapter also documents some of the successes that the people of Chennai have achieved by coming together and exercising their democratic duties including restoration of the Villivakkam Lake, the neglect of which resulted in heavy flooding of the areas around it in 2015. The chapter will demonstrate how building vibrant civil societies makes us a functional democracy, which is key to solving issues of the people—be it flood, drought or anything else.

PRELUDE TO THE FLOOD

Background of the City

Tamil Nadu is a fast urbanising state and most of the stress of this fast urbanisation has been on its capital city, Chennai. The reason for this urbanisation is twofold: visionary state leadership after independence created strong primary education and health infrastructure, far ahead of most other states in the country. At the same time, with reference to rural employment and agriculture, there was a natural disadvantage of the lack of perennial rivers, and a sustained neglect by the government in building a strong extension system for agriculture. This combination encouraged generations of educated citizens to move towards the capital city for opportunities (aspirational migration) and, simultaneously, there was a constant flow of poorer sections that moved into the city due to poverty and agrarian distress.

Chennai is a city known for its natural drainage and water harvesting structures with three large rivers flowing parallel to each other, namely the Kosasthalaiyar in the North, Coovum in the middle and Adyar in the South. The Buckingham canal was constructed by the British, extending from North Chennai to South Chennai during the famine of 1855, in order to transport food. The canal cuts across all the three rivers, and therefore acts as a buffer, carrying excess water during floods from one river to the other (Figure 14.1).

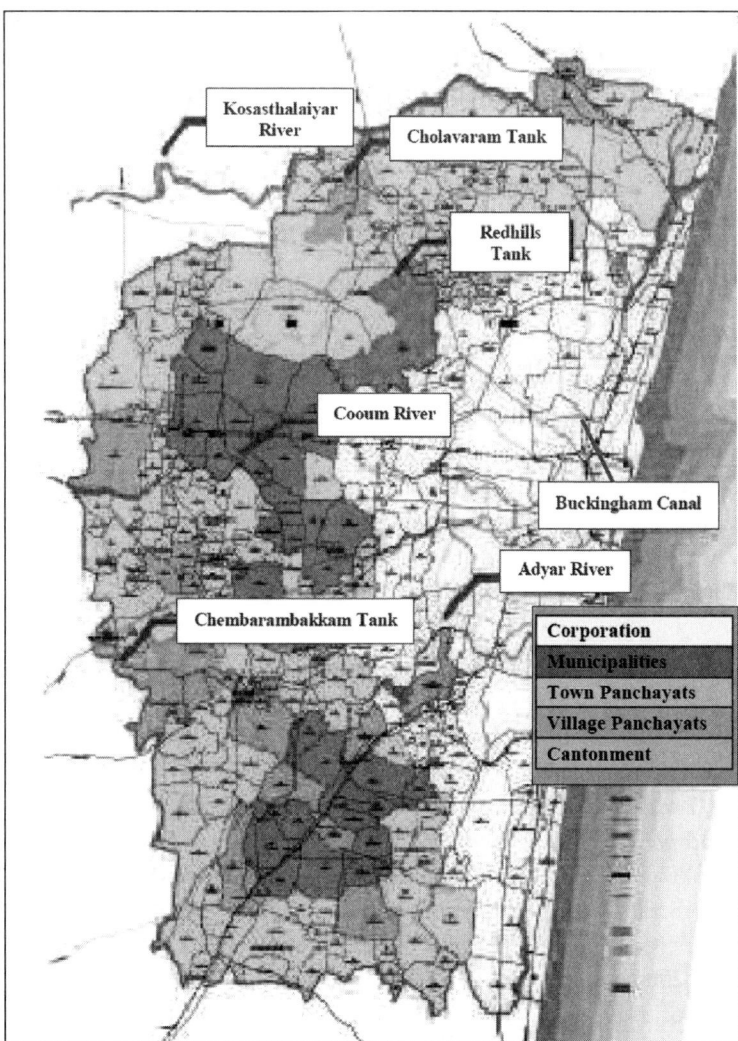

Figure 14.1 *River and Tanks in Chennai Metropolitan Area*

Source: Cited in Report of the Comptroller and Auditor General of India on Performance Audit of Flood Management and Response in Chennai and its Suburban Areas (Report no. 4 of 2017).

Disclaimer: This image is for representation purposes only.

Over the last several decades, people who migrated to the city due to distress settled along the banks of these rivers. They found occupation in the nearby areas, and lived there through multiple generations, but without formal recognition of their land tenure or entitlement to civic amenities. Over time, these settlements and communities began to be viewed as encroachers, and a strong mainstream narrative was built up, that they were barriers in the natural drainage system and needed to be removed.

However, the real danger of flooding is caused by large concrete, institutional and residential encroachments, both by the Governments of the day and by private players. These buildings mushroomed dangerously close to rivers and have encroached upon Chennai's waterbodies and watercourse *porombokes* (shared-use community resources) in the last two decades. These buildings were mammoth barriers in the natural drainage system and, as warned by experts, caused much more damage than the much-maligned thatched roofed slum households, which would wash away in strong waters anyway.

FAILURE OF URBAN GOVERNANCE

Chennai faced a heavy flood in 2005. It was a clear sign of the misplaced urban development that was ignoring the ecology of the city. However, the Tamil Nadu Government's learning, response and actions after the flood were exactly opposite to what they should have been. Instead of taking systemic efforts to secure, preserve and maintain rivers and waterbodies, the Tamil Nadu Government came up with a Government Order (G.O.) (M.S) 854 of Revenue in the immediately succeeding year, 2006, to regularise encroachments on all Government poramboke lands of an age greater than 10 years to an extent of 4 cents in rural areas, 2.5 cents in municipal areas and 2 cents in Corporation limits. This was introduced as a one-time scheme for 6 months but was extended year after year, and in effect handed over *pattas* or title deeds of waterbodies to the politician-real-estate nexus. Further, by G.O. (M.S) no. 34, this 10-year timeline was brought down to a mere 5 years. Politicians made this a full-time business. Their modus operandi was simple: encroaching upon waterbodies, and then collecting money from real estate lobbies and ordinary citizens to get the occupants pattas under the scheme.

If this rampant institutionalised encroachment was flourishing on the one side, there was more folly on the other side. The Chennai Metropolitan Development Authority (CMDA), which released its second master plan for the city in 2008, did not even have a direct system to check if the building for which plan approval is given is on a watercourse poramboke or not. As a result of all this, the city's waterbodies went through severe stress as a direct result of the actions of the state.

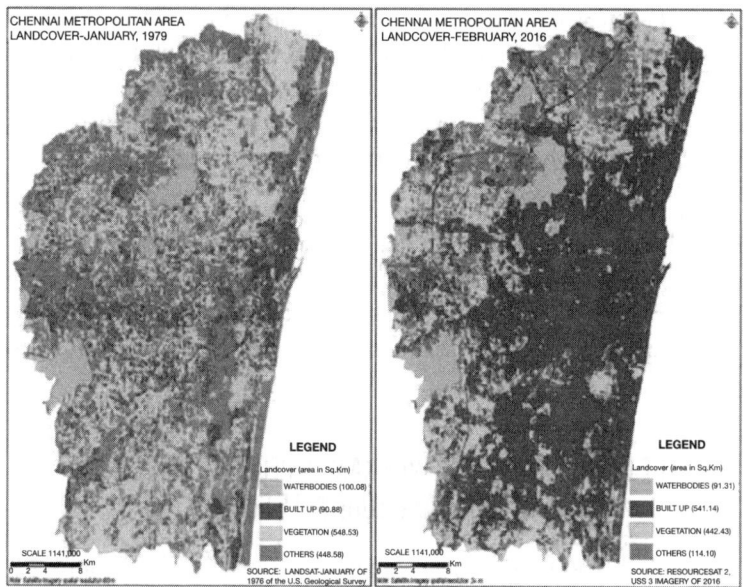

Digitally Analysed Satellite Images of Chennai Metropolitan Area (CMA)

Source: Cited in the Report of the Comptroller and Auditor General of India on Performance Audit of Flood Management and Response in Chennai and its Suburban Areas (Report no. 4 of 2017).

Disclaimer: These images are for representation purposes only.

MALADMINISTRATION OF FUNDS

Simultaneously, given the disastrous impact of the 2005 floods, there was heavy allocation of funds for flood mitigation. Under the Jawaharlal Nehru National Urban Renewal Mission (JNNURM), ₹1,448 crores

(₹14.48 billion) were allocated in 2009 for flood mitigation efforts in Chennai. If spent appropriately, these funds could have gone a long way in securing the city against the risk of flooding. However, the Comptroller and Auditor General of India (CAG) found in its audit report that there has been delay and defective planning by the State administration, leading to ill preparation for future floods.

Apart from this, a citizen's audit of the South Buckingham canal found glaring misappropriation of funds as well. Between 2011 and 2014, the canal was supposed to be expanded from 40 m width to 100 m all the way from Okkiyam Maduvu to Muthukkadu, where it reaches the sea. However, it was only extended to less than 60 m at most places. The poor work has not even been penalised and payments have been made in full to the contractors for their work.

All these administrative failures have collectively contributed towards the failure of maintenance of rivers, waterbodies and rainwater harvesting structures; in 2015, the threat of flooding was looming large with clear warning signs that the State Government —it seems alone—failed to see. The disaster that was man-made was waiting to happen.

THE BIRTH OF ARAPPOR IYAKKAM, A PEOPLE'S MOVEMENT FOR A JUST AND EQUITABLE SOCIETY

Tamil Nadu had become increasingly notorious for its corrupt leadership, and its audacious attempts to offer cash for votes, becoming known as the 'Thirumangalam Formula' (Law Commission of India 2015: 9–10). Also, large amounts of public funds that should have been used for infrastructure, employment generation and development were diverted for other uses (freebies, ushering in an era of populist politics in the state).

The aspiration for a vibrant civil society, alongside the anger arising from the utter failure in governance and the sad state of urban civic infrastructure, prompted a core group of young residents of Chennai to come together in August 2015 and form a peoples' movement,

Arappor Iyakkam (API). *Arappor* means 'the just fight' in Tamil, and the group adopted the creation of a just and equitable society as its primary vision. Realising the importance of building a vibrant civil society as the bedrock of a successful participative democracy, API stated as its key mission statements 'Focus on building a large, democratic people's movement' and 'By increasing citizen participation in governance, work towards eradicating the disconnect and power imbalance between pillars of democracy and the common people'.

The group began its efforts to build a grass-roots movement. The first priority was to lay the foundation for a transparent and corruption-free state and so, the group, along with legal experts, drafted a model Lokayukta bill for the state. API simultaneously conducted 'Know Your Rights' sessions for people in the city. These messages resonated with the civil society in Chennai, and soon, the API office was bustling with scores of volunteers working on programmes of research, outreach and civic engagement. And then the flood hit Chennai.

THE 2015 FLOOD AND ITS IMMEDIATE AFTERMATH

The first spell of huge rains came on 15 November as the result of low pressure formation in the Bay of Bengal. Within a 24-hour period, the city and its outskirts in Kanchipuram and Tiruvallur experienced almost 370 mm rainfall. The reservoirs on the outskirts of Chennai, such as Poondi, Chembarambakkam, Cholavaram and Redhills, were already at 85 per cent of their capacity. Normal life came to a standstill, with many parts of Chennai experiencing severe flooding. Low lying areas of the city, such as Mudichur near Tambaram, were under water, with residents shifting to a Government-organised camp in a nearby school for a few days.

These rains and floods were a clear warning sign to the admin-istration about their unpreparedness to handle the situation. And the worst was yet to come. The meteorological department as well as private weather forecasters such as the Tamil Nadu Weatherman clearly predicted a heavy spell of rain on 1 and 2 December 2015 well in advance. A responsible and agile State Government should

Table 14.1 *Normal and Actual Rainfall (in Millimetre)*

District	12 to 18 November 2015		19 to 25 November 2015		26 November to 2 December 2015	
	Normal Rainfall	Actual Rainfall	Normal Rainfall	Actual Rainfall	Normal Rainfall	Actual Rainfall
Chennai	104.9	449.9	82.0	217.5	53.4	347.3
Kanchee puram	59.8	452.3	66.6	238.6	46.0	459.0
Tiruvallur	67.3	414.0	54.5	180.1	41.1	342.6

Source: Cited in the Report of the Comptroller and Auditor General of India on Performance Audit of Flood Management and Response in Chennai and its Suburban Areas (Report no. 4 of 2017).

have foreseen the dangers of potential overflowing of the reservoirs, given that they were already close to 85 per cent of their capacity. The State should have made arrangements to mobilise a fully coordinated workforce under the State Disaster Management Authority with an integrated command centre, provide sufficient physical resources such as boats and other equipment for rescue operations, make pre-announcements and evacuations in low lying areas and set up proper camps and proper food and clothing reserve for the people affected. However, no such preparations were made by the State Government.

In a span of 24 hours, between 8.30 a.m. on 1 December 2015 and 8.30 a.m. on 2 December 2015, the city received rainfall of 490 mm. The low lying areas of the entire city got entirely submerged in water. Some of the worst affected were:

- Areas around the rich Pallikaranai Marshland lying almost at sea level.
- Areas in Mudichur in Tambaram lying between the source of Adyar River and the connecting point of Chembarambakkam reservoir to the Adyar River.

- Porur, Mugalivakkam and Ramapuram areas between the Porur Lake and the Adyar River.
- Low lying areas of SIDCO Nagar in Villivakkam.

The people in these areas were left inundated for days. Pictures of water filling the second runway of the Airport, leaving flights grounded, became symbolic of the flood.

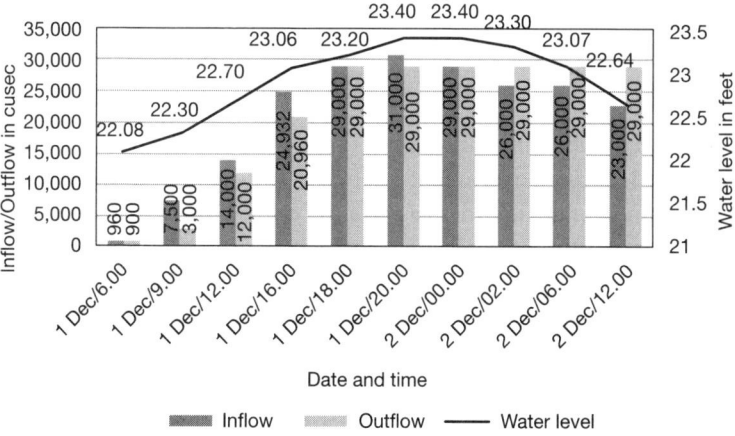

Inflow, Outflow and Water Level on 1 and 2 December 2015

Source: Cited in the Report of the Comptroller and Auditor General of India on Performance Audit of Flood Management and Response in Chennai and its Suburban Areas (Report no. 4 of 2017).

To make matters worse, the flood was worsened on 2 December, when the Government decided to suddenly open the sluice gates at Chembarambakkam Lake while it was still raining heavily. The breakdown of governance was visible. The Public Works Department (PWD) Engineer who should have taken a decision to release water from the lake before the heavy rains started did not do so as he was waiting for a go-ahead from the PWD head. The PWD Secretary and Minister were in turn waiting for a confirmation from the Chief Minister. This breakdown in governance led to heavy outflow of water from Chembarambakkam on 2 December 2015 submerging almost the entire city. And this time, the flood spared no one. Flood waters entered the homes of the upper middle class and the rich, it entered the homes of the IAS officers who had been colluding, either actively or by their silence, in perpetuating the misplaced policies of the Government. The 2015 flood was a great leveller, but it was also severely tragic—more than 500 lives were lost, lakhs of people displaced and losses to the tune of several thousand crores of rupees occurred on a single day. And the Government was still woefully unprepared to deal with the disaster it had created.

THE RISE OF CIVIL SOCIETY

It has happened time and again that wherever the Government has failed, Non-Government agencies, and people at large, have pitched in strongly in order to abate the crisis. History repeated itself in Chennai. On one side, the Government was struggling with its machinery, and getting its act coordinated. The sanitation workers on the ground were working strenuously but the lack of planning at the top had left citizens at many places stranded for help. There was a widespread power shutdown. Telephone and Internet services were largely down too.

On the other side, the civil society of Chennai responded as it had never done never before. Right from 3 December, various volunteers from the city's unaffected areas, from all over the state and from elsewhere, started rescue and relief operations. The people of North Chennai (which was not severely affected) organised boats, and several victims were rescued from their submerged homes. Supplies such as water, food, medicines and clothing, even oxygen bags were mobilised and distributed to the places of need. Surprisingly, people who were just rescued also jumped in to rescue others. Such was the spirit of Chennai. The spontaneous outpouring of compassion, unity and cooperation of Chennai's volunteers has been well received, and their efforts helped in mitigating the effects of the flood—lives were lost and property destroyed, but things would have been far worse if civil society had not responded.

API is not a development NGO. Nor did it have any experience in organising relief efforts. But it could not remain a mute spectator when its worst nightmares about the effects of maladministration had come true. While individual volunteers were already out in the field, the need of the hour was for API, as a movement, to join the rescue effort. For a start, our volunteers observed the relief operations in affected areas for a few hours, and noted that despite the best intentions, distribution was chaotic and, many times, the same people got relief items from different groups. Also, people who could not push through the crowd or wait in the queues ended up with nothing. In order to avoid these problems, API's relief effort followed a structured process. First, relief materials were packed into separate kits—family kit (blankets, torches, basic food supplies, etc.); women's' kit (clothing, sanitary products, etc.), babies' kit (clothing, milk powder, etc.). Then, a group of volunteers would go to the affected area, talk to the locals there (especially women and youth) and organise for each family to be given a token of identification. The total number of tokens issued would be tracked. Holding the token would ensure that the family got relief supplies without any anxiety about jumping the line, or materials running out. Thereafter, the local coordinators would fill in details about each family in the community—number of men, women, elders, children, etc. This would ensure independent, local volunteers vetting the list. A time would be fixed for distribution of relief, and all residents would be informed in advance to assemble. API's truck, with a mix of all kits, would be stationed, and each family would be given material appropriate to their list, without long queues or crowding. This system of census, tokens and local community involvement worked beautifully—no one was left out, everyone got what they needed and distribution efforts were seamless and hassle-free. This was a small contribution in the larger civil society mobilisation for flood relief.

BEYOND RELIEF—FOCUS ON REHABILITATION?

After the immediate relief efforts, there were several questions before civil society. Should we focus on rehabilitation of poor households? Should we adopt communities whose homes and livelihoods were destroyed and raise funds to help them? Should we work on restoration of a few waterbodies as a group? These were the common questions and a matter of extensive deliberation before different civil society groups and each one decided to proceed with what they were comfortable. Groups such as the Environmentalist Foundation of India were working on restoration of waterbodies. Other Non-Governmental agencies took up rebuilding community homes and livelihoods.

For many of us at API, we appreciated the efforts of other groups, but were not convinced to work on either of these. It was clear that this was a man-made disaster caused primarily due to the misplaced policies of the Government, abysmally poor urban planning and very probably the vested interests of corrupt public servants. We believed that driving the Government towards protecting the ecology of the city could not happen without citizen's active and sustained participation in Governance. Today, the nexus between the real estate business, politicians and bureaucrats runs deep, and there is no way citizens can remain apolitical about this and expect the Government of the day to reform itself suddenly.

Urban waterbodies possess a different character. Rural waterbodies have daily, direct usage by farmers and others for irrigation and other purposes and therefore there is self-interest of the community to protect the waterbody. However, in the urban context, a drastic distance had been systematically created between the waterbodies, and the public who depended on them—because these waterbodies were no longer used for traditional purposes, such as irrigation and drinking water, and also because the public had become disengaged from the maintenance and preservation of the waterbodies themselves. People have become completely unrelated to the waterbodies around them as they do not see a direct benefit. In fact, in many areas waterbodies have become 'invisible' to the communities around them, because they are just tracts of land with overgrown flora, or have become indistinguishable from the surrounding topography of buildings. Encroachers have taken great advantage of this disengagement over the last several decades.

INCREASED REALISATION OF CITIZENS

The flood of 2015 provided that context to the citizens in the city, as water entered most of the households. It was a direct lesson to the citizens of the city that if they do not take care of the waterbodies and waterways around them, the apathy will affect them directly. Failure to regularly and actively engage in Governance and failure to question our elected representatives and bureaucracy would lead to these disasters, and no one would be spared. There was an awakening that the duty of responsible citizens is not just to vote once in 5 years, but to participate directly in the functioning of democracy every day. Unless our democracy moves from a superficial democracy towards a functional one, the rights of the people are not going to be recognised and ensured. However, this increased realisation was still only among a section of volunteers as most of them went back to their usual daily chores after the initial relief efforts. For those who resolved to work for a change, we needed to find ways for them to engage in the governance of waterbodies and waterways. The Government of the day has generally been non-transparent, non-engaging and less sensitive to citizens' grievances. To attract the attention of the Government, and make them take the required action, would require creative and comprehensive approaches.

STRATEGY FOR CITIZEN ENGAGEMENT IN GOVERNANCE

Having resolved to make governance work, we found that the real challenge was to identify meaningful ways in which citizens can engage in a democracy. In an urban set-up, where there is near-zero public participation in policy and governance, the imperative to push through citizen engagement required different tools of democracy to be activated. API, over the course of 24 months after the flood, tried, tested and used several different tools to increase citizens' participation in governance and enforcing transparency and accountability. Even though much of this is still work-in-progress, the following sections will provide some ideas on different ways in which citizens can directly participate in a democracy and some of the successes achieved, and the learning gained through these efforts.

INFORMATION AND RTI

The first and foremost challenge for us was to eliminate informational asymmetry. We needed to understand and assimilate the information about the waterbodies around using great detail. Lack of information is a great deterrent for citizens to not engage in a democracy, and it is a great strategy of those who wish to keep citizens in the dark. After the floods, there was a lot of initial anger and several groups wanted to get involved to question the Government and do something about the floods. But a lot of them faded away as they were not clear on how to question or how to engage with the Government to solve the problem. We at API decided that even if it takes time, it is of utmost importance to systematically understand the reasons behind the flood, and work on flood prevention and mitigation, including restoration of waterbodies. As we did not have the bandwidth to cover the entire city, we decided to focus one few key areas that were severely affected. We selected four places, namely Villivakkam, the Porur–Ramapuram stretch, the Pallavaram–Chromepet stretch and areas around Pallikaranai Marshland.

The Government was not willing to release any data or maps of the waterbodies. So, we had to rely on available resources—we started with the US Army map of the city of 1954, Topo maps of 1972 and the Google Earth maps between 2000 and 2015. An open-source call for information from residents living around these areas was given. We overlaid the maps one over the other to visualise how these areas have undergone changes over the last few years, and it was clear that waterbodies in each of these areas were heavily encroached over time.

Apart from these, the RTI Act is a powerful tool in the hands of citizens. RTI is considered fundamental to the freedom of speech and expression, as lack of information denies the right of citizens to question the Government of the day. Therefore, the RTI Act was passed in 2005 and has transferred power directly into the hands of citizens.

We encouraged citizens to use this act to get information about the waterbodies around them. Centrally, we also collected maps of the waterbodies in many of these areas. This research helped citizens understand the fundamentals about some of the areas that were flooded. For example, research revealed that Mudichur got flooded because the area is at the bottom of a gradient on either side of it—the source of the Adyar River on one side and the connecting point of Chembarambakkam Lake into Adyar River on the other side. In the first place, the government should not have allowed urban settlements in such low lying areas, which had earlier been floodplains of the river. Areas around Pallikaranai were heavily flooded because Pallikaranai and its surrounding areas are almost at or below sea level. Poor understanding of urban ecology, disjointed planning of urban development and handing over of the watercourse porombokes to real estate lobbies have resulted in severe damage in the area. Online research and maps collected through RTIs showed that there are several lakes connecting Pallavaram to Pallikaranai, but now this network does not exist.

The initial information and fundamental understanding about each of these waterbodies was dissipated to the larger set of around 200 volunteers of API through a seminar organised in June 2016, and we issued a call for formation of a strong team to work on creating a 'Flood-Safe Chennai'.

CITIZEN'S AUDIT OF WATERBODIES

The next step was that volunteers visited each of these places directly and observed the physical reasons for the flood and conduct a citizens' audit of the waterways including the inlets and outlets to and from the waterbodies. In each area, a local volunteer was assigned to lead, and they completed a pre-visit and drew up a working plan for the audit. On the appointed day, several volunteers gathered to participate in the social audit. They walked around the place to gather more information about the waterbody, talked to residents around the waterbody and understood the flow of water during the flood. This audit was an eye-opener to most volunteers as they would have passed the same place almost every day but would not have noticed the devastating condition of the waterbody. They summarised their findings and observation in a report and came up with detailed recommendations for making the area flood-proof. Around 200 volunteers participated in this exercise across the city. This was heartening, as it has never been an easy task to mobilise volunteers to spend time on civic issues. But the effect of the flood in 2015 was such that there were huge number of volunteers wanting to do something for the waterways and their restoration.

A startling story emerged out of the Villivakkam audit. The entire SIDCO Nagar area of Villivakkam, adjacent to Villivakkam Lake, was stranded in the floods for more than 10 days during the December 2015 floods. In the 1970s, Villivakkam Lake had an extent of around 214 acres but it had been reduced to almost 39 acres by the time of the 2015 flood. This was because the entire SIDCO Nagar area was built right on the lake by changing the watercourse poromboke over the years. However, in 2005, when Chennai received more rain than 2015, residents asserted that the area did not see such a severe devastation. So it was clear to the volunteers who visited that some developments over the last few years seem to have caused the major devastation in 2015. Detailed conversations with the residents around the lake brought out the reasons. It emerged that the Chennai Metro Rail's earth excavated in Thirumangalam had been brought and dumped into the Villivakkam Lake, with the permission of Chennai Metropolitan Water Supply and Sewerage Board (CMWSSB), which was responsible for maintaining the lake. The excavated earth covered almost half the lake, thereby blocking the inlets from the SIDCO Nagar area into the lake. The height of the dump was anywhere between 10 and 20 feet. This dumping had taken place in 2013 and 2014. When the local residents had questioned the dumping, they were told by the administration that there is a Mofussil bus terminus that was being planned in the area, which would make it a bustling hub, and would only work in favour of the residents, and enhance the values of their properties.

The audit was not only useful for the volunteers; it was eye-opening for many local residents too, as they were not completely aware of the reasons for the 2015 flooding. People living near the lake explained how the water was flowing in the opposite direction rather than into the lake during the floods. The dump of excavated earth made sure that no water could enter into the lake, and so, the entire water from the rains flooded the SIDCO Nagar area. Ironically, at the same time as the dumping was going on, the Chennai Corporation had been spending thousands of crores every year on building storm water drains to drain the excess rainwater into the nearby waterbody throughout the city. The citizens explained how the storm water drain that should have taken the flood water into the nearby channel Otteri Nullah was choked with silt and garbage. While such storm water drains were constructed in the city at many places, they were hardly maintained at all. No desilting was done prior to the 2015 monsoon to clear the silt and garbage in these storm water drains, consequently, the storm water drains were completely non-functional during the floods.

Each leg of the audit brought about area-specific causes for the flooding, but it also emerged that there were some general overarching reasons common to all places as well. In Porur, it was clear that the development in the last decade meant that the channel connecting the Porur lake to the Adyar river was blocked at several places with encroachments and the Channel was completely filled with silt. The Pallavaram–Pallikaranai stretch had a series of waterbodies, namely Pallavaram Periya Eri, Puthur Eri, Nanmangalam Eri, Keezhkattalai Eri and Narayanapuram Eri. The wonderful drainage and water harvesting system that had been envisioned was that water had to fill in each of these lakes before entering the Pallikaranai Marshland. However, on one side, citizens who performed the audit noticed that all the channels connecting these waterbodies have been heavily encroached and mismanaged, and that some of the lakes like Pallavaram Periya Eri have been used by the Government as a dump yard for solid waste. Some residents came forward during the audit and showed us how a local politician built a badminton court in the middle of the channel connecting these lakes, thus blocking the flow of water.

On the other side, Pallikaranai Marshland itself has dwindled over the years and part of the Marshland has been used by the Corporation as a dump yard for solid waste. As a result, citizens were able to witness how water that had to flow through these channels and fill each of the lakes was not able to because of the massive encroachments and how, as a result, water entered the houses in several places around Narayanapuram and Keezhkattalai Eri. Also, the water storage capacity of Pallikaranai Marshland had dwindled, and the water flowing out from Pallikaranai Marshland to the Buckingham canal was not fast enough to act as an effective drain, because of the inadequate expansion of Buckingham canal under the JNNURM project due to corruption (as explained earlier). Instead of expanding to 100 m, at several places, they had only expanded to 50 or 60 m which was visible both during the audit and through tracking of Google Earth images over the years in which this work was carried out.

We have mentioned only a few findings here. Many citizens were shocked that they have missed observing these issues that were happening right under their noses in their local communities. The citizen's audit was revealing and empowering, as it gave confidence to the citizens that it is not just the experts who can understand these issues. Citizens realised that water management is not rocket science. It is all about common sense, and if we take the effort to understand it, each of us can.

The audit also gave citizens an understanding of how our own neglect of these waterways has led to a terrible tragedy, how these rainwater harvesting structures are a lifeline for the city's sustenance, and what needs to be done in the immediate future to avert a similar flood. The audit teams started consolidating their findings into a report and formal complaint for the Government to act upon.

PUBLIC HEARING

Representatives of citizen groups from each of the areas where audits were conducted met after the audit and shared their findings. It was agreed that a common but powerful message needs to go to the Government to push them to act. It was decided to send official representations to all concerned authorities. However, it was clear that this would not be enough, as the Government could simply ignore all complaints and representations, as they very often do. There was a strong need for the citizens to come together in a large group and collectively voice out the concerns to the Government loud and clear, in a way that the Government cannot ignore.

Governments generally conduct what is called a Public Hearing, to provide a platform to voice their concerns, whenever a new project is to be initiated in their community. The public hearing gives citizens the much-needed power in a democracy where they are directly heard by the District Collector regarding any project that will affect them, whether positively or negatively. As we were ideating on ways to make the Government take note of our report, we decided to organise a similar Public Hearing for waterbodies, but this time initiated by the citizens of the city. Apart from the citizens who participated in the audit, we gave an open call to the citizens of Chennai to study the reasons for flooding in their respective areas, and come and present their concerns in the public hearing. The public hearing was named 'Kelu Chennai Kelu'. The word *Kelu* has two meanings in Tamil. One is to question and the other is to listen. So this public hearing was about citizens asking or questioning the officials on what needs to be done in their areas, and the Government listening to the demands of the common man. All the respective departments such as the Corporation of Chennai, CMWSSB and PWD officials, along with all the elected MLAs of the Chennai district were invited for the public hearing.

The public hearing organised on 28 August 2016 saw an overwhelming response from citizens. More than 1,200 people participated in the public hearing with resident groups from many parts of the city participating in this unique exercise. While officials from many Departments were not forthcoming to face the citizen's questions and this was conspicuous by their absence, it was heartening that the Chennai Corporation had sent their Executive Engineer to participate. The ruling party decided not to send any of their representatives and the main opposition party DMK sent their MLA from the Chepauk constituency to participate.

Apart from the officials and elected representatives, a citizens' panel comprising of key, eminent people with expertise in water management and urban governance was formed to hear the grievances of the public. The panel comprised a retired IAS officer, a senior lawyer of the Madras High Court, an academic expert and a retired engineer of the PWD. The experience and integrity of the members of the panel lent credibility and gravity to the hearing itself, and ensured that the peoples' representations would be handled appropriately. Officials from the Corporation and the opposition MLA sat through the hearing along with the citizen's panel and heard the issues that people faced in each area. The time was very relevant as the citizens gave clear directions to the Government on what they expected them to do before the next monsoon set in. The Executive Engineer of the Corporation, while responding to the citizens' concerns, promised that he had noted down all the points raised, and will work towards solving them within a period of 1 to 2 months. The Chepauk MLA promised the citizens that he would raise these concerns in the Assembly and share the feedback with his fellow MLAs for direct action on the ground.

The Public Hearing was a grand success—it was a demonstration that if people came together, with facts and sufficient evidence, the Government machinery would have to take note of the issues and respond appropriately—this was direct democracy in action.

Furthermore, the panel took up the responsibility of consolidating the grievances of the public so that they could be sent to all the concerned Departments, which were absent in the public hearing for suitable action. A detailed report entitled 'Citizens' Demand on Waterways of Chennai' was released and shared with relevant departments in September 2016.

Source: API Glimpses from public hearing 'Kelu Chennai Kelu'.

ENGAGEMENT WITH GOVERNMENT

Now it was a matter of waiting. While there was hope, there were also a lot of questions on whether the Government will take the concerns of the citizens seriously and act on them.

The Chennai Corporation responded positively by deputing a team of people to inspect each of the places mentioned in the report. The Chennai Corporation had handed over copies of the report to all the concerned Assistant Engineers and had instructed them to solve the issues mentioned therein immediately. This resulted in a series of actions at various places that gave citizens a lot of positivity and hope to start with. In Villivakkam, the Chennai Corporation immediately started the work of expanding the storm water drains. In Pallikaranai, they demolished the badminton court. In Keezhkattalai, they started demolishing buildings on the channel before political pressure was applied to stop the demolition. The channel in Ramapuram that was almost at road height was desilted. The sewage pipelines that were letting sewage into Keezhkattalai channel from the nearby pumping station were dismantled. Storm water drains were desilted throughout the city. Citizens were very heartened to see the Chennai Corporation's positive response to the audit report. Even better, the Principal Secretary incharge of the Municipal Administration and Water Supply Department sent the report to the municipalities of Pallavaram and Kanchipuram Collectorate. The Assistant Engineers we met at the local level spoke to us proactively on issues that had been mentioned in the report and how they were trying to resolve them.

The critical success factor was the show of strength—the Government would not have taken the report seriously if it had been prepared by a small group of people or an organisation. They took it seriously because it was the collective voice of thousands of people in the city. The voice was so loud, and so confident, and fully supported by facts that the Government machinery had to respond.

However, there were several hiccups and issues as well. The PWD was immovable and it was difficult to even meet the Secretary to the Department. The pressure that local politicians applied on officials was so high that District Collectors, Municipalities and the Chennai Corporation could not move ahead with legal action and demolitions on several encroachments. An IAS officer explained to us privately on how it was next to impossible to do anything about large, concrete encroachments as they are immediately pressurised by many in the higher echelons of power.

All in all, the follow-up on the report was encouraging, and several areas of the city got much improved infrastructure for flood preparedness. Citizen groups got direct reassurance that their time and efforts were worthwhile, and that peoples' power was still a formidable force in our democracy.

PUBLIC INTEREST LITIGATIONS

The last but an effective step for citizens in a democracy is the Right to Constitutional Remedies known as the Judiciary. Dr B. R. Ambedkar declared the right to Constitutional Remedies as the heart and soul of the Indian Constitution. While we in India may not yet have the ideal, independent Judiciary that delivers justice quickly, crores of Indian citizens do look up to the Judiciary as the last resort for truth and fairness to prevail. In a democracy, citizens must effectively use the judiciary for the right issues.

For matters where the executive class was in fear of taking action or negligent, citizens at API decided to take them to the Judiciary after building a strong body of evidence. The Villivakkam lake was the first issue that was taken to the Judiciary. API, through the RTI Act, sought information from the CMWSSB and Chennai Metro Rail (CMRL) on the quantum of earth dumped on the Villivakkam lake. The CMWSSB had used part of the lake to build a sewage treatment plant, but this was dismantled several years back. On one side, the CMWSSB was letting in untreated sewage from the pumping station directly into the lake and, on the other side, the Metro rail earth was dumped to cover the lake. The RTI revealed that the dumping had taken place to the extent of 20 acres of the waterbody.

A Public Interest Litigation was filed in the Madras High Court by API, asking for directions to clear the debris, full ecological restoration of the lake and to hold officials who approved and executed the dumping accountable. The Madras High Court admitted the case and, noting the environmental impact of the misdeeds of the Government such as untreated sewage being let into the lake, it transferred the case to the National Green Tribunal that has been specifically set up to handle cases relating to environment. Over multiple hearings within a period of 6 months, the case was well established, and the Municipal Administration and Water Supply Department and the Chennai Corporation agreed to restore 27.5 acres of the 39 acres of the lake. They argued that 11.5 acres of the lake would be required for construction of a new sewage treatment plant.

There are two fundamental case precedents that were strongly supportive of our position. The Madras High Court, in *T. K. Shanmugam vs The State of Tamil Nadu*, on 27 November 2015, 27/11/2015 in the case, observed:

At this juncture, this Court, taking judicial notice of the fact that even during the hearing of this case, the State of Tamil Nadu is seriously affected by unprecedented floods, i.e., during November 2015, and because of that, number of people were dead and many people lost their property, is compelled to put its views that the entire loss due to the flood was due to maladministration and the prevailing practices by the authorities as almost all the water bodies and water courses were allowed to be encroached upon resulting in reduction in their flood storing and carrying capacity, forcing the water to deviate from its regular course and enter the residential areas causing devastating effects. The authorities have permitted construction of houses in the water bodies. This resulted in inundation of these areas during flood and all these houses submerged under the flood water. This shows that despite the orders of the Court, the authorities pretend to act swiftly in removing encroachments but only in a selective manner and not in a planned and determined manner…. It has become inevitable for this Court to put on record that the authorities in power cannot destroy the water bodies or water courses formed naturally for the benefit of mankind for ever and it is beyond the power of the State to alienate or re-classify the water bodies for some other purposes without compensating the effect of such water bodies.

Second, in 2015, the Supreme Court of India, in *Hinch Lal Tiwari vs Kamala Devi and Ors.*, observed and ordered that it is the responsibility of the Government to make sure that waterbodies are not put into disuse or misuse and therefore change of such watercourse from poromboke to patta land was deemed invalid:

It is important to notice that the material resources of the community like forests, tanks, ponds, hillock, mountain etc. are nature's bounty. They maintain delicate ecological balance. They need to be protected for a proper and healthy environment which enables people to enjoy a quality life which is the essence of the guaranteed right under Article 21 of the Constitution. The Government, including the Revenue Authorities, i.e., Respondents 11 to 13 having noticed that a pond is falling in disuse, should have bestowed their attention to develop the same which would, on one hand, have prevented ecological disaster and on the other provided better environment for the benefit of the public at large. Such vigil is the best protection against knavish attempts to seek allotment in non-abadi sites.

Quoting these two judgements, we contended that even if the Villivakkam lake was put into misuse, it was the Government's responsibility to protect it. Instead of protecting these resources, the Government themselves act as encroachers of the land by building Sewage Treatment Plants and dumping earth. The National Green Tribunal ordered that the Chennai Corporation must immediately start the restoration work in 27.5 acres of land and CMWSSB should not carry on any construction on the remaining 11.5 acres, and should file a status report on how that part will be restored as well. This was a significant victory for the citizens, and a successful outcome for a journey that began with the flood of 2015. The Government's restoration work on 27.5 acres has started as we write this. But the journey does not end there—it is important for the residents to be vigilant about the quality of the restoration and ensure that there is no delay or corruption in its execution. The local residents have vowed to monitor the restoration and ensure that they will never allow the lake to be encroached again.

FOLLOW-UP

Why Chennai Stinks: Citizens' Efforts to Understand and Solve the Sewage Problem

In our effort to continue our work on waterbodies, we undertook a detailed study of Sewage generation, transfer and treatment in the city of Chennai. Our social audits and field studies had made it amply clear that one of the main reasons for the disengagement of citizens from waterbodies was their disuse for drinking water, which is mainly due to untreated sewage being let into waterbodies, both by the government and by private citizens, thereby completely polluting them, and rendering the water unusable.

To solve the issues around water management and water security for the city, finding answers to the issue of sewage was an important element. As always, the first step to finding a solution was to understand the problem in detail. So a study was done, and a report, 'Why Chennai Stinks' (Arappor Iyakkam n.d.), was published. The study provides an overall understanding of the gaps in the sewerage system of the Chennai region. It involves analysis of the pumping stations and treatment plants managed by the CMWSSB, illegal sewage connections, waterbodies and current policies and systems pertaining to sewage management.

What emerged as the root cause of improper Sewage Management is gross underestimation of the quantity of sewage generated in Chennai and the incorrect assumption that there is enough capacity to treat the entire sewage generated in the city. Even with the most conservative estimates, we found that 1,073 MLD of sewage flows into our water-bodies without treatment every day. In addition to this, the report contains detailed observations and recommendations to improve Sewage Management for the city. The report was shared and discussed in detail with officials in CMWSSB, who were quite forthcoming in their response, and promised to look into the contents of the report in detail.

We followed this up with a large public gathering on sewage, called 'Sakkadai Thiruvizha' (Celebration of Sewage). Over 500 residents from all over the city came together to discuss and deliberate on sewage-related concerns in their areas. The highlight of the event was a panel discussion on Sewage, with a stellar set of panellists—we had representatives from CMWSSB, Chennai Rivers Restoration Trust (CRRT), Chennai Corporation and academic experts passionately debating the issue, possible solutions and the roles and responsibilities of all stakeholders, including the public. This was a novel experience for both the officials and the public, and we hope this is just the beginning of a long series of healthy debate and interaction between stakeholders on matters of civic importance.

Right to Information Application on Details of Waterbodies

API filed an RTI to the Chennai Corporation, seeking details of all waterbodies under its responsibility. The response, recently received, provides details of 210 waterbodies under their control, along with details of known encroachments. It is interesting to note that they have even provided the names of lakes which are fully encroached.

We believe this information is a valuable resource, as it is an official record. We have immediately published this information in the public domain, and have encouraged our volunteers to note the details of waterbodies in their respective areas, and to organise social audits to verify the information. We are also planning the next steps around the information, such as digitising the information in a searchable format, overlaying it on existing maps and initiating legal action on the lakes that have been disclosed as encroached.

Similar RTIs have been filed with the PWD and the CRRT, and their responses are awaited.

CONCLUSION

API is a fledgling people's movement, less than three years old. It is an experiment, to build from the ground up, a platform for the common people, to come together and play a decisive role in governance. It is an incubator for people's politics, and seeking to break the myth that the soul of democracy lies in electoral politics alone. In the relatively short period of its existence, the movement has gained in strength, with selfless volunteers devoting time and effort for the greater good. And we have witnessed encouraging signs—increased awareness and questioning by the citizens, increased accountability and responsiveness from the Government machinery, relevance in the urban polity and legal victories. The tools and success stories we have shared in this chapter are strong examples of what citizens can achieve in a relatively short period of time if they actively and continuously engage with issues of Governance. Being aware, being informed, asking questions and being fearless of taking on the system, while simultaneously working with it, are everyone's duty, and together, we can make a genuine difference.

The goals of improving urban governance, of building citizens' participation in democracy, of improving transparency and accountability, and of building a vibrant civil society are formidable, and can always only be work in progress.

The key is to keep at it, in a sustained way, and to continuously increase the number of people that are involved, the number of issues that is taken up and the number of institutional solutions that are achieved.

In these days of polarisation and despair, peoples' politics is a bastion of hope. An enlightened and active citizenry is key to saving democracy and making it participative, making it functional, making it real, making it work. Active citizenry has the power to transform the cynicism of watching decades of decadence and corruption into a positive, vibrant hope for a better future for all of us.

DIRECTORATE OF VIGILANCE AND ANTI-CORRUPTION—A CASE STUDY

One of the key ways in which Governments of the day subvert democracy is by making institutions of democracy non-functional. One such institution is the Directorate of Vigilance and Anti-Corruption (DVAC), which is supposed to act against corrupt public servants and corruption in public institutions. However, it is no surprise that Governments find it convenient to make such institutions non-functional and carry on with their corruption unhindered.

There are generally three types of independence that are required for such Institutions to function—financial independence, independence in recruitment/appointment and functional independence. However, the DVAC suffers from lack of independence in each of the aforementioned and is purposefully made so. As a peoples' movement fighting corruption, API feels strongly about the need for an independent anti-corruption mechanism in the state of Tamil Nadu, and has been working on it in a focused way.

To this end, API, through the RTI Act, accessed data on the functioning of the DVAC in Tamil Nadu over the last 5 years. The results were shocking. One of the important functions of the DVAC is to conduct random search in different government departments to expose graft. However, we found that the DVAC in Tamil Nadu did not even conduct a single random search in the years 2015, 2016 or until June 2017. Most of the district units were not even submitting their monthly review work to the head office. Only one of the random searches in the last 7 years resulted in a preliminary or detailed enquiry. Such a poor performance of an institution that is supposed to fight corruption in public institutions is due to the complete control of the State Government over it. The random search is often a problem for the politicians because the graft money that bureaucrats demand and collect in various offices like the Road Traffic Offices, Registrar offices, etc., travel all the way till the top and hence the Government of the day always wants to keep this institution in check. But it is the citizens alone who can turn around this situation because the economic and social effects of widespread corruption are well known and it is only in our enlightened self-interest to make this institution function effectively and independently.

Drawing on the RTI information, API came out with a video summarising the abject performance of the DVAC and launched a campaign calling out to citizens to gather in force and question the DVAC's non-performance. In a mark of protest, many citizens sent locks to the DVAC, asking it to perform or shut shop. There was an immediate reaction to our call for a gathering at a private place, with the police intervening to thwart the event. The police may have been successful in stopping the event but their stifling of democratic voices went viral on social media and was able to reach a lot more people, through the traditional press as well. Within a few days, a group of us went directly to meet the Director of DVAC, and questioned him directly on the poor performance of the Institution. The Director and the Joint Director didn't expect the pointed questions and were not able to dismiss them, as they were based on data given by their own department through RTI. The dialogue and negotiations were constructive and the Director said that he had taken charge of the Institution only a few months back, and promised to us that the performance of the Institution will improve significantly under him.

The Director did keep his word. Suddenly, we started seeing the institution becoming active and conducting random searches in many public offices. They even raided the former Vice Chancellors of a few universities. Again, when we had filed a follow-up RTI, we observed that the DVAC had conducted 61 random searches between the months of August 2017 and January 2018. This is yet another example of how active citizenry can drive institutions of democracy to function, discharge their constitutional duties and act as effective checks and balances, in the spirit in which they were formed.

REFERENCES

Arappor, Iyakkam. n.d. *Why Chennai Stinks: Citizens' Effort to Understand and Solve the Sewage Problem.* Available at http://arappor.org/public/Document/ activites/waterbodies/Arappor-Citizens-Report-Sewage.pdf (accessed on 7 February 2019).

Comptoller and Auditor General of India. 2017. *Report of the Comptroller and Auditor General of India on Performance Audit of Flood Management and Response in Chennai and its Suburban Areas.* Report No. 4 of 2017. https://cag.gov.in/sites/default/ files/audit_report_files/Report_No_4_of_2017_-_Performance_Audit_of_ Flood_Management_and_Response_in_Chennai_and_its_Suburban_Area. pdf (accessed 22 September 2019).

Law Commission of India. 2015. *Electoral Reforms.* Report No. 255. Available at http://lawcommissionofindia.nic.in/reports/report255.pdf (accessed on 7 February 2019).

About the Editors and Contributors

EDITORS

Arvind Sivaramakrishnan is a former Visiting Professor and currently a member of the Guest Faculty, Department of Humanities and Social Sciences, Indian Institute of Technology Madras, Chennai. From 2008 to 2014, he was the Senior Deputy Editor on *The Hindu*, writing editorials, specialist articles, and book reviews on international politics, public policy, and political theory; he combined his duties with teaching and research as an Associate Professor at the Asian College of Journalism, Chennai. He took his degree, a postgraduate diploma in social administration, and doctorate as well as a professional teaching qualification at the University of Southampton, where he also taught politics. Since then, he has taught at Suffolk College, Ipswich, the Centre for Economic and Social Studies, Hyderabad, Southampton Institute of Higher Education (now Southampton Solent University), and Taunton's College (now Richard Taunton College), Southampton. He has published a range of academic papers in politics, political philosophy, public policy, and related fields, and has conducted research seminars and research training sessions at universities in the European Union and India. His books include *Introduction to Political Ideologies* (2017), *Public Interest Journalism* (2014), *Public Policy and Citizenship* (2012), *Short on Democracy* (2007), and *Through a Glass Wall* (2007).

Sudarsan Padmanabhan is Associate Professor in the Department of Humanities and Social Sciences, Indian Institute of Technology Madras, Chennai. He specializes in social and political philosophy, Indian philosophy and culture, and his research focus is on the confluence of law, democracy, and ethics in the public sphere. Sudarsan is the Co-coordinator of an Erasmus+ grant, funded by the European Union (EU) and coordinated by Aarhus University, Denmark. Sudarsan was also the Co-coordinator of Interdisciplinary Bridges for Indo-European Studies (IBIES), a consortium of 19 EU and Indian Higher Education institutions funded by Erasmus Mundus, coordinated by Aarhus University. He was Principal Investigator of the EU-funded Contemporary European Study Centres Project in India during 2010–2011; this research group works on Democracy and Development and Contemporary Global Politics. With Jyotirmaya Tripathy, Sudarsan coedited *The Democratic Predicament: Cultural Diversity in Europe and India* (2013) and *Becoming Minority* (2015); with Sonika Gupta, he coedited *Politics in the Global Age: Critical Reflections on Sovereignty, Citizenship, Territory and Nationalism* (2015).

CONTRIBUTORS

Arappor Iyakkam was formed in August 2015, with a vision to achieve a **just and equitable society**. Its primary focus areas are fighting corruption in public life, disseminating awareness of citizens' rights and developing a participative democracy, by building a vibrant civil society and a large Peoples' movement. In the 3.5 years since its inception, it has taken up a number of issues and projects of public interest, and has made rapid strides in establishing itself as a player of note in governance and public affairs in Chennai city and the state of Tamil Nadu. During the **Chennai Flood of 2015**, Arappor volunteers rallied to rescue a number of stranded Chennai residents, provided information through social media to loved ones, and arranged for the distribution of relief supplies in an organised way, including needs identification survey and token system. In June 2016, Arappor launched its **"Making Chennai Flood-Safe"** project and conducted social audit of 4 large stretches of the city heavily flooded in December 2015. As a follow-up, 1,000 participants from over 20 residential areas of Chennai were invited to present their grievances and suggestions at Arappor's public hearing **"Kelu Chennai Kelu"**, to their elected MLAs, officials of the Chennai Corporation and a Panel of Experts. The Chennai Corporation initiated several actions including removal of encroachments, and de-silting of storm water drains based on the report. Arappor takes its role as a watchdog very seriously. Its work is well-researched and well-documented. Arappor Iyakkam is transparent in its finances and democratic in its functioning. In the coming years, Arappor Iyakkam will intensify its fight for a corruption-free society. Making the Government machinery work for its citizens is the only sustainable way to build a city and a country all citizens are proud of. www.arappor.org; https://www.facebook.com/Arappor/; https://twitter.com/arappor

Josephine Anthony is an Assistant Professor at the Centre for Equity and Justice for Children and Families, School of Social Work, Tata Institute of Social Science (TISS), Mumbai. Her PhD is in the area of 'Digital Divide and Equity in Education' from IIT Madras. Her field of practice and research include Vulnerable and Marginalized Children, Researching with Children and other Vulnerable Populations, and Technology and Society, with a focus on adolescent children. Currently, she is leading two field action projects, namely, Improving Quality of Life and Wellbeing of Children in Childcare Institutions in Hyderabad, Government of Telangana and 'Child Protection Fellowship' with childcare institutions in Gaya, Government of Bihar. Josephine has lead several research projects including Educational Status of Children during Post-tsunami in Tamil Nadu, Coping Patterns of Persons with Disabilities during tsunami in Tamil Nadu, Educational Status of Children of Construction Labourers in Pune, Educational Status of Migrant Children in Pune and Delhi, Status of Women and Children among Scheduled Tribes in Rajasthan and Childcare Institutions in Hyderabad. Josephine co-led SARASWATI project for TISS, which was the task leader of Social and Institutional Evaluation of Waste Water Management, an FP7 EU-India project, Department of Science and Technology, Government of India. She has published in prominent international journals and chapters in book. She was a recipient of Linnaeus-Palme Fellowship and taught in Gavle University, Sweden (2014). Before joining TISS, Josephine worked for about a decade as a social work practitioner and a researcher in urban and rural Tamil Nadu in India and as an autism therapist in USA for about 3 years.

R. Azhagarasan holds a PhD in Comparative Literature (Tamil–English Folklore) and teaches in the Department of English at the University of Madras. He writes on issues of cultural politics in national and international journals both in Tamil and English. He wrote about the Tamil translations of *Alice in Wonderland* for the 150th anniversary celebration of the book, and has translated from Tamil into English a collection of critical work by the Dalit activist Ravikumar, under the title *Venomous Touch* (2009). With Ravikumar, he coedited *The Oxford Anthology of Tamil Dalit Writing* (2012), and his Tamil translation of Catherine Belsey's *Poststructuralism: A Very Short Introduction* was published in 2009. He has also edited an anthology on the concept of Bhakti in Tamil culture. His Tamil writings appeared in 2017 as *Utpagai Unarum Tharunam (The Enmity Within)*.

A. V. Balasubramanian is the Director of the Centre for Indian Knowledge Systems (CIKS), an institution devoted to exploring the contemporary relevance and applications of Indian Knowledge Systems, particularly in the area of sustainable agriculture, and is based in Chennai. He obtained his MSc degree in Chemistry from Bangalore University and did a post-MSc diploma in Molecular Biophysics from the Indian Institute of Science, Bangalore. Later, he studied Physiology and Biophysics at the State University of New York at Stony Brook. Since 1982, he has been involved in work related to various aspects of Traditional Indian Sciences and Technologies, and trying to explore their current relevance and potential. In 1995, he founded the CIKS.

With CIKS, he has been involved in the production of educational and training material on various aspects of Sustainable Agriculture as well as research on this topic drawing upon indigenous knowledge, wisdom and practices. More recently, he has also been involved in helping farmers to set up a large number of producer companies through which various activities related to the production and marketing of organic produce are carried out, and other services are also offered to farmers. He has been a member of several Government of India committees—such as Ministry of Science and Technology, Ministry of Rural Development and Ministry of Human Resources

Development—and has been on the Editorial Board of several magazines and journals (such as the *Journal of Ayurveda and Integrative Medicine*). He also has an active interest in other areas of Indian knowledge systems including indigenous health and yoga, and the epistemology of traditional knowledge systems. For his contributions in the area of indigenous traditions of Sciences and Technologies, he was awarded an honorary doctorate by the Gandhigram Rural University, Gandhigram, Dindigul district, Tamil Nadu, in 2010.

Jagdeep Chhokar was a professor (teacher, trainer, researcher, and advisor) of Management at the Indian Institute of Management Ahmedabad from 1985 to 2006. He was also Dean and Director-in-charge there. He is now a citizen-activist for improving democracy and governance in the country, a bird-watcher and conservationist, and a lawyer. Before becoming a professor, he was an engineer–manager with the Indian Railways, and worked as an international marketing manager for four years. He has taught in several countries including Australia, France, Japan, and the USA. He is a founder member of the Association for Democratic Reforms, and founding Chairperson of Aajeevika Bureau.

M. G. Devasahayam completed MA in Economics from Loyola College, Chennai, and taught there before joining the Indian Army. He attained the rank of Major and saw action in the 1965 India–Pakistan war and counterinsurgency operations in Nagaland; he was awarded the Samar Seva and the General Service Medal and Bar. He then joined the Indian Administrative Service, and in the state of Haryana held several senior posts before becoming Principal Secretary; he also served as a Member of the Government of India Committee on agricultural policies and programs, and was later an adviser to Ashok Leyland Ltd, Sterling Holiday Resorts, the US-based Public Service Enterprise Group, and the IIT Madras Research Park. He has written four books, respectively, on the Indian Emergency, on Jayaprakash Narayan's time in jail, on the JP Movement, and on Mother Teresa. In the voluntary sector, he is a managing trustee of SUSTAIN, an associate of the Alliance to Save Energy, and convener of the Forum for Electoral Integrity.

N. Gopalaswami is the President of the Vivekananda Educational Society, which runs a group of 25 schools in and around Chennai. In 2014, he was appointed Chairman of Kalakshetra, and in 2015 was appointed Chancellor of the Rashtriya Sanskrit Vidyapeetha, the Sanskrit university at Tirupati. Gopalaswami was awarded the Padma Bhushan in 2015. After taking the Postgraduate Gold Medal in Chemistry at University of Delhi in 1965, he joined the Indian Administrative Service in 1966; he served in the state of Gujarat for 25 years before moving to the central government in Delhi in 1992. He retired as Union Home Secretary on being appointed as Election Commissioner in 2004, and was Chief Election Commissioner (CEC) from 2006 to 2009. During his time as CEC, the Commission implemented many successful innovations; the most important were photographic electoral rolls to improve accuracy and prevent impersonation, and age-cohort analyses of the rolls for their fidelity and accuracy. The many State Assembly elections conducted during his tenure, including those in Uttar Pradesh in 2007, were praised for their probity and for being free of violence and intimidation.

Chamundeeswari Kuppuswamy is Senior Lecturer at the School of Law at the University of Hertfordshire, and combines this with a role at the Vice-Chancellor's Office, leading interdisciplinary research at the University, championing research under the theme of "Global Economy," an interdisciplinary researcher, with primary interests based in international law. Her PhD (2007) is in international bio-law, applying TWAIL approaches (Third World Approaches to International Law) to intellectual property rights and human rights. Her research topics include global commons, commons governance, property rights, right to development, decolonizing international law, common heritage of mankind, access to medicines, patents, traditional knowledge, cultural heritage, bioethics, arts as method, and security.

S. Y. Quraishi is the Chancellor of IILM University Gurgaon, and a Distinguished Fellow at Ashoka University. He is a member of the board of the International Institute of Democracy and Electoral Assistance, Stockholm. Dr Quraishi was appointed as the 17th Chief Election Commissioner of India after a four-decade career in the Indian

Administrative Service. His last post in the civil service was Secretary in the Ministry of Youth Affairs and Sports. Among his books are the edited volume *The Great March of Democracy: Seven Decades of India's Elections* (2018), *An Undocumented Wonder - The Making of the Great Indian Election* (2014), *Old Delhi: Living Traditions* (2011), *Haryana Rediscovered: A Bibliography* (1985), and *Social Marketing for Social Change* (1998).

N.L. Rajah is a designated Senior Advocate and has been practicing extensively in the Madras High Court since 1986. He is a former trustee and currently advisor of the Citizen, Consumer and Civic Action Group. In 2000, he was an invitee of the US Government International Visitor Leadership Program. In May 2013, he participated in a week-long meeting of the United Nations (UNCITRAL). He is a Founding Director of the Nani Palkhivala Arbitration Centre, and a trustee of the Palkhivala Foundation. He was a member of the special committee formed by the Law Commission of India to suggest changes and amendments to the Arbitration and Conciliation Act, 1996.

With the retired Supreme Court judge D. P. Wadhwa, he coauthored the book *Consumer Protection in India* (the third edition of which, revised by Sudhanshu Kumar, appeared in 2017); his other books include *The Madras High Court: A 150-Year Journey from a Crown Court to a People's Court* (2012), and *An Iconic Splendour* (2018), on the heritage value of the Madras High Court building. In addition, he is one of the principal contributors to the book *Courts of India: Past to Present* (2016), published by the Supreme Court of India.

Trilochan Sastry is a Professor and former Dean at IIM Bangalore. He has a PhD from MIT, MBA from IIM Ahmedabad and a BTech from IIT Delhi. He is the Founder and Chairman of the Association for Democratic Reforms that works on electoral and political reforms in India. He founded the Centre for Collective Development and Farmveda that promotes farmer cooperatives in drought-prone regions. He has authored several articles and papers on a variety of subjects including democracy, agriculture, cooperatives as well as Operations Research.

Wendy Singer is the Roy T. Wortman Professor of History at Kenyon College in USA Her ongoing work on Indian democracy and the history of women in elections emerges from *A Constituency Suitable for Ladies and Other Social Histories of India's Elections* (2007). Her work-in-progress, "A Seat at the Table" (based on research funded by a Fulbright-Nehru Senior Scholars Grant) examines the history of India's policy of reservations—particularly in governing bodies—which has precedents as early as Madras in the 1920s. This project takes her back to the period of her original research on the freedom movement and peasant politics in Bihar, notably *Creating Histories: Oral Narratives and the Politics of History-Making*. Beyond scholarship, Singer teaches Indian history, not only at Kenyon College, but periodically, at Exeter University in the UK. Also since 2018, she and Sudarsan Padmanabhan at IIT Madras have been organizing Writing Workshops for engineers and others aimed at bringing scientific research to wider audiences.

Chris Terry is an expert in voting systems, voter behavior, and comparative political systems in the United Kingdom. After seven years as a researcher for the Electoral Reform Society, the world's oldest democracy organization, Chris is now pursuing a PhD at the University of Manchester, on voters in marginal seats—those seats most likely to change hands in an election, with a focus on whether those voters differ in terms of their values, demographics, view of political efficacy, and whether they receive preferential policy treatment. Chris has written for the LSE Politics Blog, and previously worked for a public affairs company in Brussels.

Index

Adi Dravida Conferences, 216
agricultural production
    assessment of external costs in UK,
        263–264
    cost estimation in USA, 262–263
Ambedkar
    head of Constitution Drafting
        Committee, 28
Anand Babu, 64
ancient privileges, 217
ancient tryst
    politics and justice between, 17–23
antinomical vestiges, 17
Arappor Iyakkam (API), 295
    birth, 294–295
Art. 243(T)(6), 45
Art. 243(D)(6), 45
Article 324 of the Constitution of
        India, 146
Association for Democratic Reforms,
        143
Attorney General of India, 145

Booth Level Officer (BLO), 67

Cabinet
    Ordinance to the President, 147
campaigning
    nature, 7
    voters' sense of identity, 7
candidate contesting elections to
        Parliament and State
        Assembly
    PIL in Delhi High Court, 144
        judgment, 144

case
    Directorate of Vigilance and Anti-
        Corruption, 316–318
caste Hindus
    Annie Besant's views, 219
    campaigned against colonial
        administrators, 219
caste question
    revival, 214
    rise, 215
caste system, 15
Central Board of Direct Taxation
        (CBDT), 157
Central Information Commission
        (CIC), 157, 160
    decision, aftermath, 161–164
Centre for Indian Knowledge Systems
        (CIKS), 256
    approach, 256–258
    field performance data, 258
    support for organic farming, 256
Chennai, 290–292
Chennai Floods, 2015, 289
    API birth, 294–295
    citizen's audit of waterbodies,
        303–306
    engagement with government,
        309–310
    failure of urban governance,
        292–293
    focus on rehabilitation, 300–301
    immediate aftermath, 295–298
    information and RTI, 302–303
    public hearing, 306–309
    public interest litigations, 310–313

rise of civil society, 298–299
strategy for citizen engagement,
    301–302
Chief Commissioners of Income Tax
    (CCITs), 157
Chief Election Commissioner (CEC),
    7, 102
Chinese Communist Revolutions,
    11
civil disobedience, 16
Commission, 7
Communist revolution, 11
Comptroller and Auditor General, 7
Conduct of Election Rules, 1961,
    142, 152
Congress party
    return, 48
Constituent Assembly of India, 7, 16,
    191
    Ambedkar debates, 10, 39
    debates, 11
    debates over representation, 198
    Jawaharlal Nehru arguments, 7
    noteworthy feature in debate, 39
    women's representation, 199
Constitution Drafting Committee, 7
    Ambedkar, as head, 27
Constitution of India, 7
    relation with political process, 28
    Article 324, 141
    challenge, 23
    language of citizenship, 197–199
    likened to holy scriptures, 23
    role in Aristotelian political
        schema, 31
    social, political or economic meas-
        ures, 29
    the language of the Gods in the
        world of men, 24
constitutional
    amendments, 48
        validity, 48
    democracy, imagining,
        10–17

mandates
    right to information in elec-
        tions, 51–57
    morality, 30
    Ambedkar consideration, 7
constitutionally permissible
    reservations
    political institutions, 41–47
consummation of union, 18
Court in Association for Democratic
    Reforms (supra), 148
courts, ECI and election law, 113–116

definition of public authority, 160
democracy, 10, 17
    blueprint, 136–139
    Dalit activists' views, 213
    end goal, 171
    good governance, 169
    Guha's observations, 36
    Lincolnian dictum, 25
    ought/ought not to be, 26–30
    problem or solution, 23–26
    regained with Emergency end,
        134–136
    separate booths for women,
        203–205
    voter's education, 62
    women involvement, 206–210
    women preparing for universal
        franchise, 199–203
    women's access to polls right to
        run for office, 205–206
democratic due process, 17
demonstration, 7
Depressed Class conferences, 216
Dictatorship of the Proletariat, 7
duty precedes rights, 12

early years, 102
education
    gender inequity in, 232
El Partido de la Red, 171
election campaigns and voting, 184

Election Commission of India (ECI),
            62, 146
    empire strike
        Article 324, 146
        SC, 145
        SLP, 145
    issued order, 148
Election Commission of India(ECI)
    empire strike, 144
Election Commission's Model Code
            of Conduct, 7
elections
    challenges and responses, 104–106
    constitutional mandates and right
            to information, 51–57
    crime, role, 172
    criminals' in legislatures, 109
    current challenges, 107–113
    FPTP, 110–111
    Indian, 172
    malpractices, 105
    muscle power, 107
    pre-independent India, 37
    use of massive amounts of money,
            172
electoral and political systems, 87, 141
Electoral Photo ID Card (EPIC), 65
electoral politics
    role of money and power, 212
electoral practices
    pre-independent India, 37–41
electoral reforms, 141, 142
    Narayanan's proposal, 41
electoral registers, 7
electoral systems, 95
Electronic Voting Machines (EVM)
    introduction in Indian elections,
            103–104
    unforeseen problems, 104
Emergency
    commences, 125–129
    dissected, 129–133
    ends, 134–136
    minions, 128

ethics and politics
    Gandhi's claim, 12
eudaimonia, 20

First Congress Maha Jana Sabha
    fourth resolution, 220
First Past the Post (FPTP), 110–111
    system, 101
First Round Table Conference, 44
first-time voters
    expectations, 179
Foreign Contribution (Regulation)
            Act (FCRA)
    political parties, 164–167
fragmentation, 75
frugal innovation, 278–280

Gandhi
    demonstration in
        socio-religious harmony in
            South Africa, 14
    hierocratic social structures, 13
    innumerable schisms, 13
Gandhian method, 14
gender equity (EI)
    relevance of HI to analyse, 236
gender inequality (GI), 235
    inclusive education, 235
    MDGs 2 and 3, 235
    SDGs 4 and 5, 235
Goswami Committee, 142
governance, 9
Government of India Act
    laws passed, 39
    Montague–Chelmsford propos-
            als, 42
government
    people's priorities, 173–175
Grammar of Anarchy, 7

Hannen Angelo, 191
    women's representation, 193–197
horizontal inequality (HI), 233
    dynamic complexities, 234

effects on well-being, 234
multidimensionality, 234
persistence, 234
relevance to analyse GI in education, 236
Hunter Commission, 243

idea of India, 119–121
abandoning, 121–123
identifiable constituencies and representatives, 87
in-process monitoring, 67
inclusive education, 235
income tax returns (ITRs), 157
India after Gandh
The History of the World's Largest Democracy, 36
India Against Corruption (IAC), 7
Indian Constitution, 9
Indian Council of Agricultural Research (ICAR), 257
Indian Councils Act of 1909, 42
Indian elections, 172
Indian EVM, 104
Indian IP academia, 274
Indian Muslims
children, 241
contributions in community, 240
minority, 236
system around, 238
women, 240–244
Indian National Congress
Constituent Assembly, 16
questioned by Ambedkar, 221
India's Patents Act, 278
Indira Nehru Gandhi vs Raj Narain, 49
Indo-Saracenic architectural form, 237
Information, Education and Communication (IEC), 64
intellectual property rights (IPRs), 268, 284–286
assessing policy, 278–283

baseline draft, 276–278
Think Tank, 273–274
draft, 276–278
policy versions, 274–276
process, 274

Jaago Re, 64
jati, 13
Jayaprakash Narayan and his Movement, 123–125

K. Krishnamurthy vs Union of India, 46
K. R. Narayanan, 222
involvement of Dr.Rajendra Prasad, 224
poignant statement, 227
speaking at Commonwealth Club of California, 227
Know Your BLO campaign, 67
Knowledge, Attitude, Behaviour and Practice (KABP), 65
Kundu's Report for Diversity Index, 247

Law as integrity, 31
Law Commission of India, 144
legal system of pre-independent India, 38
Legislative Council
Hannen Angelo, 194
Legislature, 145
liberalism, 14
Lily Thomas/Lok Prahari case, 148
petitions filed in 2005, 150
RP Act, 148, 150
subsections 3 and 4, 149
limited franchise and separate electorates, 38
Lincolnian dictum, 25

Maintenance of Internal Security Act (MISA), 128

Member of Parliament Local Area Development Scheme (MPLADS), 82
Millennium Development Goals (MDGs), 235
Model Code of Conduct (MCC), 106–107
modernism in India, 242
Montagu–Chelmsford Committee on Constitutional Reforms, 193
moral
    Lincoln's contention, 7
multi-member STV wards, 91
Municipal Council
    Hannen Angelo's agenda, 194
Muslim Educational Conference, 243
Muslim in India
    gender equity in education, 248–250
Muslim Women's Protection Bill, 244
Muthulakshmi Reddy, 191

National Commission for Minorities, 246
National IPR Policy, 271–273
National Voters Day (NVD), 69–70
nationwide survey
    ADR, 175–177
    finding, 177–179
    implications, 182–183
    income-based expectations and performance ratings, 180
    regional variations, 180–182
Nehru's brand of mixed economy, 122
None of the Above (NOTA), 104
    judgment, 152
        implementation and aftermath, 153–155
        political parties, RTI Act, 156–157
        PUCL, 152
        RTI Act, 153

Objectives Resolution, 119
observance of procedures, 7
order and progress
    J. S. Mill's views, 228
Ordinance and subsequent Act, 147
organic agriculture
    India's food security, 254–267
organic farming
    return on investment, 261–262
    difference in price, 261
    efficacy, 256
    field performance data, 258
    implications reports, 266
    support from CIKS, 256

Panchayati Raj system, 10
Pappu campaign, 64
Parliamentary Constitutional system, 10
passive sovereignty, 268–286
People's Union for Civil Liberties (PUCL) in 2004, 152
periodic elections, 105
pharmaceutical intellectual property rights, 283–284
philosopher, 21
Plato, 31
politeia, 21
political awareness
    changing, 170
politics and justice, 18
Prime Minister's New 15 Point Programme, 247
process of willing, 25
Public Information Officers (PIOs), 157
public interest litigation (PIL), 143

Quit India Movement, 123

Rashtriya Madhyamik Shiksha Abhiyan (RMSA), 231
Rashtriya Ucchatar Shiksha Abhiyan (RUSA), 231

Reforms of the Electoral Laws, 143
religious and political ideologies
    Ambedkar refused to engage, 7
Representation of the People Act,
    1951 (RP Act), 142
Republic, 17, 18
reservation, 43
    Anglo-Indians, 44, 45
    opposed by women, 194
    Schedule Castes and Schedule
        Tribes, 45
    women, 44–45
Right to Education Act 2009, 231
Right to Information Act (RTI Act),
    153, 160
right to run
    office, 192–193
rural–urban divide, 179

Sachar Committee, 246
    discussion about Muslims, 239
Sarva Shiksha Abhiyan (SSA), 231
Simon Commission, 43
Simon Commission First Round
    Table Conference, 43–44
Simple Majority system, 7
    constituency link, 81–83
    disproportionalities, 76–80
    feature, 74
    fragmentation of votes, 75–76
    reserved constituencies, 83–90
Single Transferable Vote (STV), 88,
    90
    advantages, 92–95
        far fewer votes, 93
        fixed constituency boundaries,
            92
        no safe seats, 94
        range of voter preferences, 93
        wider choice for voters, 92
    multi-member wards, 92
    proportional representation, 90–92
    Scottish local government, 91
    use, 90

social democracy, 216
social inequality, 234
Solicitor General of India, 145
Special Component Plan (SCP), 246
Special Leave Petition (SLP), 145
special schools
    reasons for establishing, 218
Standing Committee of Rajya Sabha,
    151
substantive considerations, 25
Sultanate of Delhi, 237
Supreme Court (SC)
    decision, 145
Sustainable Development Goals
    (SDGs), 235
Swaraj, 119
Systematic Voters Education and
        Electoral Participation
        (SVEEP), 64
    impact, 68–69
    lessons learnt, 70–71
    three pillars, 66

Tamil Nadu, 290, 294
Taxation Laws (Amendment) Act,
    1978, 158
The Indian Constitution
    Cornerstone of a Nation, 41
the Net Party, 171
The Republic and Nicomachean
        Ethics, 11
theory of democracy, 9
    Panchayati Raj system, 10
    Parliamentary Constitutional
        system, 10
Think Tank Committee, 273
Thirumangalam Formula, 294
titanic struggle
    history, 24
total revolution, 124
traditional knowledge, 281–283
Tribal Sub-Plan (TSP), 246
TRIPS-plus provisions,
    284–286

Union of India, 145
Union of India vs Association for
Democratic Reforms and
Another, 53
unorganized sector
definition, 170

valuation, 262
verna, 24
Vertical Inequality (VI), 233
voters education, 63

Voters Education and Electoral
Participation (VEEP)
Division, 64
voters education
partners, 67
SVEEP division, 64

Westminster system, 73
Why Emergency document, 125–129
women's lobbying, 193
Women's Reservation Bill, 206–210